"If you are looking for great recipes so you can reliably and easily make delicious, healthy meals, here you are. Peace In Every Bite is beautifully done."

John Robbins, *author of Diet For A New America, The Food Revolution, and Healthy At 100*

"What a good cookbook and health guide filled with wonderfully sumptuous sounding recipes. Two Moons has put her thoughtfulness, care, and nutritional know-how into a very useful book for people who wish to eat very healthfully."

Elson M. Haas, M.D., *Integrated Nutritional Medicine Physician and author of many books, including Staying Healthy with the Seasons, The New Detox Diet, and A Cookbook for All Seasons.*

"Peace In Every Bite conforms with all the principles of alkaline forming dietary recommendations. I can easily endorse the content of this book and applaud the author for making it available to all."

Theodore A. Baroody, N.D., D.C., Ph.D. *author of Alkalize Or Die*

"After enjoying Two Moon's food for the past 2 decades, I consider her a High Priestess of vegan culinary arts. Peace in Every Bite offers superb advice and pointers for those new to veganism as well as those who just want to dabble in healthier food choices. This book also sets the ultimate standard in vegan cookery. It is easy to use and understand, and the format and illustrations invite fun and good times in the kitchen. Bravo, Two Moons! You have given us a fantastic cookbook!"

Dr. Susan A. Schiller, Ph.D. *Professor of English at Central Michigan University. Author of Creating the Joyful Writer, and co-editor of The Spiritual Side of Writing.*

"Many of you, like me, may not have the courage as yet to have arrived at vegetarianism as a total way of eating. No matter. "Peace in Every Bite" by Two Moons, N.D., has much to offer. I found this ample +300 page book to be full of information and surprises. One of the surprises, was that I did not have to throw out all the food and utensils in my kitchen to commence a move toward veganism. For less than fifty bucks, I could supplement my pantry with more healthy grains and other food products which undoubtedly enrich any lifestyle.

The recipes are interesting, fun and for the most part, simple to prepare, but I discovered more. I find myself using the book as a source of both understanding and preparing myriad healthy products, as abundantly seen in the "Charts and Instructions" section and "Guidelines, Tips, Charts and Miscellaneous".

Throughout we are challenged, often not so gently, as in the quote from John Robbins at page 10: "If Americans reduced their meat consumption by 10 percent, enough grain would be saved to feed sixty million people. That is close to the total number of people who die of hunger-related disease each year". I like that. It is a compelling prod of conscience that encourages me to move forward without beating me into submission to accept complete veganism.

The book is simple and understandable, not demeaning or demanding. Its greatest virtue for me is in its wisdom and resources. As is stated in the blurb, "a reference book for healthy lifestyles and sustainable practices". It also has a recipe for the finest, richest chocolate cake ever to pass your lips."

Rev. James L. Meyer, MA., JD. *Roman Catholic Priest and Founder, President and C.E.O. of Chalfonte Foundation in Michigan, U.S.A.*

"Although I have yet to try every tempting recipe in Peace In Every Bite, the ones I have prepared have blown me and my family away. The Zucchini Casserole and the Eggplant Salad are just two of our favourites-so far. Also, I love the fact that the book includes many interesting chapters and great points on the lifestyle, history, and even experience of a Vegan Lifestyle. This is more than just a cookbook, and I can't wait for the next one!"

Charlotte Lawrie, *Professional Chef and Photographer, Michigan, U.S.A.*

# PEACE IN EVERY BITE

*A Vegan cookbook.... with Recipes for a Healthy Lifestyle*

Two Moons, N.D.

*We at Trafford believe that it is the responsibility of us all, as both individuals
and corporations, to make choices that are environmentally and socially sound.
You, in turn, are supporting this responsible conduct each time you purchase a
Trafford book, or make use of our publishing services. To find out how you are
helping, please visit www.trafford.com/responsiblepublishing.html*

*Our mission is to efficiently provide the world's finest, most comprehensive
book publishing service, enabling every author to experience success.
To find out how to publish your book, your way, and have it available
worldwide, visit us online at www.trafford.com/10510*

*Printed on paper with minimum 30% post-consumer recycled fiber.
Trafford's print shop runs on "green energy" from solar, wind and other
environmentally-friendly power sources.*

www.trafford.com

North America & international
toll-free: 1 888 232 4444 (USA & Canada)
phone: 250 383 6864 ◆ fax: 250 383 6804
email: info@trafford.com

The United Kingdom & Europe
phone: +44 (0)1865 487 395 ◆ local rate: 0845 230 9601
facsimile: +44 (0)1865 481 507 ◆ email: info.uk@trafford.com

10 9 8 7 6 5 4 3

This book is dedicated to all those
interested in a healthier way
of eating and living.

# ACKNOWLEDGMENTS

I would like to thank the following family members and friends, for their support, encouragement and interest in this cookbook.

**Tomas**, for being the most grateful and complimentary diner, and for his patience when I typed out recipes and the cookie jar sat empty.

**Rachel**, for all of her computer, photographic and artistic skills in getting this book ready for publishing.

**Mara**, for her constant comment, " I can't wait until your recipes are in one book," and for her help and creative suggestions in that regard.

**Aaron**, for introducing me to John Robbins Book, *Diet for a New America*, and a vegan diet, and for his dedication and help with this book.

**Joseph**, for *that* one tip concerning the degree symbol, that saved me lots of time typing out recipes.

**Jacob, Daniel, Ryan and Nik** for photographic assistance.

**Marina**, for testing out recipes in the lower altitude of northern Ontario, Canada, and always being there to answer computer questions.

**Mom**, who doesn't mind her "flower child" converting family recipes to vegan.

**Beverly**, for always asking, "how's the cookbook coming," and for her generous help and suggestions with the near finished copy.

**Dawn & Brian**, who after much apprehension on my part, brought me into the modern age of computers.

Also, for their support and friendship: Rebekah, Erin, Debora, Eirene, Susan, Julia, Paula, Phaedra and Terezinha. Nancy, for sharing her knowledge of southwest, high desert herbs and other recipes. The Warped Shepherds fiber group and Apache Creek book club members, for accommodating my vegan diet and sharing recipes. Randy and Paula in northern Michigan and Philip in Mississauga, Ontario, for their inspiring vegan barbequing. And to all those folks back in Michigan, who dedicated one night a month for five years in the nineties, to a vegan potluck and drumming circle at our home. What fun, inspiring and delicious times those were.

*I'm also deeply grateful to the following people, whose words and/or life styles have been an inspiration in my life: Phra Ajahn Yantra Amaro and the residents at the Thai Buddhist Monastery in California, The Findhorn Community in Scotland, The Tennessee Farm Community, S.N. Goenka and the Vipassana Centers, James L Meyer and the Chalfonte community, Henry David Thoreau, Gandhi, Helen & Scott Nearing, Peace Pilgrim, John Robbins, Adelle Davis, Frances Moore Lappe, Jethro Kloss, Bernard Jensen, Victoras Kulvinskas, Gabriel Cousens, Thich Nhat Hanh, Deepak Chopra, Paul Bragg, Elson Haas, Theodore Baroody Jr., Eliot Coleman, Wendell Hoffman, Ruth Stout, J.I. & Robert Rodale, Herbert Shelton, Randolph Stone, Norman Walker, Samuel West and Anne Wigmore.*

# CONTENTS

# GUIDELINES, TIPS, CHARTS & MISCELLANEOUS

# INTRODUCTION

*"If there's no love in the kitchen, there's no life in the food."*

It seems that every magazine or newspaper that you look at today, has an article or news release on eating a healthy diet. According to Ode Magazine, " Blood pressure falls just three weeks after switching to a vegetarian, or highly varied diet …a healthy diet may be the cure for acne…what you eat and drink may directly affect your complexion." [1] AARP magazine stated, " for optimal heart health choose whole grain over processed white flour…eat at least five servings of fruits and vegetables daily" [2] and, "common household seasonings do double duty as health boosters."[3]

In the process of preparing and eating certain foods, we create the possibility for that organ, generally connected with the quote, "if there's no love in the kitchen, there's no life in the food," to be positively or adversely affected. If not the heart, perhaps other organs of the body; or an enhancement or deterioration in our mental and spiritual functions. Not that food is the be all and end all to good health. Stress, environmental pollution and accident related injuries are other factors. However, food and nutrition, along with love, should be one of the first things that we learn about in life.

When I first looked into a healthier way of eating, there was only one magazine that talked about the benefits of eating whole grains, herbs and non-processed foods; and that expounded on problems with chemicals in our food and environment and the benefits of a healthier lifestyle. It was published by J.I. Rodale and later by his son Robert. The magazine has changed quite a bit over the years, (since the passing of J.I. and Robert,) but back then it was just a vehicle in a simple, non-glossy format for J.I. Rodale to publish his ideas on diet and good health. Forty years later, those ideas, which were often considered quite fanatical, are now common and accepted concepts. Problems with our health are now being attributed to chemicals in our air and food. Organically grown foods have become mainstream. Research has shown that artificial colours and preservatives can have adverse affects in our bodies, and that whole grains, herbs and unprocessed foods contribute to a healthier way of being.

When natural foods, whole grains and vegetarian cooking first entered my life in the late nineteen sixties, whole foods and vegetarian cook books were almost impossible to find. The tiny health food store that I frequented, had a sparse selection of packaged foods, and little if any produce, compared to the large cooperative and privately owned natural food markets of today. As well, soy based meat substitutes, dairy alternatives and frozen vegetarian foods were not yet being marketed.

---

[1] Ode Magazine, Volume 5, Issue 1 Jan/Feb 2007, Pg. 65-67
[2] AARP Magazine, Jan/Feb 2006, Pg. 42
[3] AARP Magazine, Nov/Dec 2006, Pg. 16

My suburban kitchen looked much as it does today, like something out of "Little House on the Prairie," with a hand operated grain mill attached to the counter, whole wheat bread rising in a large wooden bowl, jars of sprouts greening in a sunny window and soybeans bubbling on the stove, ready to be made into tofu, or mixed with veggies in a casserole dish. My young son became the local Huck Finn, as he intrigued his friends into grinding the flour. Not unlike the story of the Little Red Hen, their hard work qualified them for a share of the bread or cookies that followed.

I was on a mission; to provide my family, myself and the neighbourhood kids with healthy alternatives, and the objective of not only eating differently, but also shopping differently. My cupboards were filled with raw seeds, nuts and dried fruit, instead of artificially coloured candies and other sugary treats. Until Halloween handouts became suspect of harmful intent, I gave out nutritious oatmeal raisin cookies and popcorn balls made with organic corn and maple syrup. My basement became a food cooperative, where natural grains and other foods were purchased in bulk and divvied up between the members. My kitchen turned into a testing ground, where Fanny Farmer and Joy of Cooking recipes took on a whole new look, with the inclusion of dark whole grains and flours and natural sweeteners. I started a bakery in that little kitchen. My five, seven, and nine year old children learned mathematics by measuring the ingredients for the baked goods, ordered by friends and family and packaged in brightly hand coloured brown paper sacks. In my spare time I passed out grape boycott information in support of Caesar Chavez and the farm workers, formed a cooperative babysitting service and worked at my fiber arts of spinning and weaving.

I started compiling recipes for a cookbook even back then, but raising and home schooling my children took first place. Then in 1981, inspired by the lives and writings of Henry David Thoreau and Scott and Helen Nearing, we moved to the countryside in Michigan, where organic farming and homestead survival skills were added to my daily routine. I was as well, presented with insights into living in harmony with the Earth, and Thoreau's idea of "living deliberately, to front only the essential facts of life, and see if I could learn what it had to teach, and not when I came to die, discover that I had not lived." It was here that I practiced ways of living that had not been routinely used in our culture for some time; such as living without electricity, indoor plumbing, television and other modern conveniences.

Eventually I put my basement food co-op skills and personal experience with medicinal herbs and natural healing to work, by managing a natural foods cooperative storefront, studying for numerous health related degrees, and setting up a Naturopathic practice. The idea for the cookbook followed me down to the sunny southwest state of New Mexico, where we continue to enhance our philosophy of a self-sufficient and sustainable lifestyle, and where I've taken on the roles of architect, designer and assistant builder of our solar and wind powered homestead, and the challenges of high desert gardening. I now create my vegan recipes in a round stone kitchen, which I helped build; or in a solar oven or wood fired horno on our patio; and test my creations on my husband Tomas, and friends and family that visit.

This cookbook is the result of almost forty years of experimentation. I've personally prepared and eaten every one of the recipes in this book. In that time period I went from a floundering vegetarian diet to a devoted vegan one. I raised seven children through those floundering vegetarian years, trying my best to introduce them to a different way of surviving on this planet, and with the idea that we should eat to live, rather than live to eat. In 1992, my twenty one year old son Aaron read John Robbins book, *Diet for a New America,* and converted to a vegan diet. Soon to follow in his footsteps was his eleven-year-old sister Mara, and then myself and my partner Tomas. Experimentation in the kitchen then took on a different, more challenging and healthier course.

This cookbook is about how to have peace in every bite; by choosing the healthiest ingredients, by eating foods that are grown in harmony with nature, and do the least harm to our environment. By preparing foods which have no animal products or animal by-products, we can sit down at our dinner tables with peace in our hearts, knowing that we're contributing to the health of our planet, the well being of ourselves, family and friends, and that we're not directly or indirectly responsible for harming any animal. By eliminating unhealthy foods and habits, and by incorporating healthful foods and positive attitudes and actions, well-being can be achieved. You'll find over five hundred great tasting recipes in this book. Some, like the traditional chocolate chip cookie, rice pudding and "cheese" cake, will make you wonder why you ever thought dairy or eggs was a necessary ingredient in any baked good. The veggie loaves, burgers, stir-fries and soups will satisfy any appetite. Your diet will be more varied and more delicious than ever. (The recipes in this book were created at 6700 feet. If you live below three thousand feet, it's very important that you refer to the section on altitude adjustments.) You'll find much more than recipes in this cookbook. You'll find charts and facts on ingredients and cooking preparations, numerous sections related to healthy lifestyles, and many tips on how to live a peaceful, self-sufficient and sustainable way of life.

A vegan diet *is* much more than a meatless and dairy less diet, and it's not just about food. It incorporates a different way of looking at ourselves and the world around us. It's about discovering what philosophies on a mental, moral and spiritual level harmonize with the natural order of things, and does the least harm to our environment, the Earth and the beings that inhabit her. It's a lifestyle where we can start making connections with our actions and how they can impact everything in the world. As this quote, inspired by Chief Seattle's speech of 1854 states: "All things are connected. Whatever befalls the Earth befalls the sons and daughters of earth. Man did not weave the web of life; he is merely a strand in it. Whatever he does to the web, he also does to himself." We have to ask ourselves; what kind of a footprint are we leaving as we make our way through each day, and what sort of footprint will we leave behind for future generations.

I hope you enjoy this book as much as I have enjoyed creating it. May you always eat foods that are nourishing and promote wellness. May you walk gently upon Mother Earth, and may your lives be filled with love, true inner peace and happiness.

Two Moons

# VEGETARIAN MYTHS & FACTS

*Medical science tended to scorn a vegetarian diet, in our recent past. Extensive research and positive results have now brought about quite a different picture. Following are a few myths and facts about vegetarianism.*

MYTH: Vegetarianism is a faddish diet espoused by a small group of radical people.

**FACT**: A 1994 report by Vegetarian Times magazine stated that l2.4 million Americans called themselves vegetarians; about one third more than a decade before. Many factors have contributed to this increase, including; <u>Interest in eastern spiritual philosophy and the back to nature movement</u>: 55 sq. feet of rainforest is consumed in every l/4 pound hamburger. <u>Environmental awareness:</u> it takes 50 times more fossil fuel to produce a meat-centered diet than vegetarian. According to a United Nations Food and Agricultural Organization report, cattle emit l8 percent of greenhouse gases; contributing to global warming even more than transportation. <u>Reverence for animals & animal rights and cruelty issues:</u> 500,000 animals are killed per hour for meat in the U.S. and thousands of animals are submitted to painful experimentation for the sake of cosmetic refinements. <u>Economy:</u> A low food budget survives far better and longer on a vegetarian diet. <u>Health reasons:</u> The growing awareness of the connection between diet and health. A meat-based diet has 55% pesticide residue; compared to l% with commercial grains. Studies conducted by Seventh Day Adventists and other groups support better health and long life claims.

MYTH: Vegetarians tend to be weak and their lives are shorter.

**FACT:** When George Bernard Shaw decided to become a vegetarian in his mid twenties, physicians warned him of an early grave. Shaw lived to a ripe old age of ninety-four. Peace Pilgrim walked more than 25,000 miles for world peace; crossing America for nearly three decades. Many vegetarians are breaking athletic records. Dave Scott won the Iron man triathlon six times. Edwin Moses was an Olympic Gold Medalist, for eight years in the 400-meter hurdles. Murray Rose, as a teen, became one of the world's greatest swimmers and later starred as Tarzan. Paavo Nurmi, the "Flying Finn" set twenty world records and won nine Olympic gold medals. Ron Hilligan won Mr. America; and Gayle Olinekova was a premiere women's long distance runner. Gabriel Cousens M.D. in his book *Conscious Eating,* stated: "that a vegetarian diet helps the body function at an endurance rate that is twice that of a flesh centered diet." Dr. Joteyko of the Academy of Medicine in Paris found that vegetarians had two to three times the endurance and took one-fifth the time to recover than meat eaters. Since most vegetarians eat diets containing more fiber and less refined sugar, health problems such as heart disease and colon cancer are less likely to develop.

MYTH: A vegan diet is boring and mainly consists of eating salads.

FACT: A vegan diet generally leads to an interest in foods that were previously overlooked. A wide variety of fruits, vegetables, beans, grains, meat substitutes and dairy alternatives contribute to an interesting, colourful and healthful diet.

MYTH: Those on a vegan diet tend to be deficient in B-12, iron, protein and calcium.

FACT: Seldom has a B-12 deficiency been found in those on a vegan diet. Research indicates that those who eat less meat actually need less B-12. Fermented soy foods, nutritional yeast, spirulina and sea vegetables contain substantial amounts of B-12, plus calcium. Organically grown foods can be higher in all nutrients. Eating dairy products in excess can actually block iron absorption. Protein isn't just in meat; it's in grains, legumes and vegetables too. Eating a varied diet with substantial calories can provide plenty of protein. A study done in China, where milk products and calcium intakes are low, found lower risks of osteoporosis in women than in American women. According to the USDA publication, "Nutritive value of American food," two thirds of a cup of collard greens has 91% of the calcium of a cup of milk. By eating leafy greens, seeds, nuts, soy products and sea vegetables, enough high quality calcium can be obtained. The high phosphorus to calcium ratio in meat, fish, poultry and soft drinks can actually cause lowered calcium in the blood.

By limiting or avoiding products such as alcohol, antibiotics, tobacco, caffeine, prescription and over the counter drugs and refined sugar, which can deplete many nutrients; and by eating a variety of foods, including: raw enzyme/chlorophyll rich foods and natural, whole grain products; and by chewing foods well to help release the enzymes, a vegetarian diet can provide the nutrients necessary for a healthy body.

MYTH: Vegetarian food is expensive, hard to find and difficult to prepare.

FACT: Natural food markets and food cooperatives worldwide offer a wide selection of vegetarian fare, as well as recipes, books and information on health. Local supermarkets have started offering soy-based meat substitutes and some organic produce. Many foods can be purchased in natural food markets from bulk bins, eliminating the fancy packaging. A vegetarian diet can actually be far less expensive than a meat and dairy based diet. We tend to require less in quantity of any food which is of high quality and organically grown, because it satisfies our nutritional needs more easily. By spending a little more for organically grown foods, we support a cleaner, chemical free environment; and in the process, help sustain our own and our families good health, thus avoiding costly medical bills. Many vegan cookbooks contain recipes that are not only delicious and fun to make, but easy and quick to prepare as well.

MYTH: We need to eat meat in order to survive on Earth.

FACT: Some of Earth's largest animals, such as the elephant, rhinoceros, elk, and cow, have survived quite nicely on grass and green plants. Albert Einstein said, "Nothing will benefit human health and increase the chances for survival of life on Earth as much as the evolution to a vegetarian diet. Taking into account that meat eating is a driving force behind every major category of environmental damage, now threatening our future; erosion, fresh water scarcity, air and water pollution, climate change, deforestation, biodiversity loss, social injustice and spread of disease; not eating meat is one of the most important things we can do to save the planet.

MYTH: If we didn't eat meat we'd be over run by animals.

FACT: Most meat is farm and factory bred and raised. The numbers are only as high as the demand. Animals in the wild have a natural birth control mechanism, which reflects the carrying capacity of their environment.

---

**Some famous vegetarians:** Hank Aaron, Louisa May Alcott, Joan Baez, Alec Baldwin, Bridgett Bardott, Bob Barker, Kim Basinger, Dr. Ruth Bates, Ed Begley Jr., Milton Berle, Candace Bergan, Linda Blair, Orlando Bloom, Boy George, Buddha, Peter Burwash, Shaun Cassidy, Julie Christie, Chelsea Clinton, Charles Darwin, Leonardo DaVinci, Doris Day, Danny DeVito, Harvey & Marilyn Diamond, Bob Dylan, Thomas Edison, Albert Einstein, Ralph Waldo Emerson, Michael J. Fox, St. Francis of Assisi, Benjamin Franklin, Richard Gere, Gandhi, Stephen Gaskin, Dick Gregory, Daryl Hannah, George Harrison, Woody Harrelson, Henry Hiemlich, Dustin Hoffman, Billie Idol, J.H. Kellogg, Billie Jean King, Coretta Scott King, Gladys Knight, Dennis Kucinich, K.D.Lang, Frances Moore Lappe, John Lennon, Howard Lyman, Toby Maguire, Ziggy Marley, Steve Martin, Peter Max, Linda McCartney, Sir Paul McCartney, Yoko Ono, Natalie Merchant, Moby, Edwin Moses, Joe Namath, Sir Isaac Newton, River, Summer & Joaquin Phoenix, Leonard Nimoy, Bill Pearl, Peace Pilgrim, Plato, Natalie Portman, Pythagoras, John Robbins, Fred "Mister" Rogers, Albert Schweitzer, Peter Sellers, George Bernard Shaw, Shelley, Alicia Silverstone, Russell Simmons, Upton Sinclair, Isaac Bashevis Singer, Dr. Benjamin Spock, Ringo Star, Gloria Steinem, Leo Tolstoy, Cicely Tyson, Vincent Van Gogh, Lindsay Wagner, Alice Walker, Donald Watson, Charlie Watts, Dennis Weaver, H.G.Wells, John Wesley, Ann Wigmore, Spice Williams.

**Resource:** partially from, www.famousveggie.com (5/07)

# SHOPPING FOR THE VEGAN PANTRY

BUY ORGANIC: The basic tenet of organic farming is to grow food without chemicals. Organically grown means that the food has been grown in practical, ecological partnership with nature. Organic food processors, handlers and retailers adhere to standards that maintain the integrity of organic agricultural products. The primary goal of organic agriculture is to optimize the health and productivity of interdependent communities of soil life, plants, animals and people. Doctors are now telling us that chemical residues are having a major impact on life. Pesticides are now being linked to cancer and neurological damage in young children. Wild life is adversely affected by chemicals, as are farm workers and their families. Many diseases can be linked to the toxins in our food, water and air. When we buy organic, we support organic growers, the health and well being of our families and Earth. Organic foods are sometimes more expensive, but by reducing or eliminating the chemicals in our diet, we reduce the likelihood of spending even more money on medical care in the future.

BUY LOCALLY PRODUCED FOOD: On an average our food travels thousands of miles from farm to factory to warehouse, to the supermarket and then to our plates. Grow some of your own veggies and herbs, or support the growers in your region, by buying locally produced foods, which helps reduce the amount of energy required for transporting.

BUY PRODUCE IN SEASON: Out of season produce is expensive and is probably being shipped from other countries. Make locally grown and in season produce a part of your menu planning.

AVOID IRRADIATED FOODS: Food irradiation is the process of using high levels of nuclear waste (cobalt-60 and cesium-137) generated by nuclear reactors, which kills insect larvae and many, though not all disease organisms. However, by destroying bacteria, which ordinarily signals spoilage through foul or "off" odors or tastes, irradiation masks the presence of other food-poisoning microbes. Irradiation is often concealing unsound practices in the food industry. As well, it destroys certain vitamins in food. Some supermarkets claim that irradiation preserves foods; while many scientists are saying irradiation makes foods unsafe, changes the molecular structure of food and destroys nutrients. New studies show that ingesting radiation-exposed food can cause genetic damage, which can lead to cancer and birth defects. *(Information from the Public Citizen newsletter and the Boycott Quarterly.)*

AVOID GENETICALLY MODIFIED FOODS: Mounting scientific evidence suggests that genetically engineered foods may present serious hazards to human health and the environment. Scientists warn that GE foods may set off allergies, increase cancer risks, produce antibiotic-resistant pathogens, damage food quality and produce dangerous toxins. Environmental hazards of genetically engineered crops, recently discussed in scientific journals and the media, include: increased use of toxic pesticides, damage to soil fertility, genetic pollution of adjoining farmlands, harm to Monarch butterflies and beneficial insects, such as ladybugs, and the creation of " super pests, super weeds" and virulent new plant viruses.

OTHER ITEMS TO AVOID: <u>Always read package labels for any known allergens or meat or dairy bi-products.</u>

Aluminum pots & pans: Aluminum salts are toxic and have been linked to brain cell damage and Alzheimer's disease. Use cast ironware, glass or stainless steel instead. When using aluminum foil, always use an under sheet of parchment paper, to protect the food.

Artificial colors: Many are proven allergens or carcinogenic.

Artificial flavours: Testing done on animals reveals adverse effects.

Artificial Sweeteners: Saccharin produced cancer in rats. Many artificial sweeteners on the market have not been fully tested for safety factors.

Hydrogenated or partially hydrogenated fats: As a saturated hardened fat, it is strongly linked to heart disease and cholesterol elevation.

Monosodium glutamate (MSG): Contains many common allergens know to produce headaches and other illnesses.

Sodium nitrate and nitrite: Can form cancer-causing agents in the stomach.

White flour and sugar: White flour has been processed to eliminate the best nutritive properties found in the bran and germ. White sugar is usually processed with animal bone char and chemically bleached.

SHOP AT NATURAL FOOD STORES: Products found at natural food stores generally don't contain the above ingredients. They tend to be more supportive of organic, non-irradiated and non-genetically modified foods, spices and herbs. Many of the ingredients in this book can only be found in natural food stores.

Avoid having to choose plastic or paper, by using cloth shopping bags. In the process you'll be helping to save our natural resources. Thrift stores are the best place to find large cloth bags at reasonable prices. Choose minimally processed and packaged foods. Buy foods from bulk bins, eliminating fancy packaging. Make cloth bags or reuse plastic bags, when buying from bulk bins. And above all, remember, that you may pay more for organically grown foods or products of higher quality, but in the process you'll be supporting a cleaner environment, a healthier body, and greatly reduce or eliminate doctor and medical bills of the future.

# BASIC STAPLES FOR THE VEGAN KITCHEN

*Most of these items don't require refrigeration. Store them in large glass jars or stackable containers. If unfamiliar with any product, see the dictionary of ingredients on page 297*

**Beans:** black beans, garbanzos, great northern, kidneys, lentils, limas, mung beans for sprouting, navy, pintos, split peas.

**Breads & Crackers:** hearty whole grain breads and crackers, graham crackers for pie crust, pita pocket bread, whole wheat tortillas or chapatis.

**Condiments etc:** apple cider vinegar, ume plum vinegar, rice vinegar, tamari soy sauce, Bragg liquid aminos, miso, mustard, ketchup, horseradish, vegan worcestershire sauce, sea salt, black pepper and herbal salt substitutes.

**Dried Veggies:** agar flakes, dulse flakes, kelp powder, other types of seaweed for soups, nori sheets, mushrooms, vegetable broth powder or veggie bouillon cubes.

**Flours:** whole wheat pastry (for desserts), whole wheat bread flour, cornmeal, buckwheat and rye; and arrowroot or cornstarch for thickeners.
For wheat free baking: rice, bean and tapioca flours, potato starch and xantham gum.

**Frozen Products:** soy ice cream, vegan sausages and burgers.

**Grains and Cereals:** barley, bulgur, cracked wheat, couscous, millet, rolled oats, long and short grain brown rice, popcorn, quinoa, wheat bran, granola, dry cereals and hot cereal mixes.

**Nuts & Dried Fruits and Seeds:** almonds, cashews, pecans, pine nuts, walnuts, caraway seed, sunflower seeds, sesame seeds, pumpkin seeds, apples, apricots, dates, figs, papaya, pineapple, prunes, raisins, unsweetened coconut flakes.

**Oils:** Buy only cold pressed oils. Safflower, sunflower or canola oil for baking; coconut, olive oil, grapeseed or sesame for sautéing; flax, sesame or olive oil for salad dressings; hot or plain toasted sesame oils for seasoning.

**Pasta:** spaghetti, lasagna, macaroni, spirals, orzo, Japanese udon and ramen noodles.

**Prepared Foods:** canned beans, tomatoes, sauces, salsa, vegan mayonnaise, jams & preserves, olives, sauerkraut, pickles and salad dressings.

**Soy, Rice and Gluten Products:** tofu, tempeh, non-hydrogenated vegan soy margarine, soy yogurt, vegan cheese, soy rice or nut milks, soy or gluten based meat substitutes.

**Spices and Herbs:** (buy non-irradiated spices and herbs) allspice, asafetida (hing), basil, bay leaf, black pepper, caraway seeds, cayenne, celery seed, chili powder, chili fiesta blend, cilantro, cinnamon, cloves, coriander, cumin, curry, dill weed, fennel, garlic powder, ginger, Italian seasoning, marjoram, mustard powder, mustard seeds, nutmeg, onion powder, oregano, paprika, parsley, peppermint, rosemary, saffron, sage, sea salt, spike seasoning blend, tarragon, thyme, turmeric.

**Sweeteners:** organic unbleached raw sugar, agave syrup, blackstrap molasses, barley malt syrup, maple syrup, stevia and brown rice syrup.

**Vegetables & Fruits:** (fresh) _The following will store well in a cool pantry:_ onions, garlic, parsnips, potatoes, sweet potatoes, turnips, pumpkin, winter squash, apples, bananas and pears. _It's preferable to keep the following in the refrigerator or a very cool root cellar:_ asparagus, beets, cabbage, carrots, eggplant, kale, lettuce, peas, radishes, spinach, sprouts, summer squash such as zucchini, sweet and hot peppers, Swiss chard, avocados, grapes, melons, papaya, peaches, plums, rhubarb, strawberries and other berries.

**Other Items:** aluminum free baking powder, baking soda, cocoa, carob powder, coconut milk, coffee substitutes made from roasted and ground grains, egg replacer powder, flax seeds, green & herbal teas, nut butters, sesame tahini, tvp, xantham gum, vanilla, almond, lemon and mint extract.

---

"If Americans reduced their meat consumption by 10 percent, enough grain would be saved to feed sixty million people. That is close to the total number of people who die of hunger-related disease each year!"
John Robbins - May All Be Fed

---

# THE A-Z OF BAKING & COOKING UTENSILS

*Here's a list of some handy utensils and appliances, for ease and efficiency in the kitchen.*

APRON:  To keep your clothes clean

BAKING PANS:    Cake pans, 8 x 8 & 9 x 13 inch, and round layer pans
Bread pans, 8-9 inch
Spring form pans, 8 inch or larger
Muffin tins
Cookie sheets  (also for baking granola, rolls, pizza and scones)
Pie pans, 8 inch and larger

BEATERS:  Electric and a wire whisk.

BLENDER:  For pureeing tofu, mixing beverages and much more.

CAKE TESTERS:  Toothpicks or metal cake testers.

CANNING KETTLE:  For ease in home canning of jams, fruits and veggies.

CASSEROLE DISHES:  Ovenproof dishes with lids; at least 1 qt. and larger.

CHOPPING DEVICES:  Electric and a good chopping knife.

CITRUS JUICER:  A hand or electric one for ease in juicing.

COLANDERS:  For draining liquid from pasta and vegetables.

COOKIE & SCONE CUTTERS:  Metal cutters, especially for rolled cookies.

COOLING RACKS:  Especially for cooling baked goods such as cookies and cakes.

COMPOST BUCKET:  For all those vitamin and mineral rich veggie and fruit scraps. Keep it under or close to your sink.  When it's full, empty it on an outdoor compost pile. Cover lightly with leaves or mulch.  Turn and water it periodically to produce a nutrient rich soil for your garden.  If you're concerned about attracting critters, consider purchasing a self-contained compost unit, which is vented, has a lid and can be secured to the ground.

CROCK POT:  A handy cooking devise for simmering soups and stews without standing over the stove.  It's especially convenient for those days when you must be away from home.

CUTTING BOARDS:  Label one specifically for cutting garlic and onion.

DOUBLE BOILER:  This is especially handy for cooking gravies or melting carob or chocolate.  It prevents the mixture from burning.

FLOUR MILL:  If you do a lot of baking, a grain mill is the best way to obtain fresh flour.  Keep purchased whole grain flours in a cool room or the refrigerator.  A small electric coffee grinder and some blenders can be used for coarse grinding of grains.

FOLEY FOOD MILL:  This is an old hand cranked devise that is invaluable for making apple and tomato sauces.  It fits over a bowl and the cooked fruit or veggies are put in the mill.  When the handle is turned the sauce comes out the bottom and into the bowl; and the skins and seeds stay in the mill to be emptied into the compost.  These mills can be found at flea markets, antique stores and purchased new through various mail order catalogues.

FUNNELS:  Plastic or glass funnels, to pour ingredients into serving jars. (Such as salad dressings and sauces.) Wide mouthed funnels, for canning foods.

GARLIC PRESS:  To finely mince fresh cloves of garlic.

GRATERS & GRINDERS:  Electric and hand operated for grating veggies.  An electric coffee mill works well for grinding nuts, herbs, seeds and spices.

HOT PADS & TRIVETS:  For taking dishes from the oven and serving at the table.

ICE CREAM MAKER:  A small electric ice-cream maker will accommodate all recipes.

JUICER:  Electric—for making your own fresh fruit and veggie juices.

KNIVES:  A variety of sharp knives, including one for paring, chopping and slicing.

MEASURING CUPS:  In a variety of sizes, from at least 1/4-1C.

MEASURING SPOONS:  A set of 1/8 tsp. – 1 TB. Measurements.

MIXING BOWLS:  In a variety of sizes.

OVEN THERMOMETER:  For checking the accuracy of your oven.

PARCHMENT PAPER:  When aluminum foil is necessary, wrap first with non-toxic parchment paper.

PEELER:  For peeling carrots, potatoes, apples etc. (when necessary)

PIE CRUST RINGS:  To prevent your tender piecrust from burning.

POTATO MASHER:  An old fashioned and useful devise, for mashing veggies.

POTS AND SAUCE PANS:  A variety of sizes for soups, stews, veggies and sautéing.  Avoid aluminum or Teflon coated ones.

PRESSURE COOKER:  A very helpful devise for cooking beans, grains and more.  Saves a lot of time and energy.  See page 273 for tips on pressure-cooking.

ROLLING PIN: For ease in rolling piecrust, cookie dough and scones, etc.

SCALE:  A kitchen scale to weigh pasta, veggies, or food for canning.

SKILLETS:  For sautéing and frying.  Heavy, cast-iron skillets are the best.

SOUP KETTLES:  Which can alternate for popping corn.  A heavy stainless steel pot, with a thick or copper bottom works best.  Avoid aluminum or Teflon coated ones.

SPATULAS: <u>metal ones</u>, for moving fried or sautéed foods from the skillet.
<u>Plastic spatulas</u> for scraping food from bowls and blenders.  <u>Heat proof spatulas</u> for stirring food in pots and pans, while on the stove.

SPOONS:  Large slotted spoons  - for scooping without the liquid.
                    Wooden & metal spoons for stirring and serving

SPROUTING CONTAINERS:  jars, trays or sprouting bags; for making delicious and chlorophyll rich seed and bean sprouts.

STEAMERS:  A collapsible unit that fits in a regular pot, or a pot specifically designed for steaming.

TIMER:  To remind you when to check on or remove something from the oven or stove.

TONGS:  For serving salad and pasta.

WATER PURIFICATION SYSTEM:  Pure water is essential for good health.  There are many systems available, some that attach to your faucet or sit on the counter top; and others that connect at the water source and purify all of your water needs.  Some options are: distillers, reverse osmosis and ozonators.

WOKS:  Great pots for stir-frying and more.

# PREPARATION & COOKING TERMS

CHOPPED: Similar to diced but shapes are less precise in size.

DICED: Veggies are cut in small cubes. Finely = approximately ¼ inch  Coarsely = ½ inch

MINCED: The technique is in between that of finely diced and ground. A press can be used for garlic.

SHREDDED: A knife or a grating device is used to produce very thin, short or long slices.

SAUTEING: Cooking veggies in a hot skillet containing a little oil. Water can be substituted for the oil, although the end result will be different.

SIMMER: Food is cooked at a gentle rather than a rolling boil.

STEAMING: Cooking vegetables in a basket or unit *above* boiling water.

STIR FRYING: Basically the same as sautéing, but usually refers to being done in a wok.

MEASUREMENTS:
| | |
|---|---|
| tsp. = teaspoon | TB. = tablespoon |
| C. = cup | oz. = ounce |
| lb. = pound | pkg. = package |

"Research is now clear and sufficient that the basic dietary guidelines taught to us as schoolchildren are wrong. Based on the knowledge we have today, we cannot go on recommending a diet based on the old four food groups....Evidence has shown that most people who eat according to the old four food groups die earlier and have a greater risk of serious illness than many of those who eat differently."

*The new four food groups proposed by the Physicians Committee for Responsible Medicine are:*

1. Whole grains (5 or more servings a day)
2. Legumes (2-3 servings a day)
3. Vegetable (3 or more servings daily)
4. Fruits (3 or more servings a day)

-Neal Barnard, M.D., at the 1991 conference sponsored by the Physicians Committee for Responsible Medicine.

# INGREDIENT SUBSTITUTES

*Want to make a quick substitution?  Try these suggestions.*

BRAGG LIQUID AMINOS:  Tamari soy sauce.

BROTH OR STOCK:  Replace liquid stock with water and broth powder or bouillon cubes.

CHILI FIESTA BLEND:  Substitute Chili Medley Blend, pg. 102.

COCOA POWDER:  Use chocolate chips or 1 square/1oz baking chocolate for every 3TB. cocoa, or substitute carob for chocolate allergies, and adjust amount of sweetener.

CORNSTARCH:  Use arrowroot, potato starch or any type of flour.

CURRY POWDER:  Mix to taste: ground ginger, cumin, coriander, fenugreek, turmeric and fennel.

EGG REPLACER POWDER:  *Many desserts can be made without the use of an egg substitute.*
* 1/4 C. pureed tofu (for each TB. Egg replacer powder.)
* 1 tsp. flaxseed meal mixed with 1/4 C. hot water and set aside for 5 minutes (for each TB. replacer.)
* Add more baking powder.
* Use cornstarch for thickening puddings.
* Agar-agar flakes are effective in some cakes and pies.

GARLIC, FRESH:  1 clove = 1 tsp. minced or 1/2 tsp. dried powder.
Or use a pinch of asafetida (hing) powder, to replace garlic and onion.

HERBS:  (Fresh) Use 1/2 tsp. dry or 1/4 tsp. powdered, for each TB. of fresh.

HING POWDER (Asafetida) : Fresh or dried garlic and onion.

KETCHUP:  Use tomato sauce.

LEMON & LIME JUICE: (fresh) Use the same amount of bottled juice. One large lemon or lime = 2-3 TB. juice.

OILS:  In baking:  Soy margarine, or use all or part applesauce.
In sautéing:  Use non-hydrogenated soy margarine, vegetable stock, juice or water.

SALT: Use one of the following or a combination of: tamari soy sauce, liquid Aminos, spike, an unsalted herbal seasoning blend, or salty ume plum vinegar.

SESAME OIL: Sauté 1 TB. sesame seeds in 1/2 C. regular vegetable oil. For hot toasted, use toasted sesame oil, and add some hot pepper.

SOY MILK: Use other vegan milks made of rice, nuts, oats etc. or use 2 TB. dry soy or rice milk powder mixed with 8 oz. water. **Note**: Use <u>un</u>sweetened milks in casseroles and main dishes.

SOY SAUCE: Where soy sauce is stated in recipes, Tamari soy sauce is recommended. It is made from naturally fermented soybeans. Bragg Liquid Aminos can be substituted.

SWEETENERS: Wherever dry sweeteners are called for, an organic, unbleached cane sugar was used. Other dry sweetener options include: date sugar, succanat, turbinado sugar and fructose. Brown sugar is usually just white sugar with a little molasses added for colouring. Processed white and confectioners sugar may be refined through animal bone ash.

**Other sweetening options are:**
* Blackstrap Molasses: Very sweet with a strong flavour. Use sparingly.
* Maple Syrup, Agave syrup, barley malt and fruit juice or concentrates:
  Use 2/3-3/4 C. for every cup of dry sweetener, or to your taste preference.
* Fruit juice or pureed fruit, such as bananas or apples, can replace 1/2 or more of other sweeteners.
* Stevia, which is of plant origin, can be used. It is powerfully sweet and comes in tiny bottles of liquid or powder. Follow the bottle directions, or use: 1/3-1/2 tsp. powdered or 1/2-3/4 tsp. liquid stevia; for each cup of regular dry sweetener. Sweeten individual servings of beverages with just a drop or two. Replace only part of the sweetener in baked goods, or experiment with recipe adjustments. Stevia is well tolerated in Candida/yeast conditions.

TAMARI: Substitute Bragg Liquid Aminos, other naturally fermented soy sauces, spike, regular sea salt, or a salt-less herbal mixture.

THICKENERS: For each tablespoon of wheat flour used for thickening, use the same amount of cornstarch, arrowroot, agar flakes or powder, tapioca, rice or other flours. A very small amount of xantham gum powder (1/8-1/4 tsp.) can be used for thickening salad dressings and in wheat free baking. <u>**Note:**</u> In desserts, cornstarch works better for thickening <u>non</u>-acid fruits. Use unbleached white or whole wheat pastry flour for acid type fruits, such as blueberries.

WHEAT: Substitute: barley, buckwheat, corn, kamut, oats, rye, spelt; bean, potato, rice and tapioca flour. See guidelines for a wheat free diet, pg. 274

# INSTRUCTIONS FOR COOKING GRAINS

*Use the smaller quantity of water listed, in altitudes below 3,000 feet.*

**AMARANTH:**     Cook 1 C. amaranth in 1½-2 C. water for 20 minutes.

**BARLEY:**     Cook 1 C. barley in 2½-3 C. water for 60 minutes.

**BULGUR:**     Pour 1-1¼ C. boiling water over 1 C. bulgur and cover for 30-40 min.

**KAMUT:**     Soak 1 cup kamut in water overnight. Drain and add 2-3 cups boiled water. Cover and cook for 40 minutes.

**MILLET:**     Add 1 cup millet to 3-3½ C. boiling water. Cover, lower heat and cook 30 minutes.

**OATS:**     Cook 1 cup oat groats or oatmeal in 2-3 C. water. Groats take 20-30 minutes and oatmeal takes 10-15.

**QUINOA:**     Cook 1 cup quinoa in 2-2½ C. water, for 15-20 minutes.

**RICE:**     Cook 1 cup brown rice in 2-2½ C. water for approximately 45 minutes. Bring to a boil first, then lower the heat so that the rice simmers slowly.

**WHEAT:**     Cook 1 C. cracked wheat in 2½-3 C. boiling water, for approximately 20 minutes, or until wheat is soft.

**WILD RICE:**     Cook 1 C. rice with 2-2½ C. water for 45 minutes.

**Note:** *Grains can also be cooked slowly in a crock-pot, or quickly in a pressure cooker.*

*See the Dictionary of Ingredients on page 297, for specifics on each grain.*

# COOKING GUIDE FOR BEANS

*Soak beans overnight before cooking, unless otherwise noted. The following beans don't need to be soaked: Red and green lentils, split peas and adzuki beans. Don't cook beans in their soaking water, which contains large amounts of indigestible natural sugars. Drain beans and replace with fresh water. For age-old methods of gas prevention, add a pinch of ginger or asafetida (hing) to cooking water. When pressure cooking split peas, add 1 tsp. of vegetable oil, to help reduce foaming.*

| *(1 cup dry beans)* | *Water* | *Stovetop* | *Pressure cooker* | <u>Yield</u> |
|---|---|---|---|---|
| ADZUKI * | 3 ¼ C. | 45-60 min | 10 min. | 3 C. |
| BLACK | 3 C. | 1-1 ½ hr. | 15-20 min. | 2 ¼ C. |
| CHICKPEAS (Garbanzos) | 4 C. | 1 ½-2 hr. | 25-30 min. | 2 C. |
| GREAT NORTHERN | 3 ½ C. | 45-60 hr. | 10-15 min. | 2 1/3 C. |
| KIDNEYS | 2 ¼ C. | 60 min. | 20 min. | 2 ¼ C. |
| LENTILS * | 3 C. | 30 min. | 7-10 min. | 2 ¼ C. |
| MUNG | 2 ½ C. | 45-60 min. | 10-15 min. | 2 C. |
| NAVY | 3 C. | 45-60 min. | 6-8 min. | 2 2/3 C. |
| PINTO | 3 C. | 60 min. | 14-20 min. | 2 2/3 C. |
| SOY | 4 C. | 2 ½-3 hr. | 30-45 min. | 2 C. |
| SPLIT PEAS * | 3 C. | 45-60 min. | 8-12 min. | 2 C. |

*** Un-soaked**

## MEASURING REFERENCE & METRIC CONVERSION

**U.S. MEASURMENTS**

| | | |
|---|---|---|
| 3 tsp. (teaspoons) | = | 1 TB. (Tablespoon) |
| 1 ½ tsp. | = | 1/2 TB. |
| 2 TB. | = | 1/8 C. (cup) |
| 4 TB. | = | 1/4 C. |
| 5+ 1/3 TB. | = | 1/3 C. |
| 8 TB. | = | 1/2 C. |
| 16 TB. | = | 1 C. |
| 1 C. | = | 8 fluid ounces |
| 1 C. | = | 1/2 Pint |
| 2 C. | = | 1 Pint |
| 4 C. (2 pints) | = | 1 Quart |
| 4 Quarts | = | 1 Gallon |

**METRIC CONVERSION**

| | | |
|---|---|---|
| 1/4 tsp. | = | 1 ¼ ml. (milliliters) |
| 1/2 tsp. | = | 2 ½ ml. |
| 1 tsp. | = | 5 ml. |
| 2 tsp. | = | 10 ml. |
| 1 TB. | = | 15 ml. |
| 1/4 C. | = | 60 ml. |
| 1/2 C. | = | 120 ml. |
| 1 C. | = | 235 ml. |
| 2 C. | = | 470 ml. |
| 1 fluid oz. | = | 30 ml. |
| 1 Pint (U.S) | = | 470 ml. |

**OVEN TEMPERATURES**   *(Fahrenheit to Celsius)*

| | | | |
|---|---|---|---|
| 250° F. | = 121°C. | 375°F. | = 191°C. |
| 300° F. | = 149°C. | 400°F. | = 204°C. |
| 325° F. | = 163°C. | 425°F. | = 218°C. |
| 350° F. | = 177°C. | 450°F. | = 232°C. |

# ALTITUDE ADJUSTMENTS

*The recipes in this cookbook were developed at 6700 feet altitude. At sea level to 3,000 feet the increased air pressure makes it necessary to make some ingredient changes, especially with baking. The best way to determine the changes necessary is to follow the original recipe; and then experiment by increasing some ingredients and decreasing others, as it is difficult to give the amounts accurate for all altitudes.*

## SOME SUGGESTIONS FOR SEA LEVEL TO 3,000 FEET

- Roasting and sautéing are not affected by altitude changes.
- Decrease flour in cakes by 10-20%, or increase the liquid.
- Increase baking powder or soda by 25-50%
- Decrease liquid for pie dough by 10-20%.
- Use 25% more sweetener, or approximately 2-3 TB. more per cup of sweetener.
- Use 25-50% more yeast in bread recipes.
- Increase length of rising time for yeast breads.
- Some baked goods will have better results, if oven temperature is decreased by 15-25°.
- Use 1/4 cup less for each cup of water, when cooking rice or other grains.
- For some causes of poor results with baked goods, refer to the dessert section.
- Experiment and record your results for future reference.

## MORE TIPS FOR BAKING AND COOKING

The altitude of the land isn't the only factor which can affect the results of preparing some foods. When pertaining to fruits and vegetables, much depends on the freshness, juiciness and sweetness. Thus, any added sweetener, thickeners, or spices, might need adjusting. The recipes in this cookbook use far less sweetener than normally prescribed, allowing for the natural sweetness of fruits and grains instead. Your taste preference for salt or sweetening may be more or less. As well, the pots, pans, stove, and even the weather conditions can affect the end result. Keep this in mind when you are using any recipe. Considering that numerous studies have shown that microwaving can alter the frequency of food and destroy valuable enzymes, it's a healthier option to use the heat sources of solar, wood or gas. Use all of your senses when you cook; check for freshness and potency of dried herbs and spices, smell, taste and adjust any seasonings. Season lightly at first; it's far easier to add more than to take away. Success in the kitchen also has much to do with intuition and trial and error; so don't be afraid to experiment, and develop your own unique recipes. Above all, the most important ingredient in any kitchen is a peaceful and loving attitude.

# Breads

# YEASTED BREADS

**TIPS ON BREAD BAKING:**

* When baking at altitudes of 3,000 feet or less, refer to altitude adjustment tips on page 20.

* If yeast and other ingredients have been stored in a cold place, let them come to room temperature before proceeding with any recipe. For altitudes at sea level-3000 ft, add an extra teaspoon of bread yeast in each recipe.

* Rising time will vary depending on altitude. In lower altitudes rising will take longer.

* All bread recipes can be "sponged" as in the whole wheat bread recipe. Sponging helps to activate the mixture and reduce the amount of kneading generally required.

* Don't mix all of the flour together at once. This could produce a very dry mixture. Always add the flour gradually, adding only as much as is needed to form the dough into a smooth ball. Save some of the flour to sprinkle on the counter and knead the bread on it. Work in more flour if the dough is sticky.

* If you accidentally add too much flour, work some more liquid into the mixture until it is of desired consistency, or soft enough to form a ball.

* Wheat free breads can be made, by eliminating the wheat flours and substituting a mixture of rice, tapioca and bean flours, potato starch and xantham gum. See page 274 for "Guidelines for a Wheat Free Diet."

* For delicious un-yeasted bread, for making sandwiches and toast, see the Irish Soda Bread recipe in the Quick Breads Section.

* Another baking idea is to place the dough in a bread pan and immediately put it in a cold oven, without letting it rise to the top of the pan. Turn the oven dial to the temperature given in recipe and let the bread slowly rise and bake as the oven heats up.

## POOR RESULTS & CAUSES

<u>Overly yeasty smell and taste:</u> Too much yeast, or too long in rising. <u>Dry texture:</u> Too much flour added, or baked too long. <u>Soggy in center:</u> Insufficient baking time.
<u>Heaviness:</u> Insufficient kneading or rising time. Yeast could be dead.
<u>Loaf falls:</u> Too long in rising, or inadequate kneading. Oven could be too cold, or pan too small for size of loaf. <u>Holes or spaces in bread, especially near top of crust:</u> Insufficient time spent in kneading or forming loaf, or too long in rising.

**MAKING THE SPONGE:** The sponge is the batter containing yeast, liquid, sweetener and _part_ of the flour. (Salt can be added after sponging) Stir the ingredients together for a couple of minutes, until well combined. The consistency is that of thick cake batter. This process can be omitted, but because the sponge stretches in rising, it does decrease the hard work of kneading the dough. Sponging can be done with any bread recipe. Cover the sponge and let it sit for 30-60 minutes in a warm, draft free place. Other baked goods can be made while the dough rises.

**KNEADING THE BREAD:** If you followed the previous sponging method, make sure you add salt and additional flour before proceeding with the kneading process. Sprinkle the counter with a dusting of flour. Turn the ball of dough from the bowl onto the counter. Put the base of your palms on the dough. Push it down and away from you with a rocking motion. Add more flour if the dough is sticky. Fold and roll and push the dough, until it's smooth and elastic in feel and forms into a ball.

**BREAD DOUGH RISING:** The kneaded dough is now left to rise for an hour or more in a draft free place, or until about double in size. Lightly oil the top of dough and cover with a towel. Gently punch dough when it has finished rising, and form into desired shapes. Let dough sit 30-60 minutes longer, before baking in a preheated oven.

**BREAD SHAPE IDEAS:**
* Shape to fit the size of a lightly oiled bread pan.
* Form into a long thin, French type loaf and place on a lightly oiled cookie sheet.
* Form into one or two round loaves and bake on a lightly oiled sheet.
* Roll dough out as thin as possible in a rectangular shape. Sprinkle with chopped fruit, nuts and sweetener, and then roll and form dough into a round tube. Bake whole or cut into rounds and place cut side up on a lightly oiled cookie sheet.
* Divide dough into thin long ropes. Braid, tie knots, twist or make spirals, for pretty dinner rolls.

"To supply one person with a meat habit, food for a year, requires three-and-a-quarter acres. To supply one lacto-ovo vegetarian with food for a year requires one-half acre. To supply one pure vegetarian requires only one-sixth of an acre. In other words, a given acreage can feed twenty times as many people eating a pure vegetarian (vegan) diet-style, as it could people eating the standard American diet-style."

John Robbins - Diet For A New America

# WHOLE WHEAT BREAD

2 tsp. bread yeast
3 C. lukewarm water
1 ½ C. uncooked hot cereal mix or cracked wheat (optional)
1/4 C. sweetener
1 TB. sea salt
3-4 C. whole wheat bread flour

1. Dissolve yeast in lukewarm water.
2. Stir in cereal mix, sweetener and 2 C. of the flour.
3. This will make a slightly soupy batter, which will be covered
and let to "sponge" for at least 1 hour or longer.
4. After the 1 hour stir in the additional flour and salt, adding the flour
in small quantities, only until the mixture forms a soft ball.
5. Knead the ball of dough until smooth and elastic.
6. If you want a lighter loaf, let this ball sit another hour-to rise and then
proceed to number 8.
7. For a heavier loaf, form the ball of dough into a loaf size shape now.   Preheat oven
to 350°
8. Place dough in lightly oiled bread pan and let rise in a warm, draft free place, until the
dough reaches the top of the bread pan.
9. Bake in a preheated oven for 50-60 minutes and until loaf is browned on top.
Tap bottom of loaf when removed from pan.  It should have a slightly hollow sound when
done.  Makes 1 large loaf.

**Note:** *For a lighter loaf, eliminate the cereal mix and use an additional 1-2 cups of bread flour.  Other Suggestions:  Add ½-1 C. cornmeal or leftover cooked cereal.*

---

**TIP: Test or " proof " yeast before making bread:** *To make sure yeast is still alive, add a little sweetener and yeast to ¼ C. lukewarm water.  If it doesn't bubble or show some activity on the surface of the water, within a few minutes, then the yeast is either old and dead, or the water used was too hot or too cold.*
**To test bread for doneness:** *Turn the bread out on a cutting board, after it has baked the required amount of time.  It should sound slightly hollow when taped firmly with a finger.  The top and bottom of loaf should be browned and firm to the touch.  Cool the loaf on a rack.*
**Storing breads:** *Make sure that breads are completely cooled before bagging.  Breads can be stored for a couple of days in a cool room, but should then be refrigerated to prevent mold from developing.*

## RAISIN NUT BREAD

2 tsp. bread yeast
2 C. lukewarm water
1/2 C. sweetener
3 TB. vegetable oil
1 tsp. salt
5-6 C. whole wheat bread flour

1 TB. cinnamon
1 C. raisins
3/4 C. chopped nuts

1. Dissolve yeast in 2 C. lukewarm water.
2. Add sweetener, oil and salt.
3. Gradually beat in 3 C. of flour and set aside for 1/2-1 hour.
4. Add cinnamon, raisins and nuts, stirring well to combine.
5. Add only enough of the remaining whole wheat flour, until a smooth ball can be formed.
6. Knead ball until smooth. Let ball rise for approximately 1 hour.
7. Shape into one large or two small loaves.
8. Place in lightly oiled pan(s). Let rise to top of pan.
9. Bake in a preheated 350° oven for 50-60 minutes.
Makes l large or 2 small loaves.


## CRACKED WHEAT/OATMEAL BREAD

1 C. cracked wheat
3 C. very hot or boiled water
1 ½ C. rolled oats
2-4 C. whole wheat bread flour
1/3 C. vegetable oil

1/4 C. dry sweetener
1/8 C. blackstrap molasses
2 tsp. bread yeast, dissolved
   in 1/2 C. lukewarm water
2 tsp. salt

1. Soak cracked wheat in the 3 C. very hot or boiled water and let cool to lukewarm.
2. Add oatmeal and 2 C. flour plus all other ingredients, stirring to combine well.
3. Let this batter sit to "sponge" at least l hour.
4. Add enough additional whole wheat flour to make a stiff dough.
5. Knead dough into a smooth ball, adding more flour if necessary.
6. Let dough rise for one hour, then form into loaves or rolls.
7. Let dough rise to top of bread pans before baking 50-60 or 20-25 minutes for rolls, in a
preheated 350° oven. Makes 1 large or 2 small loaves.

"Let your food be your medicine....let your medicine be your food." - Hippocrates

## PUMPERNICKEL RYE BREAD

2 medium size potatoes (cooked)
2 tsp. bread yeast
1/2 C. lukewarm water (can use water from steamed potatoes)
1 tsp. sweetener
3 C. lukewarm water
1/2 C. blackstrap molasses
3/4 C. cornmeal
1 TB. caraway seeds
3 TB. vegetable oil
1 TB. salt
4 C. rye flour
3-4 C. whole wheat bread flour

1. Mash potato when cooled.
2. Dissolved the yeast in the ½ C. lukewarm water. Add sweetener, rest of water, potatoes, molasses, cornmeal, caraway seeds, oil and salt and mix well.
3. Add all of rye flour and half of wheat flour, stirring well.
4. Add enough additional wheat flour to form a stiff ball and knead until smooth.
5. Cover and let rise 1 - 2 hours.
6. Shape into one large lightly oiled loaf pan or form into 1-2 rounds on lightly oiled cookie sheets.  Let rise an additional 20-40 minutes.   Preheat oven to 375°.
7. Bake 50-60 minutes or until done.  Makes l large loaf or 1-2 small rounds.


## OLD WORLD RYE BREAD

2 tsp. bread yeast
2 C. lukewarm water
1/4 C. blackstrap molasses
2 tsp. salt
2 TB. caraway  seeds
2 TB. vegetable oil
2 C. rye flour
1/4 C. cocoa
2-3 C. whole wheat bread flour

Combine yeast, water and molasses.  Add salt, caraway seeds, oil, rye flour, cocoa and enough whole wheat flour, added in ½ cup increments, to be able to knead into a smooth ball of dough. Let rise 1-2 hours.  Shape into a round loaf and place on a lightly oiled cookie sheet, or bake in a loaf pan.  Let rise an additional 30 minutes, or until the dough reaches the top of pan.  Bake at 375° for 45 minutes, or until done. Makes l large round loaf.

## FRENCH BREAD

2 tsp. baking yeast
3 C. lukewarm water
3 TB. sweetener
1 TB. salt
1 C. whole wheat pastry flour
3-4 C. whole wheat bread flour

1. Dissolve yeast in the water with sweetener.
2. Stir in the salt and flour, adding one cup of flour at a time, until the mixture forms a soft ball of dough.
3. Knead the dough on a lightly floured surface until it is smooth and no longer sticky. Place the dough in a bowl, cover and let rise in a warm place, about one hour.
4. Punch dough down and form into one long, large loaf or two small narrow loaves. Cut ½ inch deep, diagonal slashes, every 2-3 inches along length of loaf. Place the loaves on a lightly oiled cookie sheet that has been sprinkled with cornmeal. Cover and let rise another 30-45 minutes.
5. To approximate the texture of commercially produced French bread, after rising, carefully spray the loaves with water, * tilting the sheet to remove excess water. Place wet loaves immediately in 400° oven. Bake for 30-40 minutes or until browned and done. Length of baking time will differ depending on size of loaves. Spray loaves again half way through baking.
Makes 1 large or 2 small loaves.
* **Note:** *Loaves can be thoroughly wetted by holding them under the kitchen sink faucet or sprayer.*

<u>Easy Garlic Bread</u>: *Mix 1/2 C. softened soy margarine or olive oil with as much granulated, powdered or fresh squeezed garlic as you prefer. Cut French bread into serving size pieces and lather each piece with margarine/garlic mixture. Put pieces back together to form loaf shape and wrap in parchment paper and then foil. Heat in 350° oven for 10-15 minute or until warm.*

---

" I am convinced that a proper diet is essential for maintaining or regaining one's physical well-being. It would seem that the converse is also true: an unbalanced diet, top heavy with fat, protein, and toxins like cigarettes, drugs and alcohol, stifles health and is the foundation of many of the diseases seen in western countries today. The time has arrived when people must take these facts and observations seriously, and re-examine their own diets and lifestyles."
Michael Klaper, M.D. - Vegan Nutrition Pure and Simple

# SOURDOUGH BREAD

**The Starter:**

In a bowl mix together 1 TB. bread yeast, and 2 C. lukewarm water. Let this sit one minute before adding 2 C. whole wheat bread flour. Stir until smooth and sticky. Let sit, lightly covered, in a warm place for 2-3 days, until frothy. After souring process, if you are not ready to use the mixture, refrigerate it in a jar, so that it's about half full. After making the bread, store the remaining starter in the fridge. If you're not going to use your starter at least one time within a two-week period, it can be stored in the freezer.

**MAKING THE BREAD:**

1 C. sourdough starter
2 C. lukewarm water
2 tsp. salt
1 TB. sweetener
4-5 C. whole wheat flour

1. If starter has been in fridge, set in a bowl and let it come to room temperature before adding remaining ingredients.
2. Add lukewarm water, salt, sweetener and flour; adding flour in one cup increments and only until dough can be formed and kneaded into a smooth, firm ball.
3. Cover ball of dough with a cloth and let it rise in a warm place for 1-2 hours, or until dough has almost doubled in size.
4. Form into one large loaf or rolls. Place in a lightly oiled bread pan. Let rise again another 30 minutes, or until dough reaches top of pan. Bake in preheated 350° oven for one hour, (20 minutes for rolls) or until golden brown and done. Makes l large loaf or 12-18 rolls.

**Replenishing starter:** *The starter is the important element of sourdough bread. Replenish starter after each cup that you take out for making bread. This way you will never run out. Add to jar containing the original starter mix; 1 C. lukewarm water and 1 C. flour, for every cup of starter that was used. Sit the jar in a warm place 8-12 hours, and then return to refrigerator.*

---

"The refined, degerminated, demineralized, and devitalized foods are a curse to humanity. The miller in making white flour takes out the vital portion, or the parts that makes a new plant---the wheat germ, and also the bran, parts that contain the minerals and vitamins which supply our bodies with blood making material."

Jethro Kloss - Back to Eden (first published in 1939)

---

# HERBAL WHOLE WHEAT ROLLS OR BUNS

2 tsp. baking yeast
1 ½ C. lukewarm water
1 TB. sweetener
1 tsp. salt
1/2 C. vegetable oil
3-4 C. whole wheat bread flour
2 tsp. dried herbs. (a combination of oregano, basil and dill)
1 tsp. garlic powder
1 TB. dry parsley

1. Dissolve yeast in warm water.  Add sweetener.
2. Add salt, oil and two cups of flour along with herbs, garlic powder and parsley.  Mix together well.
3. Add as much of the remaining flour to form a smooth ball of dough.  Knead dough on floured surface, until smooth.  Add more flour if dough is too sticky.
4. Let dough rise for about l hr.
5. Break pieces from dough, forming 12-18 dinner rolls or 6-7 burger buns.  Place on a lightly oiled cookie sheets.  Let rise an additional 30-60 minutes.
6. Bake in a preheated 375° oven for 15-20 minutes or until golden brown.
Makes 12-18 dinner rolls or 6-7 burger buns.

**Note:** *Turn any of the yeasted breads into rolls or buns.*
**VARIATION:** Plain whole wheat rolls or buns: *Eliminate the herbs.*

"Everything that goes into the mouth should be nourishing.  This is one of the most important things to consider.  What does not nourish is so much dross, which works the digestive and eliminative organs of the body for no return.  In many people, these organs are already broken down from overwork.  If you are living to eat, there is a possibility your pleasure may be short lived.  Better eat to live now."
Bernard Jensen PhD. - Food Healing For Man

# CINNAMON ROLLS

1/2 C. raisins
1 C. hot water
3 TB. vegetable oil
3 TB. sweetener
1/2 tsp. salt
2 tsp. bread yeast, dissolved in
1/4 C. lukewarm water

1½ C. whole wheat bread flour
1½ C. whole wheat pastry flour
2-3 TB. cinnamon
1/4-1/2 C. chopped walnuts or pecans
1/4-1/2 C. sweetener (optional)

1. Soak raisins in 1 C. hot water.
2. Stir oil, 3 TB. sweetener and salt into raisin mixture.
3. When lukewarm to the touch, add the yeast dissolved in ¼ C. water, and 1½ C. bread flour.
4. Stir in just enough pastry flour to knead into a smooth ball of dough.
5. Let dough rise for approximately 1 hour. Preheat oven to 350°.
6. Roll dough out into a rectangle shape, approximately 10x16 inches.
7. Sprinkle with cinnamon, chopped nuts and optional sweetener.
8. Roll dough into a round tube, starting at the narrower end.
9. Slice into 10-12 round pieces. Place cut side down in a liberally oiled cake pan. For a sweeter roll, follow the sticky bun directions below.
10. Let rise an additional 30 minutes. Bake in a preheated 350° oven for 25-30 minutes, or until lightly browned. Makes 10-12 cinnamon rolls

**VARIATIONS**: Jam Rolls: *Jam, fruit butter or preserves can be spread on dough instead of using raisins, nuts and cinnamon.* Sticky buns: *Mix in a saucepan, 1/2 C. sweetener, 1/4 C. soy creamer or milk, and 2 Tb. soy margarine. Bring to a boil, stirring constantly, until the margarine melts. Pour mixture into a 9 x 13" baking pan. Lay rolls on top and proceed with direction #10 above.*

# ENGLISH MUFFINS

* Use the recipe for whole wheat bread, pg. 24 or raisin nut bread recipe, pg. 25.
* After the ball of dough has risen, roll out about 1/2 " thick, on board sprinkled lightly with cornmeal
* Cut with 3" or larger cookie cutter, or form into 3-4 inch discs, and place 2" apart on cookie sheet. Let rise 1/2 hour.
* Bake muffins slowly on a very lightly oiled med/ hot griddle-- about 10 minutes on each side. Cool on rack. To serve, split muffins and toast. Makes 9-12 muffins.

## POCKET PITA BREAD

2 tsp. bread yeast
1 TB. sweetener
2 ½ C. lukewarm water
1 ½ tsp. salt
1 TB. oil
5-6 C. whole wheat bread flour

1. Dissolve yeast and sweetener in water.
2. Add salt, oil and 3 cups of flour, stirring to combine well. Let mixture sit for 30 minutes.
3. Add only enough additional flour to make a soft ball of dough.
4. Knead dough 5-10 minutes, or until smooth. Let dough rise 45-60 minutes.
5. Divide dough into 12 pieces, and knead each piece into a smooth ball. Let the balls sit for 30 minutes before rolling into thin rounds, approximately six inches across. Leave pieces to rise on cookie sheets lightly dusted with cornmeal, for 30-45 minutes.
6. Bake pitas in a pre-heated 475° oven, on the lowest shelf, for approximately 6-8 minutes, or until slightly browned and puffed in the middle. They will flatten when removed from the oven. Makes 12 pitas.

## BAGELS

* Use the whole wheat bread recipe pg. 24, herbal rolls pg. 29, or raisin nut bread recipe pg. 25. After the kneading and rising process, divide the dough into 9 pieces.
* Form each piece of dough into a ball. Flatten each ball to about 4 inches across, and with a finger put a hole in the center of each piece. Set bagels aside to rise for 20-30 minutes.
* In a large soup pot bring 4 quarts of water to a rolling boil. Add 2 TB. dry sweetener to the water. Drop 2-3 bagels at a time into the boiling water, and remove carefully with a slotted spoon after 2-3 minutes. Place each boiled bagel on a lightly oiled cookie sheet. Cool for 5 minutes, then bake in a preheat 450° oven for approximately 20 minutes, or until browned and firm. Makes 9 bagels.

"The average age (longevity) of a meat eater is 63. I am on the verge of 85 and still work as hard as ever. I have lived quite long enough and I am trying to die, but I simply cannot do it. One single beefsteak would finish me; but I cannot bring myself to swallow it. I am oppressed with a dread of living forever. That is the only disadvantage of vegetarianism."
- George Bernard Shaw   (1856-1950)

# VEGGIE STUFFED BAGELS

Use the whole wheat bread and bagel recipe.

**BAGEL FILLING**: *The veggies should be finely chopped, so that they don't puncture the dough.*

1 C. chopped broccoli
1/3 C. chopped carrots
1/3 C. chopped celery
1 small onion, chopped
1 clove garlic, minced
1/2 tsp. each of dry basil and oregano
Salt and pepper to taste
1 C. shredded soy cheddar

Mix all ingredients except soy cheddar together in a bowl.

**Bagels**:
1. Follow directions for making whole wheat bagels on the preceding page. Use the whole wheat bread recipe, pg. 24, eliminating the cereal mix and using all whole wheat flour.
2. Have a large pot of boiling water ready for the bagels.
3. Divide dough into four balls and roll out into 5 x 4 inch pieces.
4. Place 1/4 C. soy cheddar and 1/3 C. mixed veggies along the 4" edge of bagel, leave at least a 1/2-inch on each side empty.
5. Fold bagel dough once to connect with other edge of bagel. Pinch edges together, and roll and gently stretch bagel on a lightly floured board, until desired size is reached, being careful not to puncture the dough. Slip one end of the dough inside the other open end, and pinch to seal.
**Note:** At this point, if any veggies have broken through the dough, simply patch with more dough.
6. Immediately after pinching bagel ends together, drop them one or two at a time in a large pot of boiling water, containing 2 TB. dry sweetener. Carefully remove from water with a large slotted spoon, after 30-60 seconds.
7. Place bagels on a lightly oiled cookie sheet and bake immediately in a 400° oven for approximately 20 minutes, or until golden browned and firm. Cool for 15-20 minutes before serving. These are more enjoyable to eat if they are cooled to room temperature. Makes 4 <u>very</u> large stuffed bagels.
**VARIATIONS**: *Experiment with different combinations of veggies and spices.*

> "Formerly, vegetable proteins were classified as second class,
> and regarded as inferior to first-class proteins of animal
> origins, but this distinction has now been generally discarded."
> -From the Medical Journal, Lancet

## FOCACCIA  *Traditional Italian flat bread*

2 tsp. bread yeast
2 C. lukewarm water
1 tsp. sweetener
2 TB. vegetable oil
3 C. whole wheat bread flour
1 C. whole wheat pastry flour
2 tsp. salt
1 tsp. garlic granules

**Toppings**:
3 – 6 TB. olive oil
1-2 tsp. ground black pepper
1/2 -1 tsp. dried ground rosemary

**Other toppings Ideas:**
sliced tomatoes, sautéed mushrooms,
sliced olives, vegan parmesan

1. Combine yeast and water in a large bowl. Add remaining ingredients, adding flour cup by cup until combined and forms a smooth ball. Add more flour if necessary. Knead dough until smooth. It will be slightly sticky. Lightly coat dough with oil, and place in bowl. Cover with a towel, and sit in warm spot to rise for about 1 hour.
2. Preheat oven to 425°. If using a pizza stone, put it in the preheated oven about 20 minutes before the focaccia goes in. Lightly oil a 10"x 15" cookie sheet or two 8-9" metal pie pans, or one large 14" round cookie sheet. Sprinkle pans lightly with cornmeal. Place dough on the cookie sheet and press or roll to fill entire area of pan. Drizzle focaccia with olive oil and sprinkle with black pepper and ground rosemary. If desired, add additional toppings of your choice. Immediately bake in 425° oven 15-20 minutes, or until browned on the bottom. Serve warm or cold. Makes One-14 inch round focaccia. **Note:** *1-3 tsp.-dried herbs, such as oregano, basil, sage or Italian seasoning, can be mixed directly into the dough.*


## PIZZA DOUGH

1 ½ C. lukewarm water
2 tsp. baking yeast
1 tsp. sweetener

2 TB. Olive oil
1 tsp. salt
1 C. soft whole wheat pastry flour
2-3 C. whole wheat bread flour

1. Soften yeast in water with sweetener. Add oil, salt, pastry flour and only enough additional bread flour to produce a soft ball of dough. Knead dough until smooth. Rise for one hour.
2. To use: roll dough into desired thickness. For a crisp pizza crust, roll out as thin as possible.
3. Dough can be rolled directly on a cookie sheet or pizza pan. Add desired toppings and immediately put pizza in a preheated 450° oven for 10-15 minutes, or until dough is lightly browned and toppings are tender. Brown and crisp bottom of crust, by sliding pizza on to a preheated pizza stone, the last 5 minutes of baking. Makes two 13-14 inch pizzas.
**Note:** *See page 115 for topping ideas.*

# QUICK BREADS

**FOR MORE QUICK BREADS:** See Breakfast Section pg. 41 and Muffins pg. 51-54
**FOR CONVERTING RECIPES TO WHEAT FREE:** See pg. 274 for "Tips For A Wheat Free Diet." *When baking at an altitude lower than 3,000 feet, refer to altitude adjustment tips on pg. 20, before proceeding with recipes.*

## HERBAL SCONES or Baking Powder Biscuits

2 C. soft wheat pastry flour
2 tsp. baking powder
1/2 tsp. salt
1 TB. sweetener(optional)

2 TB. dried herbs
(a mixture of basil, sage and mint is good)
1/4 C. vegetable oil
1/2 C. soy milk

Preheat oven 425°
1. Combine flour, baking powder, salt, sweetener and herbs. Stir to mix well.
2. With fork, stir in oil until mixture is a mealy texture.
3. Add soy milk gradually, adding only enough to make a soft ball of dough.
4. Either drop by spoonfuls onto oiled cookie sheet, or roll out on a floured surface and cut into desired shapes.
5. Bake at 425° for 10-12 minutes, or until lightly browned and firm to the touch.
Makes 6 medium size scones or 10-12 small biscuits.
**VARIATIONS:** *Fruit Scones: Increase sweetener to 4 TB. and eliminate the herbs, and add 1/2-3/4C of your favourite chopped or canned fruit, or a mixture of chopped apples, raisins and cinnamon. Plain Scones or Biscuits: Eliminate the herbs. Wheat free Scones: Substitute wheat flour with 1 C. oat, barley or bean flour, ½ C. tapioca flour, ½ C. potato starch and 1 tsp. xantham powder.*

## QUICK AND EASY CINNAMON ROLLS

Use the above scone recipe, using 4 TB. sweetener, and eliminate the herbs.
Roll dough out on a heavily floured surface, forming a rectangular shape.
Sprinkle with cinnamon, raisins, chopped nuts and sweetener.
Roll into a long tube. Slice into 3/4-1" thick rounds.
Place on lightly oiled cookie sheet, cut side up. Bake at 425° for 10-12 minutes.

---

Number of people who could be adequately fed with the grain saved if Americans reduced their intake of meat by 10%: 60 million.

---

## QUICK IRISH SODA BREAD

2 C. whole wheat bread flour
2 C. soft wheat pastry flour
1 tsp. salt
1 tsp. baking powder
1 tsp. baking soda

1/4-1/2 C. dry or liquid sweetener
1 TB. egg replacer powder in 1/2 C. warm water
1 C. soymilk
1/2-3/4 C water

1. Mix flours, salt, baking powder, soda and sweetener in a bowl, and combine well.
2. Add egg replacer mixture and milk. Mix together well, adding only enough additional water to form a stiff ball of dough.
3. On a floured surface, knead gently into a smooth, round, slightly flattened ball. A 1/2" deep cross is traditionally cut in the center of the loaf.
4. Bake on a lightly oiled cookie sheet at 375° for 40-50 minutes, or until lightly browned and firm to the touch. Makes one medium-size round loaf. The bread can also be baked in two small or one large, oiled bread pan.
**VARIATION:** Quick Irish Raisin Nut Bread: *Add 1/2 C. raisins and chopped walnuts*
Wheat Free Irish Soda Bread: *Substitute whole wheat with 2 C. bean flour, 1 C. each of potato starch and tapioca flour and 2 tsp. xantham gum powder. Eliminate step three and spoon mixture into a large well-oiled bread pan or 2 small 7x4 inch bread pans.*


## TORTILLAS OR CHAPATIS

2 C. whole wheat pastry flour
2 C. whole wheat bread flour
1 tsp. salt

1/3 C. vegetable or olive oil
1 ½ -2 C. water

1. Mix flour and salt.
2. Add oil and work in with fingertips.
3. Stir in water gradually, using only enough to make a soft ball of dough.
4. Knead until smooth and set aside for approximately 20 minutes.
5. Divide dough into 12 pieces. Knead each piece into a ball, and then with a rolling pin roll each ball into a very thin circle. Stack tortillas, flouring each one so that they don't stick together.
6. Cook tortillas one at a time in a heavy un-oiled hot griddle for 30-60seconds on each side, or until the dough bubbles slightly and tortillas are lightly browned. Remove from pan and cover tortillas with a towel. Don't overcook the tortillas; as they must be pliable when being rolled up with a filling. Makes: twelve 7-8 inch tortillas.
**VARIATIONS:** Corn / whole wheat tortillas---*Replace half or all of whole wheat flour with cornmeal.*
Herbal Chapatis: *Add 1-2 tsp. dried herbs such as dill, basil, and oregano. Chapatis are traditionally puffed over an open flame, after being baked on the hot griddle.*
**Tip:** *To keep each tortilla soft, wrap in a towel while cooking the rest.*

## CORN BREAD OR MUFFINS

1 ½ C. cornmeal
1/2 C. whole wheat pastry flour
2 tsp. baking powder
1/2 tsp. salt
1/4 –1/2 C. sweetener

1/4 C. vegetable oil
1 TB. egg replacer in 1/4 C. warm water
1/2-3/4 C. soymilk

Preheat oven 400°

1. Combine cornmeal, flour, baking powder, salt and sweetener.
2. Add oil, egg replacer mixture and enough soy milk to make a moist mixture.
3. Fill lightly oiled muffin tins 3/4 full, or an 8-9" lightly oiled square pan.
4. Bake 20-25 minutes, or until lightly browned and done.


## WHOLE GRAIN CRACKERS

1 C. whole wheat pastry flour
1/4 tsp. baking soda
1/2 tsp. salt
3 TB. vegetable oil

1 TB. sweetener, optional
soy milk

*Optional additions*: 2-3 TB. sesame or caraway seeds
1/2 –1 tsp. garlic or onion powder or other herbs.

Preheat oven 325°

Combine flour, soda, and salt in a medium size bowl. Add sweetener and oil and any other optional ingredients, and mix together until crumbly. Add just enough soy milk to form a soft ball. Roll dough out on a floured surface to approximately 1/8th inch thick. Sprinkle with sesame or caraway seeds, and roll lightly to adhere seeds to dough. Cut into desired shapes and place on a lightly oiled baking pan. Bake crackers for 8-12 minutes. Cool on a rack.

**VARIATIONS:** *Different flours can be used, or a combination of wheat, rye and oat flours.* <u>Wheat free crackers</u>: *Substitute wheat flour with ½ C. bean flour, ¼ C. each of potato starch and tapioca flour and ½ tsp. xantham gum powder.*

---

**Tip for storing crackers:** *Store completely cooled crackers in a zip lock bag or sealed container, so that they don't draw moisture and become soft.*

---

## ZUCCHINI BREAD

1 ½ C. whole wheat pastry flour
1 ½ C. whole wheat bread flour
2 tsp. baking powder
1/2 tsp. salt
3/4 C. dry sweetener
2 tsp. cinnamon
1/8 tsp. nutmeg

1/2 C. raisins
1 C. chopped nuts
1 TB. egg replacer mixed with
1/4 C. warm water
2 tsp. vanilla extract
2 C. grated zucchini (3-4 small)
1/2 C. applesauce or vegetable oil
1 C. soymilk

Preheat oven: 350°
1. In a large mixing bowl combine all dry ingredients, mixing to combine well.
2. Add egg replacer mixture, vanilla, zucchini, applesauce or oil and milk, and stir just until blended.
3. Pour batter into a lightly oiled 9x5 inch loaf pan. Bake 1 hour or until tester inserted in center comes out clean.
4. Cool slightly before turning out onto a rack.
**VARIATION**: Carrot Bread: *Substitute grated carrots for all or part of zucchini.*
Pineapple Zucchini Bread: *Instead of soy milk, mix in 1 cup crushed pineapple with juice. Add additional soy milk if mixture seems too dry.*


## BANANA BREAD

1 C. mashed bananas (about 4 bananas)
1 TB. lemon juice (optional)
1/2 C. dry sweetener
1/2 C. vegetable oil
2 C. whole wheat pastry flour

1/2 tsp. salt
1 ½ tsp. baking powder
1 tsp. nutmeg
1 C. chopped nuts
¼-1/2 C. soy milk

Preheat oven 375°

1. Mix mashed bananas with lemon juice, oil and sweetener.
2. Mix flour, salt, baking powder and nutmeg in separate bowl, combining well.
3. Mix wet and dry ingredients together. Fold in nuts and ¼-1/2 C. soy milk. Pour mixture into a lightly oil loaf pan. Bake 45-60 minutes or until tester inserted in center comes out clean. Cool slightly before removing from pan. **VARIATION**: Wheat Free Banana Bread: *Instead of wheat flour, use 1 C. barley or oat flour, ½ C. each of tapioca flour and potato starch and ½ tsp. xantham gum.*

---

*Pounds of potatoes that can be grown on an acre: 20,000*
*Pounds of beef produced on an acre: 165*

---

# BOSTON BROWN BREAD

| | |
|---|---|
| 1 C. yellow cornmeal | 2 C. soymilk |
| 1 C. rye flour | 1/4 C. blackstrap molasses |
| 1 C. whole wheat bread flour | 1 C. dry sweetener |
| 1 tsp. baking soda | 3/4 C. raisins |
| 1 tsp. salt | 1/2 C. walnuts, chopped |

1. Lightly oil two metal molds. Two and three cup lined tomato sauce cans work well.
2. Blend all dry ingredients together.
3. Stir wet ingredients plus raisins and walnuts into dry ingredients.
4. Fill cans and cover loosely with first parchment paper, and then foil.
5. Place cans on wire rack * in a deep pan with water reaching 1/2 way up the cans.
6. Bring water to a boil and reduce heat, simmering slowly for 2 hours.
7. Remove from pot and cool cans slightly, before turning bread out onto a cooling rack.

**VARIATIONS**: * *The molds can also be set on 2 or 3 canning jar lids, set in the bottom of pot. Any mixture of dried fruit and nuts can be incorporated into this recipe.*
*For a* **wheat free version**, *replace wheat and rye flour with a combination of oat and barley flour or bean and tapioca flour.*

---

**Whole Grains for good health:** *Nutrients from the bran and germ of grains are necessary for proper digestion, assimilation and to metabolize carbohydrates. Without natural fibers, refined foods containing white flour products clog our intestines and interfere with the colons functioning, particularly the peristaltic action, which keeps everything moving along. Stagnation of wastes in the digestive tract can lead to numerous illnesses and dis-ease. Diet is directly related to disease. Diets have changed drastically in the past century when whole grains use to be a major source of protein, and amounted to at least 50% of our diet. White flour is deplete of nutrients readily available from the whole grain. Whole wheat flour products supply the nutrients we need and have a full-bodied nut like taste.*

---

"Flesh foods are considerably higher in phosphorous as compared to plant foods. The high phosphorous draws the calcium out of the bones. This produces a loss in bone density........A high flesh diet causes more osteoporosis in that it is high in fat. This fat blocks the calcium up take by actually forming biochemical soaps with the calcium which are then excreted by the system."
 Gabriel Cousens, M.D.  -  Conscious Eating

# EASY ESSENE BREAD

*Historically, Essene bread is one of the earliest varieties of bread. It derives its name from a recipe of the ancient Essenes, as recorded in The Essene Gospel of Peace, a 1st Century Aramaic manuscript. It is a very simple bread, requiring only wheat berries and water to make. You can add nuts, seeds, dried fruit, apples and spices if you prefer. But, plain Essene bread is delicious, with a sweet and nutty flavour. This is a very rich, and moist "wheat free" bread, not suitable for sandwiches. It's better suited as dessert bread, a nourishing hiking food, or included in a raw foods diet, if baked at the lower temperature. Those with wheat allergies can generally tolerate sprouted wheat.*

**You will need:**
* At least four days of soaking and sprout time before baking the bread
* 4 C. hard whole wheat berries
* Soaking water
* Containers for sprouting, with breathable tops
* A grinder; either hand operated or a champion juicer or food processor
* A bowl to hold the dough and a cookie sheet for the oven

**Sprouting Directions:** *If necessary, refer to sprouting section, pg. 268.*

Place berries in a sprouting container. A mesh-sprouting bag is nice, but a large jar or container with a piece of cheesecloth secured over the containers mouth will also work. To sprout berries, cover them with water for 12 hours or overnight. In the morning drain off the soaking water. Save the liquid for soups or to water your plants. Rinse with cool water twice a day. Drain the sprouts well after each rinsing and keep the sprouts out of direct sunlight, preferably in a dark place. They are ready to use when they are about 1/2 inch long. This will take about 2-3 days. Don't rinse the sprouts just before grinding, so the berries won't be too moist. Set them in the sunlight to green up, before using. When wheat is sprouted it produces a very sweet taste, so no additional sweetener is necessary.

**To make dough:**

Grind wheat sprouts in a champion juicer (using the solid plate) or in a food processor or other device. The sticky dough is ready to use as soon as it comes out of the grinder. This is the time to add raisins or other dried fruit and nuts to the mixture. With wet hands, and no added flour, shape the sticky dough before placing on a lightly oiled cookie sheet. No kneading is required, but you want to work the dough slightly to get any air pockets out, and to produce a smooth surface. It can be made into one round loaf or smaller rolls. Bake in a preheated oven 200-250° for 2-3 hours, less for rolls, or until done. The outside of bread will be firm to the touch. The inside will be quite soft and will have a firmer texture upon cooling. To preserve the goodness of the sprouts you can bake the bread at 120° for 8-10 hours. Rolls will take less time. Essene bread will keep at room temperature for a couple of days. Refrigerate for longer storage.

# Breakfast

**FOR OTHER BREAKFAST TYPE FOODS, SEE INDEX FOR:**
Cinnamon Rolls, Bagels, Rice Pudding, Potato cakes, Pep-up drink and other beverages, and the Quick Breads section.

## PANCAKES or Waffles

*In my child raising days we called these Shmancakes, and
made faces on the pancakes with raisins or other fruit, just
before flipping them. This batter can also be used to make waffles.*

Mix in bowl:
2 C. soymilk
1/2 tsp. salt
2 tsp. baking powder
Add to above:
1/4 C. oatmeal (quick or regular)
1 C. whole wheat pastry flour
1/2 C. buckwheat flour
1/4 C. cornmeal
1/4 C. oil
1/4 C. walnuts, chopped (optional)

Mix lightly, just until ingredients are blended together.
Don't over mix. If batter is too thick, add a little more
soy milk. If too thin, add more flour. The batter thickens
as it sits. Cook on a hot, lightly oiled griddle or waffle
maker. Flip pancakes when top of cakes are bubbly.
Serve with maple syrup. Makes twelve 5 inch cakes, or 4 inch
waffles.

**VARIATIONS:** *Add 1/2 C. fresh fruit (blueberries, mangos,
strawberries etc.) to the batter, or serve cooked or raw fruit on top.
Add 1 T. vanilla extract to batter.*
<u>Wheat Free Pancakes:</u> *Replace the wheat flour with ½-1 C. bean flour, ¼ C. each of tapioca flour
and potato starch, and ½ tsp. xantham gum powder.*

"I have no doubt that it is a part of the destiny of the human race, in its gradual
improvement, to leave off eating animals."
Henry David Thoreau - Walden

# SCRAMBLED TOFU

8 oz. soft tofu
2 TB. nutritional yeast flakes
2 TB. water
1/2 TB. soy sauce (tamari)
1/2 tsp. turmeric

1/2 tsp. onion powder
1 tsp. spike seasoning
pinch garlic powder
salt and pepper to taste

Crumble tofu in a medium size bowl. Sprinkle with nutritional yeast and stir gently. Stir in remaining ingredients, except salt and pepper. Pour mixture into a heated and lightly oiled fry pan. Scrape and turn until mixture is heated through. Salt and pepper to taste. Makes 2 large servings.

**VARIATIONS:** _Veggie Scramble: Here's a very yummy way to serve tofu scramble. In a separate pan, with 1 TB. oil, fry: 1/2 chopped green pepper, 1/2 C. sliced, fresh mushrooms,1 small onion, 1clove minced garlic, 1/4 C. fresh basil, (1 tsp. dry) Stir this into cooked scramble, or serve on top._

# HEALTHY BREAKFAST SAUSAGE MIX

_Here's a spicy sausage mix to have on hand for emergencies. The herbs are dried, not fresh. The burger mix is available in bulk or packaged at most natural foods store. Shake the following together in a 1 qt. jar or container._

2 C. vegetarian burger mix
2 TB. dried sage, (crumbled)
1 ½ tsp. dried thyme
1 tsp. ground fennel
¼ tsp. black pepper

1/8 tsp. cayenne pepper (optional)
1/4 C. dried parsley
1 tsp. hickory seasoned
or regular sea salt

**TO USE:** Stir 1 C. of mix with ¾-1 C. boiling water. Let mixture sit for 15 minutes. Form into patties and fry in a lightly oiled skillet, until browned on both sides; or place patties on a lightly oiled cookie sheet and bake in the oven at 350° for 10 minutes, then flip patties over and bake another 10 minutes, or until done. Makes 10-12 two-inch patties.

"Vegan diets dramatically change the amount and type of fats in the diet, which in turn, can affect the immune processes that play a part in arthritis. The omega-3 fatty acids in vegetables may be a key factor, along with the near absence of saturated fat. And patients lose weight on a vegan diet, which contributes to the improvement."

Neal Barnard M.D. - Food For Life

## SPICY SAUSAGE PATTIES

1/2 C. TVP (granules)
1/2 C. bulgur or couscous
2 tsp. dried sage leaf (crumbled or powder)
1 tsp. dried thyme leaf
1 tsp. garlic powder

1/2 tsp. black pepper
3 TB. flour
1/4-1/2 tsp. salt
1 ½ C. boiling water

1.  Mix all of the dry ingredients, except flour, until well blended.
2.  Add boiling water, cover, and set aside for 20-30 minutes, or until liquid is absorbed and bulgur has softened.
3.  When cool enough to handle, stir in the flour and form into small patties and fry in a lightly oiled pan, or bake in the oven at 350°. Flip over after 10-15 minutes, when browned, and continue baking another 10-15 minutes.  Makes 10-12 two-inch patties.

## VEGGIE BREAKFAST WRAPS   *My rendition of Nik's New Mexican wrap.*

4 large tortillas
4-6 medium size
      potatoes, cubed
1 medium size onion, chopped
1-2 cloves garlic, minced
1/2 tsp. black mustard seed
2 tsp. curry powder

1 recipe cooked tofu scramble (see previous page)
1 C. sliced and sautéed mushrooms

**Toppings:**
8 TB. soy sour cream
4-8 TB. green chili sauce or salsa
2-4 TB.  fresh cilantro or basil (chopped)

Preheat oven 350°
1.  Have the tofu scramble and mushrooms cooked and set-aside before starting.
2.  In a lightly oiled fry pan, sauté onion, garlic, mustard seed and curry, until onion is soft.
3.  Add potatoes, stirring and frying until potatoes are coated with previous ingredients.
4. Add just enough water to pan to keep potatoes from sticking. Cover and let simmer until potatoes are tender.
5.  Heat tortillas one at a time in pre-heated oven, just long enough to soften them.
6.  Along middle of each tortilla, leaving an empty space along the sides for folding, place a row of potato mixture, one fourth of tofu scramble and mushrooms, 2 tablespoons sour cream, chili sauce in an amount depending on heat preference, and a sprinkling of cilantro or basil.
7. Roll the tortilla, folding in the sides as you go.  Wrap in parchment paper and then foil.
8. Place in 350° oven for 20 to 30 minutes.   Makes 4 large wraps.
**Note:** *Adjust the degree of heat of these wraps, by the amount and type of salsa.*

# BREAKFAST BEAN BURRITOS

4 C. cooked pinto beans, (save the liquid)
1 C. cooked brown rice
1 tsp onion powder
1/2 tsp. garlic powder or 1 tsp. fresh minced
2 tsp. chili fiesta blend powder pg. 102
1/2 tsp. salt
1/8 tsp. ground cayenne pepper (Optional-depending on heat preference)
6 large whole wheat tortillas
12 TB. mild-hot salsa or green chili sauce

Preheat oven 350°
1.  Mix beans, rice, onion and garlic powder, chili blend powder, salt and optional cayenne pepper.  If mixture seems dry, add a little of the liquid from the beans.
2.  Put tortillas one at a time on the rack of a pre-heated oven; very briefly- just until soft.
3.  Place 1/6th of the bean mixture along the center of each tortilla, leaving at least an inch empty on both sides for folding.
4. Place 2 TB. salsa along the bean mixture. (Or leave out and serve on the side.)
5. Roll up tortilla, tucking in the one side after the first roll.   Continue heating and filling each tortilla until done.  Wrap each tortilla separately in a piece of parchment paper and then foil.  Place in the oven for 20-30 minutes.  Let burritos cool slightly before serving.  These are also good eaten at room temperature.  Extra salsa or green chili sauce can be served on the side.  Makes 6 burritos.

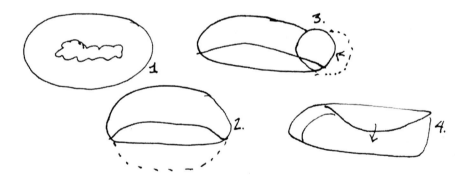

"The argument that flesh must be eaten in order to supply the body sufficient protein is unreasonable; it is found in abundance in beans, peas, lentils and all kind of nuts...It is an established fact that meat protein causes putrefaction twice as quickly as vegetable protein.  There is no ingredient in meat, which cannot be procured, in better quality in products of the vegetable kingdom."
Jethro Kloss,  - Back to Eden

# FRUIT SCONES

2 C. soft wheat pastry flour
1/2 tsp. sea salt
2 tsp. baking powder
4 TB. dry sweetener
1/4 C. vegetable oil

1 TB. almond extract
1/2 –3/4 C. fresh or canned fruit (drained)
1/4 C. chopped nuts (optional)
1/4 –1/2 soy milk, fruit juice,
   or liquid from canned fruit *

Preheat oven 425°

1. Combine flour, salt. baking powder and sweetener in a bowl.  Mix together well.
2. Add 1/4 C. vegetable oil and 1 TB almond extract. Stir with a fork to produce a mealy texture.
3. Add fruit, nuts and just enough milk or juice to form a soft ball of dough.
4. Drop large spoonfuls of dough 1-2 inches apart on a lightly oiled cookie sheet, or roll dough out about 1/2 inch thick, on a lightly floured surface, and cut with a 3-5 inch round cookie cutter, or form into one large round, and cut into triangular shapes.  Bake 10-12 minutes, or until lightly browned and firm to the touch.  Immediately remove scones to a cooling rack.  Makes 5-6 large scones

**VARIATION**: <u>Apple Raisin Scones</u>: *In place of fresh or canned fruit, use 1/2C. chopped apples, 1/8 C. raisins, and 2 tsp. cinnamon.*
<u>Cherry Almond Scones</u>:  *Use canned or fresh sweet cherries and chopped almonds.*
<u>Wheat Free Scones</u>: *Replace wheat with 1 C. oat, barley, or bean flour, ½ C. tapioca flour, ½ C. potato starch and 1 tsp. xantham gum powder.*

**OTHER IDEAS**: *Try cubed pineapple, fresh-diced papaya and mango, blueberries or any canned or fresh fruit. Adjust the amount of milk or juice depending on juiciness of fruit.*

*\* Less liquid is required when using very juicy or canned fruit.*

"Our foods have been processed and devitalized, then fortified, preserved, colored and  flavored. Consuming these over a period of time results in a prolonged deficiency which will sap our vital energies."
   Bernard Jensen PhD. - Food Healing for Man

## VEGAN FRENCH TOAST

1 pkg. (12.3 oz.) soft silken tofu          6 slices of whole wheat bread
1/4 C. soy or rice milk
1 tsp. vanilla extract
1 tsp. cinnamon powder

Mix tofu, milk, vanilla and cinnamon powder in a blender until smooth and creamy.  Dip bread in the mixture and fry in a hot, lightly oiled skillet, until browned on both sides. **Serving suggestions:** *Top with maple syrup and crushed fresh berries.* **Other Ideas:** *Substitute approximately 1/2 lb. regular soft tofu for the silken and increase milk by 1/4 cup.*

## CREPES

*This batter makes a delicate, thin pancake, which is great stuffed with your favourite fruit.  These can also be filled with cooked veggies and drizzled with light primavera sauce, pg. 160, for a delicious dinner.*

1 C. soy milk
2 TB. vegetable oil
1 TB. dry sweetener
1 C. soft whole wheat pastry flour
1/4 tsp. sea salt
3 tsp. egg replacer powder, mixed with
4 TB. warm water

1. In a medium size bowl, blend all of the above ingredients together until well combined.
2. The batter can be used immediately or covered and refrigerated until ready to use.
3. Lightly oil a hot skillet.  (A 12-inch cast iron skillet without sides works nicely.)
4. Pour approximately 1/4 cup of crepe batter into the hot skillet.  Tilt the pan so that the batter spreads out in a thin, even circle.  Cook about 1 minute or until golden.  Flip and cook other side. Stack crepes between dishtowels, until all are cooked and you're ready to serve.  These crepes can also be made ahead and stored in the refrigerator for several days, and eaten cold.
5. Serve with maple syrup, or lay cooked or raw fruit down the middle and fold or roll crepe around the fruit.  Serve topped with more fruit if desired.  Makes 6-7 six-inch crepes.

---

*" Live Simply so others might simply live."* - Gandhi

---

# WHOLE WHEAT DANISH
**_With cream cheese and fruit filling_**

2 tsp. baking yeast
1 C. warm soy creamer or milk
1/2 C. dry sweetener
1/4-1/2 tsp. crushed or ground cardamom
1 tsp. sea salt
1/2 C. vegetable oil
2 TB. egg replacer mixed w/ 1/2 C. warm water
3-4 C. whole-wheat pastry flour
1 C. fruit spread or jam (strawberry, peach, raspberry etc.)
4 oz. (approx) vegan cream cheese (optional)

1. Dissolve the yeast in soymilk. Let sit five minutes to proof the yeast.
2. Add sweetener, cardamom, salt, vegetable oil, and egg replacer mixed with water.
3. Add the flour, one cup at a time, adding only enough so that the mixture can be formed into a soft ball of dough. Knead the dough for about five minutes or until smooth.
4. Oil top of dough and set in a bowl covered with a cloth. Sit to rise in a warm place for 1 hour.
5. Gently punch dough down, and divide into two pieces. Roll each piece separately on a floured surface, as thin as possible. (approximately 12x16 inches) This is often easier if the dough is flipped over a number of times, as you roll, flouring each side if necessary.
6. Cut dough into twelve 5-inch squares. Spread 1 TB. vegan cream cheese and 1½ TB. jam down the center of each square. Fold square over to form a triangle. Seal the edges with a fork, and prick the top of each triangle two or three times with the fork.
7. Set each Danish on a lightly oiled cookie sheet. Let rise for 45-60 minutes.
8. Bake in a preheated oven at 350° for approximately 20-25 minutes and lightly browned. Makes 12-14 pastries.

**VARIATIONS:** _Fill pastry with any of your favourite fruit filling or prepared jam or preserves. The vegan cream cheese can be eliminated._

<u>Jelly Roll or Cinnamon Danish</u>: _Spread the 12x16 inch pieces of dough with: 1 TB. oil, 1/3 C. sweetener, 2 TB. cinnamon, 1/2 C. raisins (or your favourite fruit spread.) Roll up and seal the edges; or slice roll into ½-1 inch pieces and bake cut side up on cookie sheet. Bake the same as the triangles._

---

> "The way you help heal the world is you start with your own family."
> - Mother Teresa

# BLUEBERRY COFFEE CAKE

| | |
|---|---|
| 1/2 C. dry sweetener | 2 C. soft whole wheat pastry flour |
| 1/3 C. soy margarine | 2 tsp. baking powder |
| 1 TB. egg replacer | 1/2 tsp. salt |
| 1/3 C. warm water | 2 C. fresh, canned, or frozen blueberries |
| 1/3 C. soy milk | (drain the liquid off, if using canned berries) |

*Topping:*

1/4 C. dry sweetener
1/3 C. whole wheat pastry flour
1 tsp. cinnamon
1/4 C. soy margarine

Preheat oven 375°
1. Cream the 1/2 C. sweetener with margarine.
2. When sweetener and margarine are creamy smooth, add the egg replacer mixed with warm water, soy milk, flour, baking powder and salt. Beat by hand or with an electric mixer until combined well. Gently stir in the blueberries.
3. Spread mixture into a 9" lightly oiled, square pan.
4. Blend topping ingredients together until combined and crumbly. Sprinkle topping evenly on top of cake batter.
5. Bake in a preheated oven for 30-35 minutes, or until top is lightly browned and cake is done.

**VARIATIONS:** <u>Peach, Cherry or Apple Coffee Cake</u>: *Replace berries with fresh or canned and drained fruit, such as peaches, cherries or apples.*
**OTHER IDEAS:** *Use any in season fruit. Add 1/2 C. chopped nuts to the batter.*
<u>Wheat Free Coffee cake</u>: *Replace whole wheat flour with 1 C. bean flour, ½ C. tapioca flour, ½ C. potato starch and 1/2 tsp. xantham gum powder. Use oat or tapioca and bean flour in the topping.*

---

"According to the American Dietetic Association, pure vegetarian diets in America usually contain twice the required protein for one's daily need. Harvard researchers have found that it is difficult to have a vegetarian diet that will produce protein deficiency unless there is an excess of vegetarian junk foods and sweets."
Gabriel Cousens, M.D. - Conscious Eating

## PORRIDGE   Hot whole grain cereal

4 C. water                                  1/2 tsp. cinnamon
3/4 C. oat groats                           1/2-1 C. reg. rolled oats
1/2 C. mixed grains (or all groats)         1/4 C. raisins
dash of salt

Bring water, groats, mixed grains and salt to a boil.  Turn down heat and simmer slowly.
When grains are softened, (approx. 15 minutes) add cinnamon, oatmeal and raisins.  Add an
additional 1/2 cup of water if mixture is too thick.   Simmer 5-10 minutes, or until oatmeal is
soft.  Serve with soy milk and sweetener. Serves 2-4
**SUGGESTIONS**:  *Experiment with various grains and dried fruit in this hearty hot cereal.*


## GRANOLA

*The low heat method of baking this granola minimizes nutrient loss.*

6 C. regular rolled oats
1/2 C. wheat bran
1 C. unsweetened, dry, shredded coconut
1/2 C. raw sunflower seeds
1 C.  walnuts or other nuts, chopped
1/2 C. each raisins & diced papaya
1 tsp. cinnamon
1/2 C. maple syrup
1/4 C. vegetable oil
1/4 C. orange/pineapple juice (or any light coloured fruit juice)
2 tsp. almond or vanilla extract or maple flavour

Preheat oven 250° (or lower)
1. Mix everything except the maple syrup, oil, juice and almond extract in a large bowl, until
well blended.
2. Mix the syrup, oil, juice and extract together in a small bowl.  Pour this over the oat
mixture and mix with a spoon or your hands, until well combined.
3. Pour mixture into two, lightly oiled 9x13 inch cake pans.  Place in a pre-heated oven, and
bake for 60 minutes, or until granola mixture is lightly browned. Stir occasionally. If you are
using two racks in the oven, the bottom pan will be done about ten minutes before the top
one. Cool granola in the pans, before storing in a lidded container.

**OTHER OPTIONS:** *Add any of the following to your granola mixture before baking: Dried candied
ginger, pineapple, currants, pumpkin seeds, wheat or rye flakes, wheat germ, and sesame seeds.  If the
amounts are in larger quantity than the original recipe, you will need to consider increasing the oil, juice and
sweetener. Raisins and other dried fruit can also be added during last fifteen minutes of baking.*

## APPLESAUCE MUFFINS

2 C. whole wheat pastry flour
1/2 tsp. salt
1 tsp. baking powder
1 tsp. cinnamon
1/2 C. soy milk

2 TB. vegetable oil
1 C. applesauce
1/3 C. maple syrup or other sweetener
1/2 C. raisins
1/2 C. chopped walnuts (optional)
Soy milk or juice

Preheat oven 400°
1.  Stir together flour, salt, baking powder and cinnamon.
2.  Add all remaining ingredients, mixing until well combined.  Add more soy milk or juice, if needed, to make a thick mixture.
3.  Spoon the batter into 9-12 lightly oiled muffin tins.
Bake 15-20 minutes, or until done.
**VARIATION**: _Apple Muffins_: _Use chopped apples instead of sauce, and adjust liquid._

## PUMPKIN MUFFINS

1 ½ C whole wheat pastry flour
1 C. whole wheat bread flour
1/2 C. wheat bran
2 TB. sunflower seeds
1/2 C. dry sweetener
2 tsp. baking powder
1/2 tsp. salt

1/2 tsp. ground cloves
1 tsp. cinnamon
3/4 tsp. nutmeg
3/4 C. raisins
2 C. canned or home cooked pureed
    pumpkin (substitute sweet potato or squash)
soymilk to moisten

Preheat oven 400°
1.  Stir together all ingredients except pumpkin and soy milk
2.  Stir in pumpkin and enough soymilk to make a thick, moist batter.
3.  Fill lightly oiled muffin tins 3/4 full.
    Bake 15-20 minutes or until done. Makes 10-12 muffins.

"My refusing to eat flesh occasioned an inconveniency, and I was frequently chided for my singularity, but, with this lighter repast, I made the greater progress, from greater clearness of head and quicker comprehension."
- Benjamin Franklin

# BRAN MUFFINS

1 ½ C. raw wheat bran
1 C. whole wheat pastry flour
1/2 C. whole wheat bread flour
2 TB. oatmeal
2 TB. sunflower seeds (or other nuts)

2 tsp. baking powder
1/2 tsp. salt
1/4-1/3 C. dry sweetener
1/4 C. vegetable oil
¾ -1 C. soy milk or fruit juice
(use less sweetener if using juice)

Preheat oven 400°

1.  Combine all the ingredients, except the oil and soy milk.  Add only enough milk or juice to make a thick, moist batter.
2.  Fill lightly oiled muffin tins ¾ full.
3.  Bake approximately 20 minutes, or until firm to the touch.  Cool 5 minutes before removing from pans.  Makes 10-12 medium size muffins.

**VARIATIONS**:
Mint Bran Muffins:  *Add 1 tsp. extract of mint with the liquid.*
Banana Bran Muffins: *Substitute some of the soy milk or juice with mashed bananas.*
Carrot or Zucchini Bran Muffins: *Add 1C. grated carrots or zucchini, 1tsp. cinnamon, 1tsp cardamom, and just enough soymilk, to make a thick, moist mixture.*
Oat Bran Muffins: *Replace wheat bran with oat bran.*
Leftover Squash Muffins: *Add ½ C. mashed squash, in place of part of the liquid.*
Fruity Bran Muffins: *Add ½ C. or more of canned or fresh fruit.*
Wheat Free Bran Muffins: *Substitute rice or oat bran for the wheat bran and the wheat flour with ¾ C. bean flour, ½ C. tapioca flour, ¼ C. potato starch and 2 tsp. xantham gum powder.*
Tropical Coconut:  *Add 1/3 C. cubed pineapple, pecans instead of sunflower seeds, 2 small mashed bananas, and 1/3 C. coconut milk instead of soy milk.*

**TIPS & IDEAS FOR MUFFINS:** Fill muffin tins ¾ full, leaving room for the batter to rise.  Add only enough liquid to make a thick and moist batter.  Too much liquid will produce a cake like muffin, and too little will make a dry muffin.  Always cool muffins for 5-10 minutes before removing from pans.  Wheat or oat bran can replace at least a third of the flour in any recipe.  Muffins with a surprise filling: Fill the tins only half full with batter. Spoon one teaspoon of jam or preserves over the batter and cover this with the other half of batter.

## BANANA NUT MUFFINS

3 C. whole wheat pastry flour
2 tsp. baking powder
1/2 tsp. salt
1/4 – 1/2 C. dry sweetener
1 tsp. vanilla
1/4 C. vegetable oil
3 mashed bananas (1 ½ cups)
1/2 C. walnuts (chopped)
1/2 C. raisins
½-3/4 C. soy milk or fruit juice

Preheat oven 400°

1.  Mix dry ingredients together.
2.  Add wet ingredients, plus walnuts and raisins and only as much milk or juice, to make a thick, moist mixture. Spoon mixture into lightly oiled muffin tins. Bake 15-20 minutes or until done. Makes 10-12 muffins **VARIATION:** *Extra Banana flavour---use more bananas and less soy milk or juice.* Banana Apple Muffins: *Add 1/2 –3/4 cup chopped apples to batter.*

## BLUEBERRY MUFFINS

4 C. whole wheat pastry flour
1 tsp. salt
1/2 C. sweetener
1 TB. baking powder
1/4 C. oil
1 C. fresh blueberries (or canned and drained well)
1 TB. egg  replacer mixed in 1/4 C. water
1-1 ¾ C. soy milk

Preheat oven 400°

Combine flour, salt, sweetener and baking powder. Stir in remaining ingredients, and only as much milk as needed to make a thick batter.  Spoon into oiled muffin tins. Bake 15-20 minutes, or until done. Makes 12 muffins.

**VARIATION:** Cranberry Muffins *Use fresh or frozen cranberries instead of blueberries.*

# HEARTY WHOLE GRAIN MUFFINS

2/3 C. couscous
1 C. soy milk
1/3 C. rolled oats
1/2 C. wheat bran
1/2 C. whole wheat bread flour
1 C. whole wheat pastry flour
2 tsp. baking powder
1/2 tsp. salt
1/2 C. raw sunflower seeds
1/2 C. currants, raisins or other mixed dried fruit
1/2 C. sweetener
1/2 C. vegetable oil
1/2 C. soy milk or juice (or a combination of both)

Preheat oven 400°

1.  Soak couscous in 1 C. soymilk for 10-15 minutes, or until soft.
2.  In a separate bowl stir together well, the remaining dry ingredients, including nuts, fruit and sweetener.
3.  Add couscous to the dry ingredients, along with the oil and soy milk.
and mix just enough to combine.  Add more soy milk or flour to make a thick, moist mixture.
4.  Spoon into 10-12 lightly oiled muffin tins and bake 15-20 minutes, or until done.

**VARIATION:** *Substitute fresh or canned fruit for the dried.*

"By attention to diet, many diseases may be prevented, and others mitigated.  It is a just observation that he, who lives by rule and wholesome diet, is a physician to himself.  With vegetables, fruits, nuts and cereals we proved that one could maintain a healthy body as an operating base for a sane mind and a purposeful harmless life."

Helen & Scott Nearing, - Living the Good Life.

# Appetizers,
# Salads & Dressings

# FRESH SPRING ROLLS

12 large rice wrappers
2 C. fresh mung bean sprouts
1 C. shredded carrots
1 ripe avocado cut in thin slices
1 C. fresh cilantro or basil leaves
1 C. peanuts or cashews, chopped fine (optional)
Ume plum or rice vinegar

1.  Immerse two wrappers, one on top of the other, in a pan of hot water for approximately one minute, or until soft.
2.  Lay the two wrappers, still on top of one another, on a soft dishtowel, and pat lightly with a towel.
3.  On the double thick wrapper place 1/6th of all the veggie and herb ingredients, along middle of wrapper and at least 1" from sides. Sprinkle lightly with peanuts and vinegar.
4.  Roll up, folding in ends after the first roll.
5.  Cut in half crosswise and serve with soy dipping sauce, pg. 161

**VARIATIONS**: *Use pre-cooked and cooled rice vermicelli or other noodles, instead of or along with fresh sprouted mung sprouts. Substitute avocado with other veggies, such as shredded cabbage, radishes, sliced cucumbers or pickles.*

" Time and again we are queried on our sources of protein. Where, we ask in return, do the cows, elephants and rhinoceros---all sturdy creatures---get their protein needs supplied? From grass, from foliage, from green things, is the answer...they are simple creatures eating nature's way. We try to be the same: simple-living people surviving on simple food, home grown, organically grown, and simply prepared. Our foods are vital, nutritional and economical. For fifty years we have thrived on such, and plan to continue so until our last days."
Helen & Scott Nearing - Living the Good Life

## DOLMAS (stuffed Grape leaves)

15-20 canned grape leaves *
1/4 C. onion, chopped
2 TB. oil
1/2 tsp. paprika
1/4 tsp. cinnamon
1/2 tsp. dried peppermint leaves
1 tsp. dried dill weed

3/4 tsp. kelp powder
1/4 tsp. each of allspice, pepper & salt
1 C. cooked brown rice
2 TB. lemon juice
3/4 C. water

1. Rinse bottled grape leaves to remove excess salt, and cut off any stems.
2. Sauté onion in oil. Add spices, salt and pepper, stirring and cooking just briefly.
3. Remove from heat and add 1 C. cooked rice and mix together well.
4. Place 1 heaping teaspoon on each grape leaf and roll leaf up, tucking in edges. *
5. Place all leaves in an ovenproof pan.
6. Mix together lemon juice and water. Pour this mixture over the dolmas and cover.
7. Bake in a preheated 350° oven for 30 minutes. Remove cover and continue to bake an additional 5-10 minutes, or until liquid is absorbed.
8. Let cool and serve at room temperature or cold. These are even better the following day.   * Fresh grape leaves can be used. Steam briefly before using.

**VARIATION:** *Fill leaves with cooked couscous or bulgur, instead of brown rice.*

**Tip:  For rolling grape leaves:** *Take the two sides of the grape leaf where you cut off the stem, and have them meet, by slightly overlapping one side over the other, producing a solid piece of grape leaf. This will make for ease in filling and rolling the leaves, so that the rice mixture doesn't fall out.  Roll the dolmas, starting from the stem side of the leaves, and folding in the sides after the first roll.  Tuck in any outer leaves so that you end up with a neat, tight roll.*

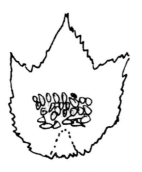
1. Overlap leaf after stem is cut off. Place stuffing on leaf.

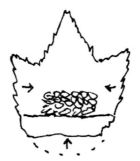
2. Roll leaf... tucking in sides.

3. Make a neat, tight roll.

"It is getting closer to nature, closer to the garden, and further from the drugstore, that we are going to have good health and salvation and a long life."
Bernard Jensen PhD. – Food Healing for Man

## NORI ROLLS

5 seaweed, nori sheets
2 C. cooked and cooled, long or short grain brown rice,
   or sushi rice, which is stickier
2 TB. rice vinegar
2 TB. sesame seeds
1 C. carrots, shredded
1 avocado, cut in strips (optional)
1 dill pickle or cucumber cut in thin strips

1.  Place a sheet of nori on waxed paper or a small bamboo mat.
2.  Mix rice with vinegar and sesame seeds in a medium size bowl.
3.  Place 1/5 of rice mixture on each nori, and with moistened hands pat rice evenly on nori sheet, leaving about 1 inch of sheet empty at top edge.
4.  Place shredded carrot, pickles and avocados from edge to edge, along center of nori.
5.  Lightly moisten the top edge of each nori sheet with water. Roll the nori starting at bottom edge and press at end to seal.  The edges are not folded in.
6.  After all nori have been rolled, cut into bite size slices. (approximately ½ inch) Use a very sharp knife.  Serve with soy dipping sauce (pg. 161) or hot wasabi. (Japanese horseradish)

**VARIATIONS**: *Any combination of veggies can be used in a nori, including: bean sprouts, tofu or tempeh, cabbage, spinach or lettuce.  These are best served the same day, but, they're still good after a day, if stored in the refrigerator.*

1. Lay nori sheet on mat.   2. Roll nori with help   3. Slice into
   Spread rice & veggies       of the mat.              desired thickness.
   on nori.

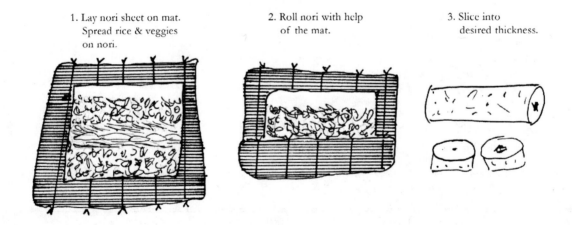

## TABOOLI
**Cracked wheat salad**

1 C. bulgur
1 ¼ C. boiling water
3/4 tsp. salt
1 tsp. fresh rosemary (1/8 tsp. dried)
1 C. cucumbers, chopped
1-3 tomatoes, diced
1/4 C. onions, diced

1 C. fresh parsley, chopped
1/2 C. fresh mint, chopped (1-2 tsp. dried)
1 C. cooked garbanzo beans (optional)
3 TB. lemon or lime juice
2 TB. olive oil
1/4 tsp. black pepper
2 TB. Ume plum vinegar

Pour boiling water over bulgur and cover. Set aside for 30-45 minutes or until water is absorbed and bulgur is cool. Add all remaining ingredients, stirring together well. Chill for a couple of hours or overnight before serving.

**VARIATION:** Wheat Free Tabooli: *Substitute cooked quinoa for the bulgur.*

## TRADITIONAL POTATO SALAD

4 medium size or 4 C. cubed potatoes, (with or without skins)
1 TB. Ume plum or apple cider vinegar
1/2 C. each: onion, green pepper, & celery, chopped
1/4 C. fresh parsley, chopped (2 tsp. dried)
1 TB. fresh dill weed, chopped (½ tsp. dried)
1/4 C. dill pickle, diced
1/4 tsp. each of salt and pepper
1 clove garlic, crushed or chopped fine (optional)
3/4 C. soy mayonnaise
paprika powder
Fresh parsley for garnish

1. Steam cubed potatoes until tender.
2. Chill quickly under cold running water and drain. Sprinkle with vinegar and set aside for 10 minutes.
3. Combine all remaining ingredients with potatoes, except paprika and parsley, mixing together well.
4. Sprinkle top of salad lightly with paprika powder, and garnish with sprigs of parsley. Chill in the fridge and adjust seasonings, if necessary, before serving.

**Other addition ideas:** *Sliced black olives.*

# GERMAN STYLE POTATO SALAD

2 lb. small red potatoes
3 TB. olive oil
2 cobs of corn, in the husk (substitute 1-2 C. canned or frozen)
2 C. tomatoes, chopped
1 small onion, chopped
1 red or green pepper
1/2 C. fresh basil, minced (1-2 tsp. dried)
2 cloves garlic, minced
1/4 C. olive oil
3 TB. Ume Plum or other vinegar

Preheat 450°
1. Cut potatoes into bite size pieces and toss with 3 TB. olive oil.
2. Put potatoes and corn in the husk (if using) on a large cookie sheet or oven pan.
Bake at 450° for 20-30 minutes, or until veggies are done. Remove husks and cut kernels from the corncob. If using frozen corn, cook before proceeding.
3. Cool potatoes and corn slightly, before adding tomatoes, onion, pepper, basil and garlic.
4. Whisk together the olive oil and vinegar and stir into the salad.  Serve warm or cold.


# TOFU "EGG" SALAD

8 oz soft tofu, drained and crumbled
2 TB. nutritional yeast flakes
1/2 tsp. each turmeric & onion powder
1 tsp. spike
1 TB. fresh parsley, chopped (½ tsp. dried)
1 TB. chopped  dill pickle
1/4 C. soy mayonnaise
1 tsp. prepared mustard
1/2 C. celery, diced

Mix all ingredients in a bowl until well combined.  Salt and pepper to taste.  Serve between slices of bread, topped with sprouts or lettuce.

---

"Wholesome food and drink are cheaper than doctors and hospitals."
Dr. Carl C. Wahl, - Essential Health Knowledge, 1966

---

## DILLY CREAMED CUCUMBERS

1 large cucumber (1-2 C. thinly sliced)
1/2 C. soy mayo
1 TB. soy sour cream
1 tsp. ume plum vinegar
1 tsp. horseradish
1-2 TB. fresh dill weed, chopped (½-1 tsp. dried)

1. Using a wire whisk, mix all ingredients, except cucumbers, until blended.
2. Stir cucumbers into sauce and serve.
**VARIATION:** <u>Cabbage Slaw</u>: *Replace cucumbers with shredded or thinly sliced red or green cabbage.*


## EASY BEET SALAD

4-5 cooked and cooled beets          Ume plum or rice vinegar
1 small onion, sliced                       salt and pepper to taste

Slice and toss beets with onions in a bowl. Sprinkle with Ume plum vinegar and salt and pepper to taste.


## WHEAT GLUTEN or TEMPEH SALAD
*This is a great salad served on a bed of lettuce or sprouts.*

2 C. (1 lb. 2 oz) tempeh or "chicken" style seitan, cut into bite size pieces
4 green onions, or one small onion, chopped
1/2 C. celery, diced
1/4 C. almonds, toasted (optional)
2 TB. parsley, fresh, chopped (1 tsp. dried)
1-2 TB. sweet or dill pickle, diced
1/2 C. mayonnaise
2 tsp. prepared mustard
2 TB. tamari
salt and pepper to taste

If using seitan, drain it well. Refrigerate the liquid it came in, for using in sauces or gravies. Combine all ingredients in a mixing bowl, adding more mayonnaise if needed, to make a creamy mixture. Salt and pepper to taste. Serve on top of lettuce, or eliminate the whole almonds and serve in a bun, topped with sprouts or lettuce.

## RICE SALAD

2 C. cooked brown long grain and wild rice mix
1- 10 oz. pkg. frozen or fresh peas, briefly cooked and cooled
3 stalks celery, sliced
3 green onions, chopped
1 green pepper, diced
1 head broccoli, florets only, cut in bite size pieces
1/4 C. olive oil
3 TB. soy sauce
2 TB. Ume plum vinegar
1 TB. curry powder
2 C. crunchy chow mein type noodles

Mix together all ingredients, except chow mein noodles. Chill in fridge before serving. Mix in crunchy noodles just before serving, so that they don't get soggy.

## QUICK SPAGHETTI SALAD

1 pound spaghetti
2 cloves garlic, minced
1 medium size onion, diced
1/4 C. pine nuts
1 tsp. dried basil
salt and pepper to taste
French dressing, (pg. 70) or your favourite dressing.

1. Cook 1 lb. of spaghetti in boiling water for 10-12 minutes, or until done. Drain and rinse with cold water, to cool down quickly.
2. Stir in garlic, onion, pine nuts and basil, and as much French dressing as preferred, tossing with tongs to coat spaghetti well. Salt and pepper to taste, and serve immediately; or cool in fridge for later. Serves 4-6

**VARIATIONS**: Quick Macaroni or spiral pasta Salad: *Substitute macaroni or spiral pasta for the spaghetti.*

"Not overeating is what I call the art of conscious eating. It is learning to take just the right amount of food and drink to support our individual needs on every level of our spiritual and worldly functioning. Researchers have shown that not overeating increases longevity.

Gabriel Cousens, M.D. – Conscious Eating

## ORIENTAL NOODLE SALAD

12 oz. Udon or linguine pasta
1 C. mung bean sprouts
1 TB. toasted sesame oil
1/3 C. crunchy peanut butter
1/3 C. water
2 TB. soy sauce
1 TB. rice vinegar

2-3 garlic cloves, minced
2 scallions, or 1 small onion, chopped fine
2 tsp. fresh ginger, minced
2 tsp. sesame seeds
1 tsp. hot toasted sesame oil
1 medium size carrot, grated
1/4 C. fresh basil, chopped

1.  Cook pasta in boiling water.  Cook until al dente, approximately 8-10 minutes.  Drain and rinse under cold water.
2.  Toss pasta and mung sprouts with 1 TB. toasted sesame oil.
3.  Combine all remaining ingredients in a bowl, except carrot and basil.  Mix with a whisk until smooth and creamy.
4.  Toss pasta/sprout mixture with the carrots, basil and peanut sauce. Chill and serve cold.
Serves 2-4
**SUGGESTIONS:** *This salad can also be served hot.  Eliminate rinsing the pasta with cold water, before proceeding with remaining instructions.  It can be served topped with sautéed veggies.*


## ZESTY VEGGIE PASTA SALAD

8 oz. pasta twists or other pasta
3 C. cut up veggies (a mixture of summer squash, beans, asparagus, snow peas etc.)
12 oz. jar marinated artichoke hearts
1 C. vegan cheese, diced (optional)
1/2 C. diced fresh tomatoes
1/4 C. olive oil
1 TB. Ume plum vinegar
1 TB. rice or cider vinegar
1 tsp. dried oregano (1TB. fresh, chopped)

1. Cook pasta and rinse with cold water.
2. Steam the 3 C. mixed veggies, just briefly (approximately 3-5 minutes).
3. Mix veggies and pasta with all remaining ingredients.  Marinade in the refrigerator for at least one hour before serving.  Serves 4

For more pasta salad recipes: See "Quick Green Pasta"- pg. 91,  and Vegetable Tofu Lo Mein, pg 89.  in the main pasta section. Serve both cold

## ORZO SALAD with Vegan Feta

*Orzo is small pasta shaped like rice.*

2 C. orzo
1 C. shitake mushrooms, chopped
1/3 C. oil cured black olives, pitted & sliced
1/2 C. cucumber, chopped
1/2 C. red onion, sliced
3/4 C. red pepper, chopped
1/4 C. fresh parsley, chopped (1 tsp. dried)

1 C. soy feta (pg. 153)
1/3 C. olive oil
3 TB. Balsamic vinegar
1/2 tsp. salt
1/8 tsp. black pepper
1 tsp. dried oregano
1 clove garlic, minced

Cook orzo in plenty of boiling water, 8-12 minutes, or until tender. Drain in a wire mesh colander, then rinse in cold water and drain again. Set aside to drain well.
Sauté mushrooms in about 2 TB. water, until soft. Set aside to cool.
Mix olives, cucumber, onion, pepper, parsley, cooled mushrooms and vegan feta with cooled and well-drained orzo.
Mix olive oil, vinegar, salt, pepper, oregano and garlic in a small bowl and whisk together well. Stir oil mixture into the orzo mixture. Serve salad at room temperature or cold.
Serves 4-6

## NACHO SALAD

*This salad is a complete meal in itself. Serve it with warmed tortillas.*
*Host a nacho salad party and have each guest bring one of the ingredients for this dish.*
*Readjust the amounts needed depending on number of guests.*

1 large bowl of lettuce & sprouts
4 C. cooked pinto beans
2-4 avocados, chopped
2-3 tomatoes, chopped
1 C. olives, sliced
1 C. cilantro, chopped
1-2 medium size onions, sliced or chopped

1 large cucumber, chopped
4 C. meatless ground, browned
2 C. vegan cheddar, grated
1 bottle salad dressing
1 large bag corn chips
2-4 C. salsa sauce
2 C. soy sour cream

**To construct salad:** Place a bottom layer of lettuce and sprouts in individual bowls or plates. On top of lettuce place desired amount of the remaining ingredients, except corn chips, salsa sauce and sour cream. Toss with some salad dressing and top with a handful of crumbled corn chips, and a spoonful or two of salsa and sour cream. Serves 8-10 people, depending on appetites, and additional dishes served.
**VARIATIONS:** *Add any of your favourite chopped veggies.* **Suggestions:** *chopped broccoli and cauliflower, sliced pickles and radishes, shredded cabbage.*

## EASY ORIENTAL MUNG BEAN SALAD

2 C. sprouted mung beans             ½-1 C. Oriental sesame dressing (pg. 71)
2 large radishes, sliced
1 medium size carrot, grated
1 C. purple or green cabbage, sliced or chopped
1 medium size tomato, chopped

Mix all ingredients together in a bowl, except the dressing. Toss salad with desired amount of dressing and serve.  Serves 3-4

### Additional ideas:
*Turn this recipe into a* <u>*Autumn Harvest Delight,*</u> *by adding raw grated zucchini, chopped broccoli, fresh basil, arugala, green peppers, diced cucumbers, parsley, cilantro, dill weed and some sprouted lentils and sunflower seeds. Add more sesame dressing if necessary.  Top the salad with a few edible nasturtium or borage flowers.*

## MINA'S CHICKPEA SALAD

*A favourite French River, family reunion dish.*

4 C. cooked chickpeas            1/4 C. white wine vinegar
1 green pepper, diced             2 TB. lemon juice
4 green onions, chopped (optional)     1/2 tsp. dried basil
1 small red onion, diced         1/2 tsp. dried oregano
1/2 C. diced celery              1-2 cloves garlic, minced
1/2 C. olive oil

Mix all ingredients and marinade several hours before serving.

**VARIATION:** *Add chopped red pepper for colour.*

<u>Mixed Bean Salad</u>: *Use only 1 cup of chickpeas and 1 C. each of kidney, navy and pinto beans; or any of your favourite beans.*

---

*"If you don't pay for the best foods you will pay a doctor."*
*Bernard Jensen Ph.D. - Food Healing For Man*

---

## QUINOA & BLACK BEAN SALAD

1 C. quinoa,
1 C. cooked black beans
1/2 C. corn
1/2 C. each of red onion & red pepper, chopped
1 tomato, chopped
1 clove garlic, minced
1/4 C. fresh parsley, chopped (1 TB. dried)
1 tsp. dried basil
3 TB. each of olive oil & apple cider vinegar
salt and pepper to taste

Cook the quinoa in 2½ C. water for approximately 15 minutes, or until tender and water is absorbed. Toss the cooled quinoa with the black beans and all remaining ingredients, except the oil, vinegar, salt and pepper. Mix the oil and vinegar together in a small jar, and pour over the veggie/bean mixture. Mix together well and salt and pepper to taste.


## BEAN & KAMUT SALAD

1/2 C. each of uncooked kidney & pinto beans
1/2 C. kamut grain
1/4 -1/2 C. fresh parsley (1 tsp. dried)
2 tsp. dried oregano
1 tsp. each dried dill weed & basil
2 cloves garlic, minced
1/4 tsp. salt
1/8 tsp. black pepper
1 medium size red onion, chopped (or 4 green onions)
1-2 medium size tomatoes, chopped
1/4 C. olive oil
1/4 C. apple cider vinegar

Soak beans and kamut overnight in a pot containing 4 cups of water. Drain in the morning and add 4 cups of fresh water to the pot. Cook for 60 minutes, or until beans are tender, or 20 minutes in a pressure cooker, letting the pot cool down naturally before opening it. Drain beans and kamut and rinse in cold water. Add beans and kamut with remaining ingredients, except the oil and vinegar, and mix together well. Mix oil and vinegar together in a separate container. Stir oil and vinegar mixture into bean and kamut mixture. Add more salt and pepper if necessary and refrigerate. This salad can be put together the day before you plan to serve it.

Harvest Salad, Pg. 68 ~ Goddess Dressing & Lemony Flax Oil Dressing, Pg. 72

# CHINESE STYLE EGGPLANT SALAD

1 recipe oriental salad dressing (pg. 71)
1 large eggplant
1/4-1/2 C. fresh cilantro leaves, chopped
3-4 green onion (use the green part too)
    (or substitute regular onion, chopped fine)

Peel and cut eggplant into bite size pieces, about 3/4 inch. Steam very briefly, until tender but not soggy. Remove eggplant from steamer and set aside to cool. When cool, toss the eggplant with enough dressing to coat all pieces. Sprinkled with cilantro and onions and marinate in fridge for at least one hour before serving.

# LAYERED SALAD

*This is a vegan spin on an old-time favourite.*

4-6 C. lettuce * chopped, and sprinkled generously with spike or herbal seasoning.
1 C. green pepper, sliced or diced
1 medium size red or yellow onion, sliced
1 C. celery, sliced
1 pkg. (1-2 C.) frozen peas (uncooked) or use fresh shelled
1/2 C. water chestnuts, sliced
1½ C. soy mayonnaise mixed with 1 TB. vegan worcestershire sauce
  (mayonnaise is spread over the top of veggies to edge of bowl)
Your favourite vegan cheese, grated and sprinkled on top of the mayonnaise mixture.

Put the ingredients in the order they are listed, in a large clear glass-serving bowl. The glass bowl allows for the colourful layers to be seen.
Cover and refrigerate 4-6 hours, or overnight. When ready to serve, sprinkle with your choice of toppings. Be sure to dip down to the bottom when serving.

**Toppings:** dried soy bacuns or fried and crumbled meatless bacon, chopped tomatoes and sliced or chopped avocados
* **Note:** *A combination of lettuce greens and spinach can be used.*

World famous health nutritionist, Paavo Airola, PhD., has proclaimed, that overeating of even health foods was one of the main causes of ill health, and that under eating was the most important health and longevity secret.

## SPINACH SALAD

1 pound fresh spinach
1 medium size onion, grated
1/2 C. olive oil
3 TB. lemon juice
1 garlic clove, minced
1/4 tsp. each of salt and pepper
2-3 medium size tomatoes, cut in bite size pieces

Wash spinach and drain. Cut into bite size pieces and toss with onion. Mix together oil, lemon, garlic, salt and pepper. Pour oil mixture over spinach and onion, and toss until well mixed. Garnish with the tomato pieces.

**VARIATIONS:** *Sprinkle with a handful of soy bacuns or other garnishes, such as: sliced olives, water chestnuts, tamari roasted sunflower seeds, vegan feta and bean or seed sprouts, and toss salad with Oriental Salad Dressing, see pg.71.*

## GREEK SALAD WITH ARUGALA

2-3 handfuls of mixed salad greens
1 handful of fresh arugala greens
1 cucumber, cut in small pieces
2 medium size tomatoes, chopped
1 small red onion, sliced fine
10 black oil cured olives, sliced
1/2 C. or more of vegan feta cheese (pg. 153)

Mix chopped salad greens, arugala, cucumber, tomato and onion together in a salad bowl. Top with olives and vegan feta cheese. Sprinkle with dressing.

**Dressing:**
Shake together in a jar, or serving container: 1/2 C. olive oil, 3 TB. lemon juice or vinegar, 1/2 tsp. dried oregano, 1/2 tsp. dried basil, 1/2 tsp. salt and black pepper.

**Other Salad Ideas:** Harvest Salad: *Add any of the following to the above salad: sliced carrots, grated zucchini, chopped broccoli, mung, lentil or radish sprouts, toasted sunflower seeds, diced chives, chopped green peppers, grated raw beets, shredded cabbage, fresh basil and nasturtium or borage flowers.*

> **SALAD TIP:** *A combination of shredded cabbage and sprouts, or all sprouts, makes a good substitute for lettuce.*

## TOMATO SALAD

5 medium size tomatoes

2 C. mixed greens

4 scallions, thinly sliced

1 TB. chopped fresh parsley

**Dressing:**

1/2 C. olive oil

2 TB. lemon juice

1 TB. fresh basil, chopped  (1 tsp. dried)

1/2 tsp. finely chopped garlic

1/2 tsp. salt

1/4 tsp. black pepper

Slice tomatoes and lay them on top of mixed greens.  Mix dressing ingredients together. Pour dressing on top of tomatoes.  Sprinkle with scallions and parsley.  Can be prepared in one large salad bowl or on individual serving plates.

## SPICY CUCUMBER & TOMATO SALAD

1 C. tomatoes, chopped

1 C. cucumbers, cut in bite size chunks

1/2 C. red onion, sliced

1-2 small green chili peppers, minced

3 TB. cilantro leaves, chopped

1 TB. Ume plum or other vinegar

2 TB. lemon juice

Mix veggies and cilantro in a serving bowl.  Stir together vinegar and lemon juice and pour over salad. Toss salad to coat the veggies.

**VARIATION:** _Asparagus salad:_  *Instead of or in addition to tomatoes and cucumber, use asparagus, steamed 5 minutes, cut into 1-1 ½ inch pieces and chilled quickly in cold water.*

"There are people all over the country today planting organic gardens.  Good food only comes from soil that has been properly cared for and composted to keep the mineral balance high...We must have this kind of food, because when we are lacking minerals and vitamins, we are on our way to dis-ease, ill health, ailments----all sorts of physical problems."

-Bernard Jensen, Ph.D.- Food Healing For Man

# SALAD DRESSINGS & TOPPINGS

## SWEET N' SOUR SALAD DRESSING

3/4 C. olive oil
1/2 C. apple cider vinegar
2 TB. lemon or lime juice
2 TB. maple syrup
2 tsp. prepared mustard
1/2 tsp. paprika
1 tsp. each dried basil & dill weed
1/2 tsp. cardamom powder
2 cloves garlic, minced (or ½ tsp. powder)
1/8 tsp. xantham gum

Mix all ingredients in a jar, and shake vigorously to combine well.   Shake before serving.

## FRENCH DRESSING

1 C. olive oil
3/4 C. ketchup
1/4 C. water
1/4 tsp. garlic powder
1/4 tsp. celery salt
1/8 tsp. cayenne pepper
1/2 C. apple cider vinegar
2 tsp. prepared horseradish

2 ½ tsp. prepared mustard
1 tsp. paprika
1 tsp. dried basil
1 tsp. dried oregano
1 tsp. worcestershire sauce
2 TB. sweetener (optional)

Mix all ingredients together and serve.

**VARIATIONS**:  Creamy French Dressing:  *Add 1/2 C. or more of soy sour cream or soy mayonnaise.*

"It takes less water to produce a year's food for a pure vegetarian (vegan) than to produce a month's supply for a meat eater."
        John Robbins  - Diet for A New America

## SIMPLE OIL AND VINEGAR DRESSING

3/4 C. olive oil
1/4 C. apple cider vinegar or lemon juice
1/4 C. catsup (optional)
1 clove garlic, minced or squeezed

1/2 -1 tsp. sea salt
1/2 tsp. paprika
1/4 tsp. black pepper

Shake all ingredients in a jar and serve.


## ORIENTAL SALAD DRESSING

1/4 C. sesame oil
1/8 C. toasted sesame oil
1/4 C. vegetable oil
1/4 C. rice vinegar
1/8 C. Ume plum vinegar
2 TB. soy sauce

1/2 tsp. garlic powder
1/2 tsp. prepared mustard
1 tsp. horseradish
1/2 tsp. ginger powder
1 TB. ketchup or tomato sauce
1/8 tsp. xantham gum (optional)

Mix all ingredients together in a jar or container and serve.

**VARIATION**: <u>Creamy Oriental Dressing</u>; *add 1/8 C. sesame tahini, and 1/8 C. sour cream to above mixture.*


## NANCY'S RASPERRY VINEGAR DRESSING

1/2 C. olive oil
1/2 C. raspberry vinegar
2 tsp. sweetener
1 TB. prepared mustard
1 tsp. lemon pepper
1/8 tsp. xantham gum
salt to taste

Mix all ingredients together and serve.

## GODDESS DRESSING

1/2 C. olive oil
1/4 C. tahini
1/4 C. apple cider vinegar
1 TB. soy sauce
1 TB. lemon juice
1/2 tsp. garlic granules (1 fresh clove, minced)
1 tsp. dried parsley
1/3 C. water
1/4 tsp. sea salt
1/8 tsp. xantham gum

In a blender, mix all ingredients together until smooth and creamy. It will thicken more after refrigeration. Thin with water or lemon juice if necessary.

## LEMONY FLAX OIL DRESSING

1/4 C. flax oil
1/4 C. lemon juice
1/4 tsp. dried basil
1/4 tsp. dried dill
1 clove garlic, minced (¼ tsp. dry)
1/8 tsp. salt and pepper (or to taste)
1 tsp. Braggs Liquid Aminos
1/8 tsp. xantham gum  (optional)

Mix all ingredients together until well combined.
**Substitution idea:** *Replace part or all of lemon juice with lime juice, and all or of part flax oil with olive or grape seed oil.*

## TAMARI SUNFLOWER SEED SALAD TOPPING

Dry roast raw sunflower seeds in a heavy un-oiled skillet, over medium heat. When lightly browned, sprinkle with tamari soy sauce. Stir to coat seeds, then remove from heat and cool. Sprinkle on salads. **VARIAITON:** *Seeds can also be sprinkled with granulated garlic. Most nuts are great roasted this way.*

# Soups

## SPLIT PEA DAHL

2 C. yellow or green split peas  
6-8 C. water  
1 C. carrots, finely chopped  
1 large potato, cubed small  
1 clove garlic, minced (optional)  
4 TB Cilantro (fresh)

1-2 tsp. Garam Masala spice  
1 tsp. turmeric  
Dash cayenne, optional  
1-2 tsp. salt

1. Cook split peas in 6 cups of water until mushy, approximately 1 to 1 ½ hours, or 8-12 minutes in a pressure cooker with 1 tsp. of vegetable oil. Immediately cool down pressure cooker by putting the pot under cold running water.
2. Transfer peas to a soup pot and add carrots, potatoes, and garlic, and remaining 2 cups of water. Simmer approximately 20 minutes, or until veggies are soft. Stir often to prevent the soup from burning.
3. Add spices and salt at last 5 minutes of cooking. Add more water if a thinner soup is preferred. Salt and pepper to taste. Serves 4-6

## CANADIAN SPLIT PEA SOUP

*A vegan rendition of an all time favourite. Traditionally it was made thick enough so that a spoon could stand upright in the bowl. Add more liquid if you prefer it thinner.*

2 C. yellow split peas  
1 ½ C. onions, chopped  
1/2 C. celery, chopped  
8 C. water  
2-3 tsp. salt

1 C. potatoes, cubed small  
1 C. carrots, chopped fine  
1 TB. dried parsley (3 TB. fresh)

Simmer all ingredients until peas are tender, approximately 1 to 1 ½ hours. Or cook peas in a pressure cooker with 1 tsp. oil, for 8-12 minutes. Immediately cool down pressure cooker by holding lid under cold water; then transfer peas and remaining ingredients to a soup pot, and simmer about 20 minutes or until veggies are soft. Thin the soup if desired, with more water. Salt and pepper to taste.

**VARIATION:** Indian Curry Split Pea Soup: *At last 10 minutes of cooking, add 1-2 tsp. curry powder, 1/2-1 tsp. ginger powder, and 1 tsp. dry basil.*

# LENTIL SOUP

1½ C. dried lentils
5-7 C. water
2 TB. broth powder (optional)
2 garlic cloves, minced
1/2 C. onions, chopped
1 C. potatoes, diced
1/2 C. carrots, diced
1/2 C. chopped Swiss chard (optional)
1/2 tsp. each of turmeric and ground cumin
½-1 tsp. each of dried thyme and ground coriander
1/4 tsp. each of ground cardamom and black pepper
1/8 tsp. cayenne pepper, or to taste (optional)
1 TB. lemon juice
Salt to taste

1.  Place lentils, 5 cups of water, broth powder, garlic, onions, potatoes and carrots in a soup pot.
2.  Bring to a boil and simmer for 30 minutes, or until lentils are soft.
3.  Add remaining ingredients and simmer an additional 5-10 minutes, adding more water if necessary.  Salt to taste and serve.

# BARLEY TOMATO SOUP

4 C. water
1-28 oz. can (3 cups), diced tomatoes, or spicy spaghetti sauce
1-2 garlic cloves, minced
1 large onion, chopped fine
1/3 C. uncooked barley
1/2 C. fresh mushrooms, chopped or sliced
1/2 tsp. dried dill weed
1/2 tsp. dried basil
1/4 C. chopped fresh parsley (2 TB dried)
salt and pepper (to taste)

Put everything except the dill, basil, parsley, salt and pepper in a soup pot.  Cover pot and bring to a boil. Turn heat down and simmer slowly for approximately 1 hour, or until barley and vegetables are tender.  Add dill, basil and parsley the last 10 minutes of cooking.  Salt and pepper to taste.  Serve.

**Note:** *This soup is ready to serve in 25 minutes, if cooked in a pressure cooker. It thickens more as it sits, so more water may need to be added for thinning.  Adjust seasonings if necessary.*

# HEARTY ITALIAN VEGGIE BEAN SOUP

4-6 C. water or vegetable stock
2 C. cooked navy beans
1 C. onions, chopped
2 garlic cloves, minced
2 C. mixed veggies (carrots, mushrooms, celery, corn, cabbage etc.
    chopped into bite size pieces)
3 C. diced tomatoes, or sauce
1 C. potatoes, cubed small
1/2 tsp. each of dried basil, oregano, summer savory
1/4 tsp. each of dried thyme, rosemary, marjoram, sage
2 TB. soy sauce
1 tsp. black pepper
salt to taste

1. Put 4 C. of the water and all other ingredients, except the dried herbs, soy sauce, pepper and salt in a large soup pot.
2. Bring to a boil and simmer approximately 30 minutes, or until vegetables are tender.
3. Add all remaining ingredients and simmer an additional 10-15 minutes, adding remaining l-2 cups of water, if soup is thicker than you prefer.  Salt to taste and adjust seasonings if necessary.

**VARIATION:** *Substitute <u>lima beans</u> or any other bean for the navy beans.  Add 1/4 -1/2 C. uncooked barley with the water. <u>Minestrone Soup:</u> Add a half-cup of uncooked macaroni or other small pasta, during last 12 minutes of cooking, and add more water or stock if necessary.*


# TOMAS'S POTATO LEEK SOUP

7 C. water
3 TB. broth powder
3 large potatoes, cubed small
3 leeks, sliced in thick rounds
1/2-1 C. bok choy or cabbage, chopped
1 tsp. dried tarragon leaf
salt and pepper to taste
1 heaping tsp. cornstarch mixed with 1/4 C. water

1.  Put all ingredients except tarragon, salt and pepper, and cornstarch mixture in soup pot.
2.  Bring to a boil, then lower heat and simmer until potatoes are tender.
3. Add remaining ingredients and simmer an additional 5-10 minutes, or until soup is slightly thickened.  Serves 2-4

## ORIENTAL HOT N' SOUR SOUP

4 C. water
2 TB. broth powder
2 TB. soy sauce
1/2 tsp. salt
1/4 tsp. each of asafetida (hing powder) & black pepper
1/2 C. sliced shitake mushrooms
1 tsp. ginger (fresh chopped) or 1/2-1 tsp. dry ground
1/2 C. veggies, such as chopped Swiss chard, broccoli, carrots, snow peas
1/2 C. celery, diced
1/4 C. water
2-3 TB. cornstarch
1/4 pound tofu, cubed small
2 TB. rice vinegar
1 tsp. hot or regular toasted sesame oil

1. Place all ingredients up to and including the celery in a medium size soup pot.
2. Bring to a boil and simmer 5-10 minutes, or until veggies are tender.
3. Mix 2-3 TB. cornstarch (3 if you like a thicker soup) with the 1/4 C. water.
4. Add tofu, rice vinegar, and cornstarch mixture to soup pot, and cook 3-5 minutes, or until soup thickens. Stir in sesame oil and serve in individual bowls. Serves 2-4
**ADDITIONS OR SUBSTITUTES**: *dried mushrooms, bamboo shoots, water chestnuts, diced bok choy.*

## SAVORY MISO SOUP

5 C. water
2 TB. broth powder
2 garlic cloves, minced
1 C. mushrooms, sliced
1-1 ½ C. chopped greens, such as cabbage or Swiss chard
3 TB. light miso paste
2 TB. soy sauce
1/4 C. onions, sliced, or chopped green onions
1 medium carrot, diced
1/4 C. seaweed, (arame or hizi, or your choice)
2 TB. parsley, fresh chopped or 2 tsp. dried
1/4 pound tofu, cubed small

Combine all ingredients in a soup pot and bring to a boil. Turn heat down and simmer about 10-15 minutes. Makes approximately 4 servings.

# THAI COCONUT NOODLE SOUP

4 C. water
3-4 TB. broth powder
2 garlic cloves, minced
2 tsp. ginger, fresh minced (½ tsp. powder)
1 small onion, sliced
2 C. sliced veggies (a mixture of mushrooms, carrots, Chinese or regular
    cabbage, broccoli, celery, etc. - whatever you have on hand)
1/4 C. each of fresh chopped cilantro and basil, or 1-2 tsp. dried basil.
3 TB. soy sauce
1 small chopped tomato (optional)
1/4 lb. oriental rice sticks or noodles
1 -14 oz. can coconut milk (or substitute water)
hot cayenne pepper, optional (to taste)
Fresh cilantro or basil for topping

1.  Simmer water with broth powder, garlic, ginger and onion for 10 minutes.
2.  Add all remaining ingredients except coconut milk, cayenne pepper and herb topping.
3.  Bring to a boil, then reduce heat and simmer approximately 10 minutes, or until noodles are soft, and veggies are tender, but still crisp,
4.  Stir in coconut milk and cayenne, and simmer an additional 5 minutes.  Salt and pepper to taste.  Serve sprinkled with fresh chopped cilantro or basil.   As a main meal, this recipe makes enough for 2 very large servings.

**Additions:** *Add any mixture of fresh, or in season veggies, and 1/4 lb. cubed tofu.*

**VARIATION:** Vietnamese "Pho" Noodle Soup: *Add 4 star anise, ¼-1/2C cubed tofu and substitute 4-6 slices of ginger in step one. Eliminate the coconut milk and add 2 additional cups of broth. Cook noodles in a separate pot and pour broth and veggies over the noodles, in individual bowls, when ready to serve.  Garnish each serving with fresh cilantro or basil and optional topping of fresh mung bean sprouts.*

" A research study in New England compared typical meat eaters, lacto-ovo vegetarians and vegans.......All the subjects were fairly young, ranging in age from twenty to forty seven. The average meat eater cholesterol level was 173, which is lower than the average American, but not unusual in a young population.  The lacto-vegetarian averaged 150. And the vegan's averaged, - believe it or not---135. A Harvard Research study found about the same thing."
    Neal Barnard, M.D.  - Food for Life,
    How the New Four Food Groups Can Save Your Live.

## GARLICKY BEAN SOUP

1 TB. oil
1 medium size onion, (1 cup) chopped or sliced
1 C. shitake or other mushrooms, chopped
1 large head of garlic, about 10 cloves
3 C. vegetable broth
1 C. carrot, chopped
2 ½ C. cooked pinto, or other beans
3 C. fresh or canned stewed tomatoes or sauce

1/4 tsp. cumin powder
1/2 tsp chili fiesta blend-see pg.102
1 tsp. dried Italian herb blend,
    or oregano
1 tsp. sea salt
1/2 tsp. black pepper
lime juice (optional)

Heat oil in a soup pot. Sauté onion and mushrooms until soft. Add all remaining ingredients except lime juice, and cook until carrots are soft. Adjust seasonings if necessary. If desired serve with a splash of lime juice. 4-6 servings.

## FRENCH ONION SOUP

1 TB. oil
3 large onions, sliced thin
5 cloves garlic, minced
1/2-1 TB. unbleached white flour
3 C. vegetable stock *

1/4 tsp. dried thyme
1/4 tsp. pepper
1-2 TB. tamari
salt to taste

1. In a soup pot cook onions in oil over medium heat, for about 10 minutes. Stir often. Add garlic. Cook 5 more minutes.
2. With a whisk mix flour with 1/2 C. of vegetable stock and add to remaining 2 ½ C stock. Add stock mixture and remaining ingredients to onions and garlic. Simmer another 5-10 minutes. Add more liquid for a thinner soup. Salt to taste and serve. Serves 4

**SUGGESTIONS:** * *Instead of vegetable stock, use 3-5 TB. vegan broth powder mixed with 3 C. water. For a more authentic version of this soup; add small pieces of toasted bread sprinkled with vegan parmesan, just before serving.*

---

"The vegetarian manner of living, by it's purely physical effect on the human temperament, would most beneficially influence the lot of mankind."
- Albert Einstein

# HARVEST CORN & TOMATO SOUP

1 TB. oil
1/2 small onion, diced
1-2 garlic cloves, minced
2 ½ C. vegetable stock
    or 2 ½ C. water with 2-3 TB. broth powder
½ - 1 tsp. dried sage
1/2 tsp. each salt & pepper
1 C. canned, frozen or fresh corn kernels
2 C. tomatoes, diced
1 TB. cornstarch in 1/4 C. water

1. In soup pot sauté onions and garlic in oil until soft.
2. Add vegetable stock, sage, salt and pepper, and bring to a boil.
3. Add corn, tomatoes and cornstarch dissolved in water. Cook and stir 5-10 minutes or until tomatoes are soft, and liquid has thickened slightly. Adjust seasonings if necessary.
Serves 4

# SEASONED SEITAN VEGGIE SOUP with orzo

4 C. water
3-4 TB. broth powder
2 cloves garlic, minced
1 small carrot, diced
1/2 C. celery, diced
1 C. bok choy, chopped
3/4 C. diced seasoned seitan

1 TB. Hizik seaweed, crumbled
1/4 tsp. Dulse flakes
1/4 C. uncooked orzo
1 TB. soy sauce
1/8 tsp. ginger powder
1/4 tsp. crushed dried sage
Salt & pepper to taste

Combine water and all remaining ingredients. Stir and cook until orzo is soft, approximately 15 minutes. Salt and pepper to taste. Serves 4

"Vegetarians have the best diet. They have the lowest rate of coronary disease of any group in the country."
            Dr. William Castelli - Farmington Heart Study

# CREAMY COCONUT SQUASH SOUP

2 TB. oil
1 TB. fresh ginger, minced
1/2 C. onion, chopped
2-3 garlic cloves, minced
6 C. winter squash, or a mixture of squash and yams
    cut into 1/2" or smaller cubes
2 medium size, potatoes, diced small
4 C. water
4 TB. broth powder
2-3 tsp. dried basil
1 tsp. each of dried parsley & turmeric
14 oz. can coconut milk
1 ½ TB. curry powder
1 TB. each of soy sauce & spike seasoning
salt and pepper to taste
fresh cilantro or basil for topping

1.  In a large soup pot, sauté ginger, onion and garlic in oil until soft.
2.  Add squash, potatoes and water mixed with the broth powder.
3.  Simmer soup for 15-20 minutes or until veggies are tender.
4.  Place 1/3-1/2 of the soup in a blender and process until smooth.
5.  Return blended soup to pot and add all remaining ingredients, except fresh cilantro.
6.  Simmer an additional 5-10 minutes.
7.  Salt and pepper to taste, and serve sprinkled with chopped cilantro or basil.
Serves 4-6

**SUGGESTION:** *Substitute liquid vegetable broth for the water and broth powder.*

"Plant based diets provide a good balance of nutrients to support a healthy pregnancy and are superior to diets containing milk and other animal products.................Support for a vegan diet comes from a study of 1700 pregnancies at the Farm, a large vegan community in Tennessee. The study showed a record of safety that would delight obstetricians..............a vegan menu is preferred for nursing women too. A plant based diet reduces levels of environmental contamination in breast milk, compared to that of meat eaters."
Neal Barnard, M.D.
- Food For Life, How the New Four Food Groups can save your Life.

# TRADITIONAL CREAM OF VEGGIE SOUP

1/2 C. onions, chopped
1-2 cloves garlic, minced
1 TB. oil
3 C. <u>unsweetened</u> soy milk
1 tsp each of spike and tamari
2-3 C. mixed veggies (see suggestions below)
1 C. soy milk
3 TB. cornstarch or flour
Salt & pepper to taste

1.  In soup pot sauté onion and garlic in oil.
2.  Add 3 C. soy milk, spike, tamari and mixed veggies.
3.  Bring to a boil, then turn heat down and simmer until veggies are soft.
4.  Mix remaining 1 C milk with cornstarch, and combine together well.  Add cornstarch mixture to soup pot.
5. Simmer until soup is thick.  Salt and pepper to taste. If desired, thin with more milk.
Serves 4
**Veggie Suggestions:** *chopped or sliced mushrooms, asparagus, celery, corn, peas, potatoes*
**VARIATION:** <u>*Cream of Mushroom Soup*</u>*: Use 2-3 cups chopped mushrooms instead of the mixed veggies.*

# POTATO COCONUT SOUP

4 C. water
2 TB. broth powder
3 C. potatoes, cubed small
3/4 C. onions, chopped
2 cloves garlic, minced
3/4 C. celery, diced
2 tsp. fresh ginger, minced

3/4 C. mushrooms, chopped
1/2 tsp. spike
1/8 tsp. cayenne pepper
1 tsp. dried basil
1-14 oz. can coconut milk
fresh chopped basil (optional)
salt & pepper to taste

1. Cook potatoes, onions, garlic, celery, ginger and mushrooms in water with broth powder.
2. When potatoes are soft, add spike, cayenne, dried basil and coconut milk.
3. Simmer 5-10 minutes until soup is hot.  Salt and pepper to taste, and serve with a sprinkling of fresh chopped basil leaves.  Serves 4

**TIP:** *Adjust amount of milk in cream soups, for a thinner or thicker soup.*

## CREAMY POTATO & CORN SOUP

1 TB. oil
1 medium shallot or onion, chopped
2 cloves garlic, minced
2 C. potatoes, diced
3 C. unsweetened soy milk
1-2 TB. unbleached white flour
1/4 C. water
1 C. canned corn, un-drained (or use fresh corn.)
1/4 C. fresh parsley or cilantro, chopped
1/2 tsp. salt and pepper
1/8 tsp. kelp powder (optional)
1 TB. tamari
1/4 tsp. thyme
1 medium size tomato for topping, diced

Heat oil in a soup pot and add shallot and garlic. Sauté approximately 5 minutes. Add potatoes and soy milk. Cover and cook about 10 minutes. Whisk the flour with 1/4 C. water and add to the pot with all remaining ingredients, except the diced tomato. Cook and stir until potatoes are soft and mixture is slightly thickened. Serve individual bowls of soup topped with diced tomatoes. Makes 2 very large or 4 small servings.
**VARIATION:** Potato & Corn Chowder: *Increase flour by 1-2 TB. for a thick chowder.*


## CREAMY COCONUT/VEGGIE CHOWDER

6 C. unsweetened soy milk
3 TB. broth powder
2 cloves garlic, minced
2 tsp. fresh ginger, minced
4 C. potatoes, cubed small
1 C. mushrooms, sliced
5 TB. unbleached white flour

1 TB. tamari, soy sauce
7 oz. (approx. 1 C) coconut milk
1/2 -3/4 C. peas
1 tsp. Spike seasoning
1 ½ tsp. dried basil
fresh chopped basil, optional
salt & pepper, to taste

Mix 5 cups of the milk with broth powder, garlic, ginger, potatoes and mushrooms. Bring to a boil, and then reduce heat and simmer until potatoes are tender. Whisk the 5 TB. flour with the remaining 1 C. soy milk and add to the pot with all remaining ingredients, except the fresh basil, salt and pepper. Stir until chowder has thickened. Salt and pepper to taste. Serve this thick chowder with a sprinkling of fresh chopped basil. Makes 4 -6 servings.
**VARIATION**: *Experiment with different veggies and seasonings.*

# GAZPACHO

**A cold veggie/tomato soup, best served on a hot summer day.**

4 C. cold water
2-3 large ripe tomatoes, (2-3 cups) chopped fine
1 green pepper, (1 cup) minced
1-2 cloves garlic, minced
1 C. mixture of fresh chopped herbs: chives, parsley, basil, tarragon, oregano etc.
1 medium size onion, sliced thin
1 cucumber, (1 cup) diced
3 TB. olive oil
3 TB. lemon juice
1/2 tsp. paprika
1 TB. Braggs Liquid Aminos or soy sauce
1 tsp. fresh hot pepper, minced
1/2 tsp. salt and pepper (or to taste)
parsley or cilantro for topping

Mix all ingredients, except parsley or cilantro topping, together in a large bowl, and chill for a couple of hours or overnight. Serve sprinkled with chopped fresh parsley or cilantro.
Serves 4-6

# SPICY MEXICAN BEAN & VEGGIE SOUP

2-3 C. cooked pinto beans
3 C. stewed or diced tomatoes
3 cloves garlic, minced
1 medium size onion, chopped
1/2 C. each celery and green pepper, diced
3/4 C. carrots, chopped
1 C. mushrooms, chopped
2 ½ C. water
2 TB. veggie broth powder
1 C. fresh cilantro, chopped
2-3 tsp. chili fiesta blend powder (see pg. 102)
1/2 tsp. dried oregano
Salt & pepper to taste
Cilantro for topping

Mix all ingredients except salt and pepper and cilantro topping, in a soup pot. Simmer 20-30 minutes or until veggies are soft. Thin soup with more water if desired. Salt and pepper to taste and serve topped with fresh chopped cilantro. Serves 4

## MEXICAN TORTILLA SOUP

4 small corn or wheat tortillas,
1 small onion, chopped
2 garlic cloves, minced
1 TB. oil
2 C. diced, canned or fresh tomatoes
1/4 C. chopped, fresh cilantro
2 C. vegetable stock *
1 C. tomato sauce

1-2 tsp. chili fiesta blend powder (pg. 102)
1/2 -1 tsp. dried marjoram
1/2 C. Vegan Monterey Jack, shredded
Vegan sour cream
Fresh cilantro, chopped
Avocado, diced (Optional)
1 lime (substituted bottled lime juice)
Salt & pepper to taste

1. Cut tortillas into bite size strips. Bake strips in a 400° oven until lightly browned and slightly crisp, 5-10 minutes. Set aside to cool.
2. In a soup pot sauté onion and garlic in oil until soft. Add the tomatoes, 1/4 C. cilantro, stock, tomato sauce, chili fiesta blend powder and marjoram. Simmer 10-15 minutes. Salt and pepper to taste.
3. Divide tortillas and shredded vegan cheese among 4 soup bowls. Ladle soup into bowls. Garnish with a dollop of sour cream, fresh chopped cilantro, diced avocado and a squeeze of lime juice. Serves 2-4
**Note:** * *In place of stock use 4 TB. broth powder and 2 C. water. Use more or less liquid depending on desired thickness of soup.*

## VEGGIE SEAWEED SOUP

*This is a light soup to serve before the main course.*

5 C. water
2 TB. broth powder
1/2 TB. fresh ginger, minced
1/8 tsp. asafetida (hing) powder
1/3-1/2 C. dried seaweed
4-6 green onions, (with tops) chopped

1 C. green cabbage, chopped
1 small carrot, chopped
2 medium size potatoes, cubed small
1 TB. tamari
1 TB. fresh cilantro, chopped
salt & pepper to taste

1. Bring water, broth powder and ginger to a boil, then simmer for approximately 5 minutes.
2. Break seaweed into bite size pieces. Add seaweed and all remaining ingredients except cilantro and salt and pepper, to the broth mixture. Simmer until veggies are tender.
3. Taste broth and add salt and pepper if necessary. Serve with a sprinkling of fresh cilantro. Serves 4-6

**VARIATIONS:** *A variety of vegetables can be used in this soup; such as snow peas, broccoli, mushrooms or chopped chives. Substitute 1 chopped medium sized onion for the green onions.*

## POSOLE   Mexican Corn Soup

*This is a traditional New Mexican soup, which is very simple to make. Serve it in small bowls with tamales or other Mexican fare. The posole corn takes a long time to cook, even in a pressure cooker.*

1 C. dry posole corn (soaked overnight)
(Or use frozen)
water
1 small (1/2 C.) onion, chopped
2 cloves garlic, minced
1 TB. oil
1-12 oz. pkg. (approx. 1 ½ C.)
meatless ground

1 tsp. each dried oregano & cumin
1/2 tsp. salt
1 C. diced tomatoes
2 tsp. chili fiesta blend powder, pg. 102
1/16-1/8 tsp. cayenne pepper
3-5 C. water
salt and pepper to taste
fresh chopped cilantro

1. Pressure cook the corn in the recommended amount of water for your cooker, for approximately 40-60 minutes, or until corn is soft. Let the cooker cool down naturally. Save the water in cooker. Don't strain the corn. (It will take approximately two hours to cook the corn using the conventional stovetop method.)
2. Sauté onion and garlic, until soft, in a skillet with the 1 TB. oil. Add the meatless ground and cumin and oregano. Stir and fry until well mixed. Add sautéed mixture to the corn and left over water in the pressure cooker, or transfer all ingredients to a soup pot.
3. Add salt, tomatoes, chili fiesta powder, cayenne pepper, and 3 cups of water. Simmer for approximately 30 minutes or until the ingredients are well blended and hot. Salt and pepper to taste, and adjust seasonings. Add more water if soup is too thick. Serve sprinkled with chopped cilantro. Serves 2-4. *Other Additions: chopped red green sweet or chili peppers.*

## SPICY GREEN CHILI SOUP   *easy & quick to prepare*

3 C. water
2 TB. broth powder
5 cloves garlic, minced
1/2 C. onions, diced
4 large potatoes (4 C. small cubes)

1-15oz can mild-medium green enchilada sauce
1/4 C. chives, minced (optional)
1/2 C. each corn kernels & chopped, fresh cilantro
1 tsp. salt
1/2 tsp. each black pepper & ground cumin

In a medium size soup pot add water, broth powder, garlic, onions and potatoes. Cook 5-10 minutes or until potatoes are tender. Add remaining ingredients and simmer until mixture is well combined and hot. Serves 4-6

> "Veganism isn't just a strict vegetarian diet; it is a complete philosophical viewpoint. It is a practical outlook, simple to understand and aspires to the highest environmental and spiritual values. I am sure it holds the key to a future lifestyle for a humane planetary guardianship."
> Howard Lyman - X-cattle rancher and author of Mad Cowboy

# Main Dish
# Pasta

## PAD THAI

1 pound uncooked udon or linguine pasta
2 C. mung bean sprouts
1 TB. oil
2 garlic cloves, minced
2 tsp. fresh ginger, minced
1 C. sliced mushrooms
2 C. mixture of snow peas, broccoli and carrots
1/4 pound extra firm tofu, cubed
1/4 C. water
1/3-1/2 C. tamari
2 TB. lime juice
1/8-1/4 tsp. (or to taste) cayenne pepper (optional)
3 TB. cilantro, chopped

1/4 C. peanuts or cashews, chopped
4 scallions or chives, chopped (optional)
fresh basil or cilantro, chopped

1.  Cook noodles until tender. (Proceed to step 2) Drain pasta when done and mix with 1 cup uncooked bean sprouts. Set aside.
2.  While the noodles are cooking; sauté garlic, ginger and mushrooms until soft, in the 1 TB. oil.  Add snow peas, broccoli, carrots and tofu. Add ¼ cup water to the pan. Cover pan and steam until veggies are hot but still crisp.
3.  Add tamari, lime juice and optional cayenne pepper to cooked veggies in pan.
4.  Immediately add cooked noodles and cilantro to sir fry. Using tongs, toss and combine noodles with sauce and veggies.
5.  When the noodles are hot and coated with the tamari, lime juice sauce, remove from heat and serve on individual plates. Top each serving with chopped nuts, scallions, fresh chopped basil and remaining uncooked bean sprouts. Served with an appetizer, such as fresh spring rolls, this meal will serve 4.

**VARIATION:** *See page 63 for Oriental Noodle Salad with a peanut butter sauce.  Serve it hot with sautéed veggies.*

---

"The politics of milk is responsible for the common belief that "milk is the perfect food," and it determines the cost of the milk you drink.  Milk has no valid claim as the perfect food.  As nutrition, it produces allergies in infants, diarrhea and cramps in the older child and adult, and may be a factor in the development of heart attacks and strokes."
        Frank A. Oski M.D.  & John D. Bell   - Don't Drink your Milk - 1977
    (The frightening new medical facts about the world's most overrated nutrient)

---

## SPAGHETTI WITH CREAM SAUCE

1 lb. uncooked spaghetti
2 C. unsweetened soy milk
2 TB. cornstarch
1 tsp. tamari
salt, pepper and spike to taste
2 TB. oil
1 C. sliced mushrooms

1 small onion, chopped
3 cloves garlic, minced
1/4 C. pine nuts (optional)
1 tsp. dried oregano
1/4 C. chopped fresh parsley or basil (optional)
Vegan parmesan

1. Cook pasta approx. 10-12 minutes or until done.
2. While the spaghetti cooks, combine soymilk and cornstarch in a saucepan. Use a whisk or beater to combine them together well. Over medium heat stir the sauce until it comes to a boil. Reduce heat and simmer and stir until thickened. Stir in tamari, salt, pepper and spike during last few minutes of cooking.
3. While the sauce is simmering, heat oil in a skillet and sauté mushrooms, onion and garlic. When veggies are tender, stir in the nuts and oregano. Keep the sauce and veggies warm while cooking the pasta.
4. Strain the pasta when done and put it in a large bowl, or back in the pot it was cooked in. Pour the sauce over it and use tongs to toss the pasta with the sauce.
5. Divide pasta on individual plates. Spoon sautéed veggies on top, and sprinkle with vegan parmesan and chopped fresh parsley or basil. Serves 2-4

## VEGETABLE TOFU LO MEIN

*This dish is very easy and quick to prepare, and delicious served hot or cold.*

8 oz. linguine, udon, or ramen noodles
3 TB. oil
1 clove garlic, minced
1/4 tsp. dried basil
1 TB. fresh ginger, minced
1/2 lb. extra firm tofu, cubed
1 medium carrot, cut in small sticks

1/4 lb. snow peas (optional)
1/2 C. green pepper, thinly sliced
4 TB. tamari, soy sauce
3 TB. toasted sesame oil *
8 oz. mung bean sprouts
fresh cilantro for topping, chopped
chopped cashews or peanuts

1. Cook noodles just until tender. Drain and toss with 1 TB. toasted sesame oil. Set aside.
2. In a wok or skillet sauté garlic, basil, ginger and tofu in 3 TB. oil, for about 5 minutes.
3. Add Veggies and stir until combined. Veggies should be somewhat crisp when served.
4. Add cooked noodles, tamari and remaining 2 TB. sesame oil. Continue to toss the pasta, until the noodles are hot and coated with the soy sauce and oil. Serve topped with bean sprouts, cilantro and a sprinkling of chopped cashews. Serves 2-3
    * If you like it hot, use some _hot_ sesame oil, or add some hot pepper to the recipe.

## CREAMY GARLIC PASTA

1 pound penne or spiral pasta
1- 12.3 oz. Pkg. silken firm tofu
(or substitute regular soft tofu)
1 TB. vegetable oil
4 TB. water
3-5 cloves garlic, minced
1 TB. tamari

1 tsp each dried basil & oregano
salt & pepper to taste
2 TB. oil
8 oz mushrooms, sliced
1 small onion, sliced
2 TB. fresh chopped basil

1.  In a blender mix tofu, 1 TB. oil, water, 2 cloves of garlic, tamari, basil and oregano, until smooth.  Add salt and pepper to taste.  Set aside.
2.  In a skillet heat 2 TB. oil and sauté mushrooms, remaining garlic, and onion until tender.
3.  Cook noodles per package directions, approximately 8-12 minutes in boiling water. Drain. Mix sauce with noodles, stirring well to coat evenly.
4.  Serve topped with sautéed veggies and a sprinkling of fresh basil.  Serves 2-4

## QUICK N' EASY PASTA FOR TWO

3 C. (10-12 oz.) uncooked penne, spirals, or corkscrew pasta
1 TB. oil
2 cloves garlic, minced
1/3 C. sliced onion
1 ½ C. mixture of sliced or chopped vegetables  (mushrooms, broccoli, snow peas etc.)
1/2 C. grated carrot
1-2 TB. tamari
1-2 tsp. dried basil

Sauce:
1/3 C. olive oil
1 TB. lemon juice
1 tsp. spike

salt & pepper to taste
vegan parmesan
fresh basil, chopped (optional)

1.  Cook pasta in boiling water for 8-12 minutes, or until done.  Drain.
2.  While pasta cooks; sauté garlic, onion, and mixed vegetables in 1 TB. oil, for approximately 5 minutes.
3.  Add grated carrot, tamari and basil, combining well.  Keep warm until pasta is done.
4.  To make sauce; Combine olive oil, lemon juice and spike.  Mix sauce into hot pasta. Salt and pepper to taste.
5.  Serve pasta on individual plates, topped with sautéed veggies, vegan parmesan and fresh basil.  Makes 2 large servings.

# SPAGHETTI CARBONARA

12 oz. spaghetti
2¼ C. <u>un</u>sweetened soy milk
2 TB. cornstarch
1-2 cloves garlic, minced
4 slices meatless bacon *
4 TB. vegan parmesan
1/2 tsp. salt
1/4 tsp. black pepper
1/2 - 3/4 C. fresh arugala, chopped (optional)
2-4 sprigs fresh basil (optional)

1. Cook spaghetti in boiling water until tender.   Make sauce while spaghetti cooks, by beating together soy milk, cornstarch and garlic in a saucepan. Stir mixture while bringing to a boil.  Reduce heat and simmer until thickened (about 5 minutes).
2. While sauce simmers, fry meatless bacon in lightly oiled skillet, until crisp.   Remove from pan and cool slightly before crumbling or breaking into small pieces. Set bacon aside.
3. Remove thickened sauce from heat and immediately add 2 TB. of the  vegan parmesan, salt, pepper and the chopped arugala, stirring  until well combined.
4. Pour sauce over well-drained spaghetti, and use tongs to toss the spaghetti to coat it evenly.  Serve on individual plates sprinkled with the meatless bacon, the remaining vegan parmesan and a sprig of basil.  Serves 2
* *Eliminate #2 direction and substitute 2-4 TB. dry soy bacun bits for the meatless bacon, adding them when tossing the pasta with the sauce.*


# QUICK "GREEN" PASTA

1 pound spaghetti or pasta of choice
1 recipe Pesto Sauce (see pg. 156)
vegan  parmesan
1/4 C. pine nuts

1.  Cook pasta 8-12 minutes, or until done.
2.  Pour pesto over hot pasta and toss with tongs or fork to combine well.
3.  Sprinkle with soy parmesan and pine nuts.  Serves 2-3

**VARIATIONS:**   *This dish is also delicious served as a cold pasta salad.   It can also be served topped with a scoop of sautéed veggies of your choice. Also see <u>Creamy Green Pesto Pasta</u>: pg. 157*

# CREAMY COCONUT CORKSCREWS

3 C. corkscrew pasta (or spirals, noodles, etc.)
2 C. veggies, a mixture of snow peas, mushrooms, sliced onions and carrots *
1 TB. vegetable oil or water
1 C. coconut milk
3 TB. soy milk
1 TB. each cornstarch & tamari
1 tsp. dried basil
salt and pepper to taste
Fresh basil, chopped (optional)

1. Cook pasta in boiling water until done.  While pasta cooks sauté the 2 cups of veggies in oil or water, until tender but still crisp.
2. While veggies are sautéing, mix coconut milk, soy milk, cornstarch, tamari and dried basil in saucepan. Mix well with a wire whisk.  Cook over medium heat, stirring until mixture is smooth and very thick. Salt and pepper to taste.
3. Drain pasta well.  Stir in the creamy sauce.
**To serve:**  Top with the lightly sautéed veggies and chopped basil. Serve with a green salad.
Serves 2-3
**Tip:** *Just double or triple the amount of ingredients for more servings.*
**SUGGESTIONS:** *The corkscrew pasta only takes approximately 8 minutes to cook.  The sauce can be made ahead in a double boiler, and kept warm while the pasta cooks.  * Use any combination of your favourite veggies, or try: broccoli, chopped red pepper, minced garlic and ginger.*

# SPAGHETTI WITH TOMATO SAUCE

| | |
|---|---|
| 4 TB. oil | 4 C. chunky tomato sauce |
| 1 C. chopped onions | 1 TB. each, dried oregano & basil |
| 2 cloves garlic, minced | sea salt to taste |
| 2 green peppers (chopped) | 1½ lb. spaghetti |

Sauté onions, garlic and green pepper in oil.  Add remaining ingredients except spaghetti, and simmer sauce 15-30 minutes, or until desired thickness is reached. Cook spaghetti in boiling water until done. Serve with tomato sauce.  Serves 4
**OTHER ADDITION IDEAS:** *Sliced mushrooms, black olives, oat burger balls pg. 138*

---

" Food is man's only truly reliable medicine and foods do cure, just the same as wrong foods and drinks may kill us."
    - Bernard Jensen PhD. - Food Healing For Man

---

## MACARONI & "CHEESE"

12 oz. macaroni elbows
1-12.3 oz pkg. soft silken tofu
1/4 –1/2 C. <u>uns</u>weetened soy milk
1¾ C. shredded vegan cheddar

4 TB. soy margarine
1 C. whole wheat bread crumbs.
Salt and pepper

Preheat oven 375°
1. Bring a large pot of water to a boil.  Add macaroni and cook about 10 minutes, or until tender. Drain macaroni.
2. While macaroni cooks, mix tofu in a blender until smooth.  Put the creamed tofu in a saucepan.  Add 1/4 cup soy milk, vegan cheddar and 3 TB. of the margarine.  Simmer and beat with a wire whisk for about five minutes, or until cheddar melts.  Salt and pepper to taste.
3. Combine macaroni and cheddar sauce.  Stir together well and add the remaining ¼ cup milk if the mixture seems dry.  Place mixture in a lightly oiled 1 ¾ qt. casserole dish. Sprinkle breadcrumbs over the top and dot with remaining 1 TB. margarine.   Bake approximately 20 minutes, or until the top is browned and macaroni is heated through. Serves 4-6


## MOM'S MACARONI CASSEROLE

3 C. macaroni or spirals
1 TB. oil
1 clove garlic, minced
1 medium size onion, chopped
1/2 C. celery, chopped
1/2 red & 1/2 green pepper, chopped
1 C. meatless ground
1 C. mushrooms, sliced or chopped
1/2 tsp. each of salt, pepper, dried basil

1 C. soy cheddar, grated
1/2 C. tomato sauce
1½ C. dry bread crumbs
1/2 TB. vegan parmesan
1 TB. soy margarine
paprika powder

Preheat oven 350°
1. Cook pasta in boiling water until tender, but not overcooked.  In skillet heat oil and sauté garlic and onion until soft.
2. Add celery, pepper, meatless ground, mushrooms, salt, pepper and basil.  Sauté until everything is well combined and mushrooms are soft.
3. Lightly oil a 1 ¾ qt. casserole dish.  Layer 1/3rd of macaroni in bottom of dish.  Top with 1/3rd of sautéed veggies and 1/3rd grated cheddar. Repeat two more times.  Top last layer with tomato sauce, breadcrumbs, vegan parmesan, and dabs of soy margarine. Sprinkle lightly with paprika.  Bake uncovered for 30 minutes, or until topping is browned.  Serves 4

## PASTA WITH ALFREDO SAUCE  *Very easy and quick to prepare*

1/2 C. soy mayonnaise
1 tsp. tamari
1/2 tsp. dried basil & dried parsley

1/4 tsp. spike seasoning or sea salt
water
8-12 oz. pasta

Combine mayonnaise, tamari and spices.  With a whisk add just enough water to make a thin, smooth sauce. Salt and pepper to taste.  Stir this sauce into 8-12 oz. of cooked and drained pasta.  Top with vegan parmesan and sautéed veggies if desire.  Serves 2
**Note:** *Simply double or triple the sauce ingredients and quantity of pasta, to make 4-6 servings.*

## QUICK ORZO & VEGGIES
*This is very simple to prepare, requiring about 15 minutes from start to finish, if the vegetables are cut up ahead of time.*

1 TB. oil
1–2 cloves garlic, minced
1 small onion, chopped
1 C. mushrooms, chopped
1 small zucchini, diced
1 small carrot, diced

1 TB. fresh basil, chopped  (½ tsp. dried)
1 C. orzo pasta
2 C. water
2 TB. vegan broth powder
1 TB. tamari
1/4 tsp. black pepper

In a heavy skillet or wok, sauté garlic, onion and mushrooms in oil, until soft.  Add zucchini, carrots and basil and continue cooking and stirring 2-3 minutes. Add <u>un</u>cooked orzo, along with the 2 C. water mixed with broth powder, tamari and pepper.  Cover pan and simmer on low heat for 8 minutes, or until the orzo is tender.  Salt and pepper to taste. Serves 2-3.
**SUGGESTION**: *Consider varying the herbs and spices in this dish for a different flavour, or add a teaspoon of curry powder for the taste of India.* **Additions:** *small cubes of tofu*

---

This food is the gift of the whole universe—the Earth, the Sky and much hard work. May we live in a way that is worthy of this food...transforming our unskilled states of mind; especially that of greed.  And may we only eat foods, which nourishes and promotes wellness.  May we accept this food for the realization of the way of understanding and love.

---

# "RICOTTA" LASAGNA SWIRLS

8 cooked lasagna noodles
1-2 C. spinach, or Swiss chard, washed and chopped fine
1 lb. tofu
1/3 C. olive oil
1 tsp. each of; garlic granules, onion powder, basil & oregano
2 TB. vegan parmesan
Salt and pepper to taste
3 C. tomato or spaghetti sauce

Preheat oven 350°
1.  Have lasagna cooked and set aside.
2.  Steam chopped spinach until limp but not mushy, about 2-3 minutes.
3.  Crumble tofu and mix with olive oil, garlic, onion powder, basil, oregano and parmesan.
4.  Mix spinach with tofu mixture and salt and pepper to taste.
5.  Coat each noodle along length, with 3-4 TB. of tofu/spinach mixture, and roll up.
6.  Spread a thin layer of tomato sauce in a 9 x 13 inch baking pan, and place lasagna rolls on top.
7.  Pour remaining tomato sauce over the spirals, and bake uncovered at 350° for 20-30 minutes.  Serve sprinkled with vegan parmesan and a sprig of fresh parsley.  Serves 2-4

**VARIATION:** <u>Stuffed Manicotti Shells</u>: *Use large, cooked manicotti, pasta shells instead of lasagna. Cook the pasta shells until tender but firm, 6-8 minutes. Rinse in cold water and drain before stuffing with veggie ricotta mixture.  Bake the same as lasagna swirls. Makes approximately 14-16 stuffed shells. Serve with a tossed salad.  Serves 4*

" Anthropologists and zoologists say that the anatomy of the human body is nearest to that of the vegetarian animal---not the carnivore.  About 21 pounds of grain is needed to produce 9 pounds of meat.  The failure of one major country's crop would likely cause a famine in much of the world.  Natural, pure and whole organic food is healthier.  Digestion of it is easier and it is needed in smaller quantities.  Much energy is needed to digest heavy meat meals.  The body can remain cleaner on vegetarian diets...Meat is very expensive, and its purity and sanitation questionable.
       "Bernard Jensen, PhD.  - Food Healing for Man

# MUSHROOM & SPINACH LASAGNA

**Pasta & Veggies:**
12-16 cooked lasagna noodles
1 lb. spinach, washed and chopped
1 lb. (approx. 2 C) mushrooms, sliced
1 medium size onion, chopped
2-4 cloves garlic, minced
1 green pepper, chopped
1 TB. olive oil

**Sauce:**
4 C. spaghetti or tomato sauce
3 tsp. dried oregano
3 tsp. dried basil
Salt & Pepper

**Topping:**
1 C. grated vegan mozzarella cheese

**Soy Ricotta filling:**
1 lb. firm tofu
2/3 C. soy mayonnaise
2 tsp. onion powder
1 ½ tsp. garlic powder
1 tsp. salt
1 TB. chives, chopped (optional)

Preheat oven 350°
1. Have lasagna cooked and set aside.
2. Lightly steam spinach until limp, but not mushy.
3. Sauté mushrooms, onion, garlic and green pepper in 1 TB. olive oil, until soft. Remove from heat. Stir in cooked spinach. Set aside.
4. **Making ricotta filling & sauce:** In a medium size bowl, crumble tofu. Mix: mayonnaise, onion and garlic powder, salt and optional chives with tofu, and set aside. If using unseasoned tomato sauce, mix it in a separate bowl and season to your taste preference, or use a combination of dried basil, oregano, thyme, onion, garlic, salt and pepper.
5. **To Assemble:** In a 9 x 13 inch baking pan spread a thin layer of spaghetti or seasoned tomato sauce.
6. Layer 1/3rd of lasagna noodles on top of sauce. Spread 1/2 of soy ricotta, half of veggies and 1/3rd of remaining tomato sauce. Sprinkle 1 tsp. basil and oregano on top of sauce.
7. Continue with layers in similar fashion. The third and last layer of noodles will be spread with sauce, herbs, and the one cup of grated vegan cheese only. Bake uncovered for 30-45 minutes. Let cool slightly before serving.
**OTHER IDEAS:** *Add ½-1 cup of meatless ground to the spaghetti sauce.*

---

" The man with a hoe is the man close to the soil.
He keeps himself well by living the natural life."
- Bernard Jensen PhD.

---

# CREAMY BASIL LASAGNA

*This is a pleasant change from the traditional tomato version. The sauce is pale green in colour.*

12-16 cooked lasagna noodles
3 TB. soy margarine or olive oil
2 cloves garlic, minced
4 TB. flour
3 C. unsweetened soy milk
3/4 C. canned or fresh prepared pesto (pg. 156)
1 lb. tofu
1/3 C. olive oil
1/2-1 tsp. dried oregano
1/2 tsp. sea salt
1/4 C. vegan parmesan
1 lb. washed & chopped spinach
1/3 C. grated vegan mozzarella

Preheat oven 350°

1. Cook enough lasagna noodles to make three layers in a 9 x 12 inch pan. While noodles cook, prepare sauce and soy ricotta.

2. **Creamy basil sauce:** Melt margarine or oil in saucepan. Add garlic and cook until soft. Stir in the flour and add milk in a slow stream, using a wire whisk to blend mixture together. Cook until thick. Stir in pesto and remove from heat. Salt and pepper to taste.

3. **Soy ricotta filling:** Crumble tofu. Stir in the 1/3 C. olive oil, oregano, salt and parmesan.

4. Lightly steam spinach.

5. **To assemble:** In a 9 x 12 x 2 inch (approximate size) baking dish, pour a very thin layer of basil cream sauce.
6. Lay 1/3 of noodles over sauce. Spread 1/3 of soy ricotta filling on top of noodles and 1/2 of steamed spinach and 1/3 of remaining basil sauce.
7. Repeat the same way with two more layers of noodles. Third layer has no spinach. Pour remaining basil sauce over last layer, and sprinkle with vegan mozzarella.
8. Bake uncovered for 35 minutes or until top is light brown and lasagna is bubbly. Let cool slightly before cutting and serving.

**VARIATION:** *Add 1 cup sautéed sliced shitake or other mushrooms with the spinach.*

> "The only way we can find peace in our own hearts, is by changing ourselves, not by changing the world."

# VEGGIE POTATO LASAGNA

1 large eggplant, peeled & sliced into 1/2 inch rounds
1½ -2 pound, or about 7 medium size potatoes
2 large green peppers, chopped
6 cloves garlic, minced
1/2 tsp. salt and pepper
12-16 lasagna noodles
4 C. seasoned spaghetti or tomato sauce
3 C. (10 oz pkg.) grated vegan mozzarella
2 tsp. dried basil or oregano (or a combination of both)

Preheat oven 350°

1. Bake eggplant slices in a 350° oven, in a covered pan 15-20 minutes, or until tender.
2. Cut potatoes into quarters and steam until tender. Save water.
3. Sauté green pepper in a lightly oiled pan until soft.
4. Mash potatoes with garlic and 1/2 C. water from steaming. Add salt and pepper.
5. Cook lasagna noodles in boiling water until tender.

**To Assemble**:
1. Lightly oil a 9 x 13 inch-baking pan. Spread a thin layer of spaghetti or tomato sauce in bottom of pan.
2. Lay four noodles on sauce. Spread potato mixture along each noodle, using about 1/3$^{rd}$ of potato mixture for entire layer.
3. Lay half of eggplant and half of green pepper on potato mixture, followed by 1/3$^{rd}$ of sauce and 1/3$^{rd}$ of mozzarella. Sprinkle with 1 tsp. dried basil.
4. Repeat next layer same as first.
5. Third layer: noodles, potatoes, sauce, and top with remaining one-cup vegan mozzarella.
6. Cover with parchment paper and aluminum foil. Bake in 350° oven for 45-60 minutes. Allow lasagna to sit at least 10 minutes after taking out of oven, before serving.

**VARIATIONS**: *Use sliced zucchini instead of the eggplant. It's not necessary to pre-cook the zucchini.*

"....Given the millions of undernourished or starving people in the world, it would be best if we became vegetarians—raising would be converted to crops and if the crops would be shared bountifully with the hungry."
Bernard Jensen PhD. - Food Healing For Man

# Entrees

## MEXICAN CHILI

*A one-pot meal*

5 C. cooked pinto beans, or combination of beans
1 medium size onion, chopped (approx. 1 C)
1 green pepper, chopped
2-3 cloves garlic, minced
1 C. chopped mushrooms
1-12 oz. (1 ½ C.) kernel corn (un-drained)
1-28 oz (3 ½ C.) diced tomatoes
1/2 C. TVP granules
1 C. vegetable stock or water
1 TB. chili fiesta blend powder (see pg. 102)
1-3 tsp. cumin powder
1½ tsp. dried oregano
1½ tsp. dried basil
cayenne pepper, to taste
1 tsp. salt, or to taste

1. In a soup pot sauté in 2 TB. water: the onions, green pepper, garlic, and mushroom, until soft, about 5-10 minutes.
2. Add all remaining ingredients except cayenne and salt.
3. Stir, while bringing ingredients to a boil. Lower heat and simmer covered for 20-30 minutes, adding more stock or water if necessary.
4. Salt and pepper to taste and adjust seasonings if desired. Serves 4-6

**TVP** or textured vegetable protein is made from soybeans. It comes in several forms, small granules, flakes and chunks. TVP contains potassium, amino acids, calcium and magnesium and is low in sodium, and has no cholesterol. The granules can be used as a "hamburger" substitute in chili, stews and soups. It can also be used as the main ingredient in patties, sausages and meatless balls and loaves. **TO RECONSTITUTE TVP:** Add directly to soups and stews, or pour approximately 3/4 cups of hot water over 1 cup of TVP, and set aside for 5-10 minutes, or until TVP is soft.

## QUICK N' EASY TOSTADAS

*Hungry? Want something simple to prepare? Try these delicious and simple open faced tostadas.*

8 crispy corn tostado shells
1½ -2 C. dried refried beans (or substitute canned or fresh cooked)
Boiling water to cover beans (if using dried refries)

**Optional toppings:** sliced olives, shredded vegan cheese, chopped green peppers, chopped onion, sliced avocado, sliced and cooked mushrooms,

**Toppings:** Salsa sauce, soy sour cream, fresh chopped cilantro (optional)

Pour boiling water over dried beans and cover until soft. Add more water for desired consistency. Smooth refries while still warm over tostados shells, which have been lightly warmed and toasted in a dry fry pan. Sprinkle each shell with your choice of optional toppings, then add salsa sauce, a dollop of sour cream and a sprinkling of cilantro leaves.
SERVES 4

## NEW MEXICAN NACHOS

*Serve this dish by itself, or with a bowl of soup for a heartier meal.*

1 large bag of corn chips
1-2 C. refried beans
1 C. shredded vegan cheddar
1/2 C. sliced olives

1-2 chopped tomatoes (optional)
mild - hot salsa
vegan sour cream

Preheat oven 350°

Lay corn chips on a large cookie sheet. Drop spoonfuls of beans on top. Sprinkle with vegan cheese, olives, and tomatoes. Bake in a 350° oven, 5-10 minutes, or until the cheddar melts, and the beans are warm. Serve topped with salsa sauce and dabs of vegan sour cream.

---

*REFRIES: Are well-fried beans, not beans that have been fried twice. To make refries from scratch: Heat 4 TB. oil in a large skillet or pan. Add 4 cups of cooked pinto beans, one cup at a time, along with 1-2 minced cloves of garlic. Mash each cup into a thick paste. Add water or broth if mixture needs thinning. Use in open-faced tostadas or enchiladas.*

---

# MEXICAN TAMALE PIE    *Spiced beans with a cornmeal topping*

**Beans:**
2 small onions, chopped
2 cloves garlic, minced
2 TB. oil
4 C. cooked pinto or kidney beans
1-16 oz diced tomatoes
1-4 oz. can mild green chilies, chopped (optional)
cayenne pepper and salt to taste

**Topping:**

1+ 1/3 C. cornmeal
1 tsp. salt
2 tsp. chili fiesta blend powder (or see below)
1/2 tsp. baking soda

1 TB. egg replacer in 1/2 C. water
1 C. unsweetened soy milk
1/2 C. vegetable oil
1 ½ C. kernel corn

Preheat oven 350°

1. **Beans:** In a soup pot sauté onions and garlic in oil. Add beans, tomatoes, chilies, pepper and salt. Cook until bubbly.

2. **Topping:** Combine in separate bowl: cornmeal, salt, chili powder, soda, replacer, soy milk and oil. Mix together well then stir in corn.

3. **To Assemble:** Pour bean mixture into a lightly oiled 8" x 12" pan. Spoon cornmeal topping over the beans. Bake uncovered for 30 minutes or until topping is light brown.

---

**TIP:** If you're unable to find Chili Fiesta Blend Powder, here's a similar blend you can make: **Chili Medley Blend:** Combine *8 tsp. mild chili powder, 5 tsp. cumin powder, 1 tsp. ea of garlic and oregano and 1/8 tsp. each of coriander, cloves and allspice.*

---

"We are the only animal who continues to drink milk after weaning. Pasteurized dairy products are very mucus inducing. Cataract, respiratory disorders, arthritis, arterial degeneration, allergy, commonly result from eating pasteurized dairy products. Pasteurized milk is as deadly as meat, yet so many vegetarians take this path of slow suicide."
    Viktoras Kulvinskas, M.S. - Survival into the 21st Century

## TAMALES

*Tamales are similar to a dumpling filled with beans and salsa or green chili peppers. They're steamed inside dried cornhusks, which are available at international markets and some grocery stores. Serve them with steamed rice and a salad. They are very filling. Masa Harina flour can be found at most natural food stores.*

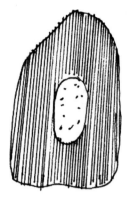

16 dried cornhusks,
   soaked in cold water for 30-60 minutes. *
2 C. masa harina, corn flour
3/4 tsp. salt
1/3 C. vegan margarine, softened
1½ C. vegetable stock or water
1 C. cooked beans, salted and spiced if desired
1/2 C. shredded vegan cheddar
salsa sauce (mild-hot)
roasted green chili strips (optional)

   *\* The soaking softens the husks for folding. Fresh husks can also be used. Care should be taken when stripping them from the corn. Cut around the base of the corn or stalk, so that the husks will come off in solid pieces. Soaking is not necessary with fresh cut husks.*

**Masa Dough:**
Mix corn flour and salt together in a bowl. Add margarine and slowly add stock or water, and with an electric beater mix until smooth. Add only a little stock at a time, and just enough so that the mixture is soft, very thick, and holds its shape on a spoon.

**To form tamales:**
Lay cornhusks out flat on your workspace. Put approximately 1-2 tablespoon of masa dough along center of husk, leaving about ½" or more of the husk empty along the sides and enough space along the top and bottom of husk for folding. Top masa with 1 TB. salted beans, a little vegan cheddar and a teaspoon or more of mild to hot salsa, and chili strips, if using. Top this with another tablespoon or more of masa dough. Amount depends on size of cornhusk. Fold long sides of cornhusks together and fold over to secure. Fold top and bottom of husk in, to produce a square "package," and tie it with a narrow strip of cornhusk, or just fold in narrow end and sides, covering the masa mixture, and leave wide end unfolded, and set upright in the steamer with open end up. Lay tamales in a steamer unit or basket with water in the bottom of unit. Steam tamales for 45-60 minutes. Makes approximately 17 tamales.

**Other Ideas**: <u>**For folding**</u>: *The husks can be rolled lengthwise and tied at both ends with thin strips of cornhusk.* <u>Meatless ground filling</u>: *Use prepackaged meatless ground or 1 C. TVP granules soaked in 3/4 C. hot water. Sauté in fry pan: 1 small chopped onion, 2 cloves minced garlic, and 1/2 of a chopped green pepper. Mix with 2 tsp. cumin powder, 1/2 tsp. oregano and 1/2 C. tomato sauce or salsa and meatless ground. Fill masa dough with this mixture.*

# ENCHILADAS

8 large whole wheat or corn tortillas
1 C. chopped onion
1 green pepper, chopped
4 cloves garlic, minced
1/8 tsp. hot pepper (or to taste)
1 TB. chili fiesta blend powder (pg. 102)
2 tsp. dried oregano
1 tsp. cumin
1 ½ C. corn (optional)
4-5 C. cooked pinto or other beans
1/2 tsp. salt
2 TB. lime juice
2 TB. fresh cilantro, chopped (optional)
1 ½ C. shredded vegan cheddar
4-5 C. green or red enchilada sauce *
Soy sour cream for topping

Preheat oven 350°
1. In an oiled pan, sauté onion, green pepper, garlic, hot pepper, chili blend powder, oregano, and cumin, until veggies are soft.
2. Add optional corn, beans, salt, lime juice and cilantro with veggies and mix well. Remove from heat.
3. Briefly put tortillas in a warm oven to soften, making them easier to roll.
4. Fill tortillas along the center with ¾-1 cup of veggie/bean filling, (depending on the size of tortillas) and 1 TB. vegan cheddar, (leave at least 1" on the sides empty if you want to tuck them in.) Roll each tortilla, tucking in sides if desired.
5. Put a very thin layer of enchilada sauce in the bottom of two lightly oiled 9 x 12 inch baking pans. Place four tortillas side by side, seam down, in each pan.
6. Bake covered at 350° for 20 minutes.
7. Pour remaining enchilada sauce on top of tortillas and sprinkle with the rest of vegan cheddar. Continue baking without the cover, for an additional 5 minutes, or until sauce is hot and cheese is soft. Serve with a dollop of soy sour cream and a side order of salad and brown rice. Makes 8 servings. **Note:** *Use mild to hot enchilada sauce, depending on your heat preference.*

"In order to regain and maintain the proper balance of health, most of the food we eat must contain live, vital, organic elements. These elements are found in fresh, raw vegetables, fruits, nuts and seeds."
N.W.Walker D.Sc. - Fresh Vegetable & Fruit Juices

# VEGGIE PASTIES

*These veggie filled pastries, called pasties, are traditional Upper Michigan fare. They can be served with a salad, for a complete meal. They also pack well in lunches and can be eaten warm or cold. Makes 4 large or 6-8 small to medium size pasties.*

## The Filling:

| | |
|---|---|
| 1 TB. oil | 3/4 C. water |
| 1 small onion (1/4 C. chopped) | 1 TB. veggie broth powder |
| 1 garlic clove, minced | 2 tsp. cornstarch |
| 1/2 C. each mushrooms, green pepper, | 1/4 tsp. salt & pepper |
| and carrots, chopped | 1/2 tsp. dried dill weed |
| 1 large potato, (1 ½ C. small cubes) | 2 tsp. vegan Worcestershire sauce |
| 1/2 C. cooked and sliced, vegan sausage (optional) | 2 TB. fresh parsley, chopped |

1. In a skillet sauté onions, garlic and mushrooms in oil, until soft.
2. Add green pepper, carrots, potato cubes and vegan sausage. Cook and stir for 5 minutes.
3. In a small bowl mix 3/4 C. water with remaining ingredients, using a whisk or beater to combine until smooth. Pour mixture over the veggies. Cook and stir until the sauce thickens and coats the veggie mixture. Cover pan and simmer until potatoes are soft. Remove from heat and let mixture cool to room temperature while making the pastry.

## The Pastry:

1 C. whole wheat pastry flour
1 C. whole wheat bread flour
1/4 tsp. salt
1/3 C. + 1 TB. vegetable oil
1/3 C. water

Mix flours and salt together in a mixing bowl. Stir oil into the flour with a fork until mixture is crumbly. Add water, mixing to form a soft ball of dough. Divide pastry into 4-6 balls. Roll each ball of dough on a floured surface, into a round circle or a square.

## Assembling the Pasties:

Preheated oven: 350°
Place a scoop of veggie mixture in center of circle or square of pastry, about a half cup for the large pasties. Carefully fold one side of dough over, forming a half moon or triangular shape. A spatula may be useful so that the dough does not tear. Pinch dough together with your fingers or a fork and prick the top two or three times with the fork. Brush each pastie with olive oil, and transfer them with a spatula to a lightly oiled cookie sheet. Bake 20-25 minutes, or until crust is browned. Let these pasties come to room temperature before eating. Serve with a lettuce and sprout salad. Makes 4 large or 6 medium size pasties.

## CURRY TOFU & SNOW PEAS  *Serve this stir-fry with brown rice or noodles*

1 lb. firm tofu
2 TB. tamari
1/4 C. oil
1-2 cloves of garlic, minced
1/2 medium onion, sliced
1 C. broccoli florets
1/4 C. parsley or cilantro, chopped
1/4 lb. snow peas (about 2 C.)

1/4 C. water
1 C. fresh basil, chopped
1 C. coconut milk
1½ tsp. cornstarch
1-2 tsp. curry powder
1-2 tsp. spike
1/4 tsp. ground pepper
hot pepper, to taste (optional)

1. Set tofu in a colander covered with a cloth and a heavy weight, such as a brick or jug of water . Let tofu sit for at 20-30 minutes, so that water is squeezed out and tofu has flattened slightly.
2. When tofu has flattened, cut into bite size pieces and place in a small bowl. Sprinkle with tamari.  Heat the oil in a wok or heavy pan, and brown tofu pieces in the hot oil, 3-4 minutes on each side, or until lightly browned. Remove from oil with slotted spoon and set aside. (Save the soy marinade)
3. Add garlic and onion to the wok and sauté until soft.  Add broccoli, parsley and peas along with tofu, water and 1/2 C. of the basil.  Cover wok and simmer 3-5 minutes.
4.  With a whisk or beater, mix coconut milk with cornstarch, curry powder, spike, pepper and tamari from marinade, and add to wok.  Simmer and stir a few minutes longer; just long enough to thicken the sauce.  Adjust seasonings if necessary.  Serve sprinkled with remaining 1/2 C. chopped fresh basil. Serves 2-4


## POTATO & CAULIFLOWER CURRY

4 TB. oil
4 C. potatoes, cubed
1 C. onions, chopped
1-2 C. cauliflower florets
pinch of Asafetida
3/4 tsp. turmeric powder
1 tsp. chili fiesta powder (pg. 102)

1 tsp. curry powder
1 tsp. ground cumin
1/2 tsp. salt
hot pepper, to taste (optional)
1½ C. water
½ C. fresh or frozen peas
fresh cilantro

Heat the oil in a large skillet or pot.  Fry potatoes and onions, 5-10 minutes, until slightly browned.  Remove from pan and set aside.  Sauté cauliflower in the same pan.  Remove and set aside.  Add asafetida and the remaining spices to the pan, along with 1 cup of the water.  Simmer briefly, and then return the potatoes, onions and cauliflower to the pot, along with the fresh or frozen peas.  Cover and cook 10-20 minutes, or until the potatoes are tender. Add additional ½ C. water if necessary.  Salt & pepper to taste. Sprinkle with cilantro, and serve with brown rice.  Serves 3-4 **VARIATION:** *Substitute snow peas, sliced mushrooms or broccoli florets for the cauliflower.*

## INDIAN POTATOES & PEAS

| | |
|---|---|
| 4 TB. oil | 1 tsp. chili fiesta powder (see pg.102) |
| 1 C. finely chopped onion | 2 tsp. cumin powder |
| 5 C. potatoes, cubed ½-¾inch | 1 C. peas  (frozen, fresh or canned,) |
| 1½ C. water | 1 tsp. salt |
| 3/4 tsp. ground turmeric | 1/2-1 tsp. garam masala blend |
| | 1/8 tsp. cayenne pepper (or to taste) |

Heat oil in a large skillet.  Add onions and fry until lightly browned.  Add potatoes, 1 C. of water, turmeric, chili fiesta powder and cumin. Stir together well and cover pan.  Cook over medium-low heat, about 20 minutes; or until the potatoes are tender.  Stir often to prevent sticking.  Add remaining 1/2 cup of water to the skillet, if necessary, to produce a thin sauce.  Add peas, salt, garam masala and cayenne the last five minutes of cooking.  Serve with brown rice.  Makes 4 large servings.

## CURRY SNOWPEA STIRFRY with cashews

*This is an easy and quick recipe, requiring about 10 minutes of cooking time.*

| | |
|---|---|
| 1 TB. oil | 3/4 C. water |
| 1/2 C. mushrooms, sliced | 1½  tsp. cornstarch |
| 1 garlic clove, minced | 3/4 C. coconut milk |
| 1/2 TB. ginger, minced | 2 TB. tamari |
| 1/4 C. raw cashews | 1-2 tsp. curry powder |
| 1 ½ C. snow peas | 1 tsp. spike seasoning |
| 1/4 C.  chives, chopped fine (optional) | 1 pinch or more of cayenne pepper |
| 1/3 C. carrots, cut in ½ inch long, thin sticks | fresh basil or cilantro |

In a wok or large fry pan, sauté in the oil: mushrooms, garlic, ginger and cashews, until mushrooms are tender.  Add peas, chives, carrots and water to pan.  Cover and simmer approximately 5 minutes, or until veggies are tender.  Beat cornstarch into the coconut milk and add to the veggies, along with tamari, and curry.  Simmer about 5-10 minutes, or until thick. Add spike and cayenne and sprinkled with chopped fresh basil or cilantro.  Serve with noodles or rice.  Makes 2-3 large servings.

"There is no kind of cooking, either in a kettle or in the bake oven, that preserves the life giving properties better than closing the foods up tight in a steam pressure cooker...at the same time it is a great fuel saver."    Jethro Kloss, - Back to Eden

## SWEET N' SOUR VEGGIES WITH PINEAPPLE

1/2 C. water
1 TB. vegan broth powder
1½ TB. tamari
2–3 TB. ketchup or tomato sauce
2 TB. rice vinegar
1 TB. sweetener
1/4 C. pineapple juice
1 TB. cornstarch

1/2 C. mushrooms, sliced
1-2 TB. dry parsley (1/4 C. fresh)
2 tsp. fresh ginger, minced
5 C. mixed veggies (snow peas, carrots, broccoli, etc.)
1/2 C. pineapple cubes & 1/4 C. juice
Dash or two of cayenne pepper (optional)

1. Mix first row of ingredients together in a small bowl, using a wire whisk. This is the sauce.
2. In wok or heavy skillet, sauté mushrooms in small amount of oil until tender. Add parsley, ginger and all remaining veggies, pineapple cubes and 1/4 C. juice. Cover and steam about 4-6 minutes.
3. Add the sauce to the veggies in pan, and cook only long enough to thicken the sauce. The veggies should be crisp. Add optional cayenne pepper and salt to taste. Serve with rice or noodles.
**VARIATION:** <u>Tofu or Seitan Sweet n' Sour</u>: *Add 1/2-3/4 C. tofu or seitan to dish, and reduce the amount of veggies.*


## CREAMY GINGERED ASPARAGUS STIR FRY

1 TB. fresh ginger, minced
1-2 garlic, minced
3/4-1 C. mushrooms, sliced
1/2 C. water
1 C. <u>un</u>sweetened soy milk
2 TB. cornstarch
2 TB. tamari soy sauce

1/8 tsp. salt and pepper
2 tsp. dried basil
1/2 C. celery, sliced
2 C. asparagus, cut in 1 ½ " pieces

1. Simmer ginger, minced garlic and sliced mushrooms in the 1/2 C. water until soft.
2. While this mixture simmers, mix in a small bowl: soymilk, cornstarch, tamari, salt, pepper and basil. Combine well with a wire whisk.
3. When garlic, ginger and mushrooms are soft, add celery and asparagus along with soy milk mixture.
4. Simmer for 5-10 minutes, until the sauce thickens and the veggies are done but crisp. Adjust seasonings to taste and serve over steamed rice or pasta.
**VARIATIONS:** *Experiment with different combinations of in season veggies.*

# HOT N' SPICY EGGPLANT

*Serve this stir-fry with steamed brown rice or on top of Udon noodles.*

1 eggplant (approximately ¾ pound) peeled and cut in cubes or strips
olive oil for sautéing
2 cloves garlic, minced
1 TB. fresh ginger, minced
1 small onion, sliced
1/2 red pepper, cut in strips
1 C. chopped bok Choy (optional)
3/4 C. water
1 TB. veggie broth powder
1 TB. tamari
1 TB. prepared Szechwan sauce
1 tsp. toasted sesame oil
1 ½ tsp. cornstarch
Salt & pepper, to taste
2 TB. fresh basil or cilantro chopped (optional)

1. Sauté eggplant in the olive oil, until brown on both sides, and soft but not soggy.
2. Remove eggplant from pan.
3. Add garlic, ginger, onion, red pepper and bok choy to pan and sauté until soft. Stir in cooked eggplant and set heat to low.
4. In a small bowl mix water with broth powder, tamari, Szechwan sauce, sesame oil and cornstarch, whisking together well. Add broth mixture to veggies in pan. Bring mixture to a boil, then lower heat and simmer until the liquid has thickened. Salt and pepper to taste. Serve sprinkled with fresh chopped basil or cilantro. Serves 2-4 *Easily multiplied.*

"The journal of the American Medical Association in 1961 estimated that 97% of heart disease could be prevented by a vegetarian diet. Research statistics show that a high flesh diet causes ten times more heart attacks in the 45-65 year old population than a diet of fresh vegetables, fruits, nuts, seeds and grains."
Gabriel Cousens, M.D. - Conscious Eating

## THAI COCONUT STIR FRY

*This recipe has many creative possibilities, depending on the variety of veggies used.*

2 cloves garlic, minced
1 TB. fresh ginger, minced
1/2 C. sliced onion
4 C. sliced & chopped veggies
(a mixture of broccoli, celery,
 mushrooms, snow peas)
8 oz. tofu, pressed * and cut into cubes

1/4 C. water
1½ C. coconut milk
2 tsp. cornstarch
3 TB. tamari
1/4-1/2 C. fresh cilantro leaves
1/8+ tsp. hot red pepper (optional)
fresh basil, chopped

1. In lightly oiled wok or large skillet, sauté garlic, ginger, and onion, until soft.
2. Add all remaining veggies and tofu, cooking and stirring approximately 2-3 minutes, or until well combined.
3. Add 1/4 c. water to wok, cover and simmer slowly while preparing the coconut sauce.
4. With a whisk or beater, combine the coconut milk, cornstarch, tamari, cilantro, and hot red pepper together in a bowl, until well combined.
5. When the veggies are cooked but still crisp, add the coconut milk mixture. Simmer 1-2 minutes or until the sauce is bubbly and slightly thickened. Adjust seasonings if necessary and sprinkle with basil. Serve with brown rice or noodles. Serves 4.
**Note:** * *See page 137 on pressing tofu.*

---

**TIP:** Try cooking with **Frozen Tofu** for a different texture. To freeze tofu: Drain tofu, and then cut into small cubes. Place cubes in a zip lock bag or freezer container. Store in the freezer until ready to use.

---

## CAJUN BLACK BEANS AND RICE

2 C. uncooked brown rice
4 ½ C. water with dash of salt
1 ½ C. chopped onion
1 C. green pepper, chopped
2-4 cloves garlic, minced
1 can (28 oz) or 4 C. fresh-diced tomatoes
1 C. water

hot pepper, to taste (optional)
2 TB. broth powder
1 tsp. each, chili blend powder, *
dried oregano, ground cumin
1/2 tsp. each, thyme, salt and pepper
2 C. cooked black beans
1/2 C. fresh cilantro, chopped

**RICE:** Put rice and 4 ½ cups water on stove to cook while preparing the beans. When rice comes to boil turn down and simmer approximately 45 minutes or until rice is soft and water is absorbed.
**BEANS:** In lightly oiled soup pot sauté the onions, green pepper and garlic until soft. Add all remaining ingredients except cilantro and simmer covered for 30 minutes, stirring occasionally. Add cilantro at last 5 minutes of cooking. Serve on top of the cooked brown rice. Serves 4-6 **Note:** * *See chili blend powder, pg. 102*

# EGGPLANT PARMESAN

*Three soy cheeses create a truly delicious classic dish. Serve with rice and a salad,*

1 large onion, chopped
4 cloves garlic, minced
2 TB. olive oil
6 C. chunky tomato sauce
1 tsp. dried basil
1/2 tsp. salt & pepper
1 large eggplant, peeled and cut into ¼ inch round slices
Olive oil, for sautéing eggplant
1/2 C. vegan Mozzarella, shredded
1/2 C. vegan Monterey jack, shredded
1/2 C. vegan Parmesan

Preheat oven 350°

1. In a skillet sauté the onion and garlic in 2 TB. oil, until tender.
2. Add tomato sauce, basil, salt and pepper.
3. Simmer uncovered for about 10 minutes.
4. Fry eggplant pieces in oil, until browned on both sides but not mushy.
5. Cover the bottom of a 9 x 12 x 2 inch-baking dish with 1 cup of tomato sauce mixture.
6. Lay half of the eggplant on top of sauce. Sprinkle slices with ½ of mozzarella and jack cheese, and approximately ½ of remaining sauce.
7. Repeat in similar fashion for one more layer. Final layer is sprinkled with parmesan. Cover and bake in preheated 350° oven for 30 minutes. Uncover and bake another 5-l0 minutes. Serves 4-6

**Note:** *If you're using an especially large eggplant, increase the layers to three, and divide the sauce and vegan cheese accordingly.*

---

". ...Milk is *not* a wholesome and health-promoting source of calcium. Be wise and get your calcium from the same place that the cow gets hers; out of the greens, grains and legumes that grow so beautifully from the earth."
Michael Klaper M.D.- Author & International Lecturer
Vegan Nutrition; Pure & Simple

## ZUCCHINI CASSEROLE

2 TB. oil
1 C. chopped onion
2 cloves garlic, minced fine
6 C. (about 4 small) zucchinis
   (chopped or grated)
1 tsp. dried oregano
1/2 tsp. salt

2 C. vegan cheddar, shredded
1/2 C.  parsley, chopped ( 1-2 TB. dried)
2 TB. lemon juice
1 tsp. oil
1/3 C. chopped walnuts or pecans
1 C. soft bread crumbs
1 TB. vegan parmesan

Preheat oven 350°
1. Heat 2 TB. oil in a heavy skillet.  Add onions and garlic and sauté until tender.
2. Add zucchini, oregano and salt to pan.  Cover and simmer on low for 5-10 minutes.
Take off of heat and stir in the vegan cheddar, parsley, and lemon juice.
3. Pour mixture into a lightly oiled 2 qt. ovenproof, casserole dish.
4. In the same skillet, heat l tsp. oil and brown the walnuts and breadcrumbs.  Sprinkle
breadcrumb mixture on top of zucchini mixture.  Sprinkle crumbs with vegan parmesan.
Bake uncovered for 30 minutes or until mixture is bubbly and crumbs browned.  Serve with
rice or potatoes and a salad.  Serves 4-6


## MUSHROOM/ASPARAGUS STROGANOFF

*This recipe has many creative possibilities, with the addition or substitution of various vegetables.  Serve it
over pasta or brown rice.*

1 lb. asparagus cut in 1 inch pieces
1 C. soy sour cream
1/2 C. plain soy yogurt
1 tsp. Worcestershire sauce
1 TB. tamari
1/2 C. water
1/2 tsp. salt & 1/4 tsp. pepper

2 TB. oil
1/2 lb. mushrooms, sliced
1 clove garlic, minced
1 tsp. dried onion granules
1 tsp. dried oregano
2 TB. fresh parsley  (1 tsp. dried)

1.  Lightly steam asparagus for approximately 5 minutes. Remove from steamer.
2.  Mix soy sour cream, yogurt, worcestershire sauce, tamari, 1/4 C. of the water and salt
and pepper together in a separate bowl, and set aside.
3.  Sauté mushrooms and garlic in the oil.  Add remaining 1/4 C. water, onion granules,
oregano, and steamed asparagus.  Simmer and stir approximately 1-2 minutes, or just until
spices and veggies are combined.
4.  Stir soy sour cream mixture into the veggies and simmer only long enough to warm the
sour cream and yogurt.  Thin with a little water if necessary.  Salt and pepper to taste.
5.  Serve immediately on a bed of rice or mixed with cooked pasta.  This is enough sauce
for 3 C. of pasta or 1 lb. of  spaghetti noodles.
**VARIATION:** *Eliminate asparagus and use all mushrooms.*

# VEGGIE STEW WITH HERB DUMPLINGS

9 large potatoes, cubed
1 yam or sweet potato, cubed (optional)
2 large carrots, sliced
1 C. sliced mushrooms
1 C. cabbage, coarsely shredded
1 medium size onion, sliced
3 cloves garlic, minced
1-12 oz. pkg. meatless ground
1 tsp. each dried dill weed, paprika, & salt
1/2 tsp. each mustard seed & black pepper
water

1-2 C. cooked beans,
　　black or navy (optional)
2 TB. vegetable broth powder *
2 TB. cornstarch or flour
1/4 C. water

1. Place all above ingredients, except the cooked beans, broth powder, cornstarch and 1/4 C. water in a large soup pot. Pour water into pot to reach half way up to top of veggies. Bring to a boil and then turn heat down, and simmer covered.
2. While veggies are cooking make the dumplings.
3. When veggies are almost tender, (approximately 30 minutes) mix broth powder and cornstarch with the 1/4 C. water in a small bowl. Whisk them together well before adding to the veggies, along with the cooked beans. Stir to combine ingredients.
4. Place spoonfuls of herb dumplings on top of cooked veggies. Cover pot and simmer 12-15 minutes, or until dumplings test done with a toothpick or knife. Serves 4-6

**VARIATIONS**: *You can use any variety of veggies in this stew. Experiment with the spices too.*
*\* Substitute vegetable stock for the powder and water, or use vegetable bouillon cubes.*

## HERB DUMPLINGS

2 C. whole wheat pastry flour
1 TB. baking powder
1/4 C. dried parsley
1/2 salt

2 TB. oil
1 C. plain soy milk

Mix together flour, baking powder, parsley and salt. Add oil and mix with a fork. Add milk and stir together well. The batter should be very thick, and hold its shape on a spoon. Drop by large spoonfuls on top of hot stew, and cook covered 12- 15 minutes or until dumplings are done.

> "And with such a (vegetarian) diet, they may be expected to live in peace and health to a good old age, and bequeath a similar life to their children after them."
> - Socrates

## SPICY HARVEST STEW

2 C. water
2 C. green cabbage, chopped
2 ½ C. tomatoes, chopped
1 C. celery, diced
1-2 cloves garlic, minced
2 C. cubed potatoes
1 C. sweet potato, cubed

1 C. sliced onion
1-2 C. crumbled soy sausage
1 tsp. paprika
1/2 tsp. each of dried basil, thyme,
dill, salt & pepper
1 C water mixed with 1 TB. cornstarch

Put two cups of water in a heavy soup pot. Add all remaining ingredients except dried spices and 1 C. water mixed with cornstarch. Simmer approximately 30 minutes, or until veggies are tender. Add more water if necessary. It should reach at least half way up to top of veggies. Add spices and the additional cup of water whisked with cornstarch. Simmer until liquid has thickened slightly. This stew can also be topped with herb dumplings. See previous page for recipe. Serves 2-4

## SAVORY MILLET VEGGIE STEW

1/4 C. millet
1 C. water
2 tsp. oil
1 medium size onion, chopped
2 cloves garlic, minced
1 C. mushrooms, chopped
1-2 C. water
1 C. diced tomatoes or sauce
1½ C. potatoes, cubed

1/2 C. sweet potato, cubed
1/2 C. celery, diced
1/2 C. cooked chickpeas
1/2 C. carrots, diced
1 tsp. dried basil
1 ½ tsp. ground coriander
1/2 tsp. dried dill weed
1/4-1/2 tsp. salt & pepper
1 TB. lemon juice
fresh basil or parsley, chopped

1. In a medium size soup pot cook millet in 1 C. water for approximately 15-20 minutes or until soft.
2. While millet cooks; sauté onion, garlic and mushrooms in 2 tsp. oil. Add this mixture to the cooked millet, along with 1 cup of water and all remaining ingredients except the lemon juice and fresh basil.
3. Add lemon juice during last five minutes of cooking. Cook until potatoes are soft. Thin stew with additional water, if necessary. Serve sprinkled with fresh basil.
Serves 2-4

# QUICK HUNGARIAN STYLE GOULASH

1 medium size onion, chopped
2 clove garlic, minced
1-12 oz pkg. meatless ground *
3-4 C. shredded cabbage
2 C. kernel corn, un-drained if canned
1/2 C. diced celery
2 C. cooked beans, (navy, pintos or other)
6 medium size potatoes, cubed small
4 C. diced tomatoes w/ liquid
1 tsp. cumin, paprika, salt & pepper
1 ½ tsp. each of chili fiesta blend, spike, oregano
2-3 C. water

In a large pot or pan sauté onion, garlic and meatless ground in small amount of oil, until veggies are soft. Add all of the remaining ingredients. Cover and simmer until potatoes and other veggies are soft. Adjust seasonings to taste. Serve in shallow bowls. Sprinkle goulash with ground paprika. Traditionally this is served over noodles, but his recipe is substantial on its own. Serves 6
**Note:** * *You can substitute 1 C. reconstituted TVP for the meatless ground.*

# PIZZA    Makes 2-13 inch pizzas

**Dough:**
1 ½ C. lukewarm water
2 tsp. baking yeast
1 tsp. sweetener

2 TB. olive oil
1 tsp. salt
1 C. whole wheat pastry flour
2-3 C. whole wheat bread flour

Soften yeast in water with sweetener. Add oil, salt, pastry flour and enough additional flour to make a soft ball of dough. Knead dough until smooth. The dough can now be frozen for later use or let rise for an hour, or used immediately. Roll out to desired thickness on pizza pans that have been sprinkled with cornmeal. Spread dough with your favourite toppings. Bake in a preheated 450° oven, for 10-15 minutes, or until crust is browned. Makes two-13 inch pizzas.

**Toppings:**  spicy tomato sauce, a combination of dried basil and oregano or pizza seasoning mix, shredded, vegan mozzarella, your choice of toppings such as: sliced olives, onion, garlic, cooked mushrooms, green pepper, meatless ground or sliced vegan sausage.
**OTHER IDEAS:** Basil Pesto Pizza: *Use Basil Pesto sauce, pg. 156, instead of tomato sauce.*
Crust Ideas: *Short on time to make the yeast dough?  Use pita bread or tortilla shells instead.  Bake in a 350° oven for 10-15 minutes, or until toppings are hot.*

# VEGETABLE QUICHE

**CRUST:**

1¾ C. whole wheat pastry flour

1/4 tsp. salt

1/3 C. vegetable oil

3-5 T. water

Blend flour, and salt.  Add oil and mix with fork until crumbly.  Add only enough water so that the mixture can be formed into a smooth ball.  With fingers pat mixture into a 9-inch quiche or pie pan. Prick the dough with a fork.  Partially bake the crust at 375° for approximately 5 minutes.

**QUICHE FILLING:**

1 TB. oil

1-2 cloves garlic, minced

3 C. sliced veggies, such as zucchini, broccoli florets, carrots, peas, asparagus, tomato, mushrooms

1/4 C. fresh basil, minced  (l tsp. dry)

12 oz container of soy sour cream

2 TB. cornstarch

1/2 C. vegan parmesan

1 C. vegan Monterey Jack, grated

1 tsp. salt

l/2 tsp. black pepper

1/8 tsp. turmeric

Preheat oven 375°

1. Heat oil in skillet.  Add garlic and sauté until tender.
2. Add veggies and basil. Sauté and stir for about 5 minutes.  Remove pan from heat.
3. In a bowl combine with a whisk, the sour cream, cornstarch, vegan parmesan, ½ C. of the Monterey jack, salt, pepper and turmeric.  Fold in the slightly cooled veggies.
4. Pour mixture into the partially baked quiche crust, and spread evenly to edges. Sprinkle with remaining 1/2 C. Monterey Jack.
5. Bake uncovered for approximately 30 minutes, or until crust is light brown and filling is set.  Cool slightly before serving.

**Note:** *This quiche is also delicious when eaten cold.*

---

" Vegetarianism, ..........is much more than a meatless diet.  It is a way of life, and one day the human race will discover that way."
                    Bernard Jensen PhD.- Food Healing For Man

# GREEK SPANAKOPITA

1/2 lb. fresh or frozen phyllo that has been thawed
1/2 C. melted soy margarine
1 lb. fresh spinach, chopped
1 medium size onion, diced fine
3 TB. olive oil
1½ -2 tsp. dried dill (or substitute ¼ C. fresh)
1 lb. extra firm tofu
3 TB. each of Ume plum vinegar & rice vinegar
1/2 tsp. sea salt
4 TB. olive oil
1/2 tsp. each of dried oregano and black pepper

1. Wash and lightly steam spinach, just until it wilts, 2 minutes.
2. Drain spinach and set aside.
3. Sauté onions in 3 TB. olive oil. Remove from heat and combine with spinach and dill.
4. Crumble the tofu and gently stir in the vinegar, salt, olive oil, oregano and black pepper. Taste and adjust saltiness if necessary. Mix tofu with the spinach mixture.
5. Cut phyllo sheets to fit in a 9 x 12 inch baking dish. Brush one side of six sheets with melted margarine. Place the sheets margarine side up, one on top of the other, in the lightly oiled baking dish.
6. Spread the entire tofu/spinach filling over the phyllo. Butter six more phyllo sheets and lay each piece, on top of the other, margarine side up, over the filling. Pour any remaining melted margarine over the top sheet of phyllo.
7. Bake uncovered at 375° for approx. 30-40 minutes or until golden brown. Cool 10 minutes before cutting into squares. Serve with a lettuce salad and rice. Makes 8 servings.

**Note:** *Ume plum vinegar is very salty. If you use all rice vinegar, you will need to add more salt.*

"Health is cumulative. It doesn't come overnight. You have to make it, little by little. Disease comes little by little. Disease comes when we have brought bad habits into our lives and then our health gradually breaks down. To invite a bad habit into our lives is like asking a thief to spend the night on our living room sofa. The room will not be the same in the morning. Some good things will be gone. Good health comes as an accumulation of doing the right things each day."
Bernard Jensen Ph.D.  - The Healing Mind of Man

# GREEK MOUSSAKA
*Serve this spicy eggplant dish with Greek salad and brown rice*

1 large or 2 medium size eggplants
Salt & olive oil

**Sauce:**
1½ C. chopped onion
5 cloves garlic, minced
1 TB. each of dried basil & oregano
2 tsp. cinnamon
2 TB. olive oil
2 C. chunky tomato sauce
2 TB. tamari
Salt & pepper to taste

**Topping:**
1 pound soft tofu, crumbled
1/3 C. water
1 TB. light miso paste
1/2 tsp. nutmeg
1/2 tsp. turmeric
1/16 tsp. cayenne pepper (or to taste)
Salt  & pepper to taste

1.  Slice eggplant into rounds, approximately 1/4 in. thick. Sprinkle with salt. Place slices on lightly oiled cookie sheet.
2.  Brush eggplant lightly with olive oil, and place in a preheated 350° oven for 15-20 minutes, or until partially cooked but tender. Set aside while making sauce and topping.

**Making sauce:**
1. Sauté onions, garlic, and spices in 2 TB. olive oil until soft.
2. Add tomato sauce and tamari and simmer 10 minutes. Salt and pepper to taste. Remove from heat.

**Making Topping:**
Add tofu, water, miso and spices in blender, and process until smooth and creamy. Salt & pepper to taste

**TO ASSEMBLE:**
1.  Preheat oven to 350°
2.  Lightly oil an 8 x 12 inch-baking dish.  Smooth half of sauce over bottom of pan.
3.  Place one half of eggplant slices in dish. Spoon remaining sauce over eggplant.
4.  Top with remaining layer of eggplant.  Spread tofu topping evenly over eggplant and to sides of pan.  Bake uncovered for approximately 30 minutes, or until eggplant is tender and topping is lightly browned.  Serve with brown rice.  Makes 6 servings.

# VEGETABLE POT PIE

1 TB. oil
2 cloves garlic, minced
1/4 C. scallions or onions, chopped
1 C. mushrooms, sliced
1 C. celery, chopped
1/2 C. carrots, sliced
1 C. fresh green garden beans, chopped *
1/2 C. peas *
1/2 C. red or green peppers, chopped
2 C. potatoes, cubed
2 TB. fresh basil, chopped ( 1 tsp. dry)
1/2 tsp. dried thyme
2 tsp. dry parsley

**Gravy:**
1 C. <u>un</u>sweetened soy milk
2 C. water
3 TB. vegan broth powder
1 TB. tamari
1/3 C. unbleached white flour
1/4 tsp. salt

**Biscuit Crust:**
2 C. whole wheat pastry flour
1/2 tsp. salt
2 tsp. baking powder
1 TB. dry sweetener
1/4 C. vegetable oil
1/2 C. soymilk

Preheat oven 400°

1.  In a large pot or wok sauté garlic, onions and mushrooms in oil until soft.  Add all the remaining veggies and herbs in first row and stir together well.  Simmer on low heat while preparing the gravy.
2. **Gravy:**  In a medium size bowl, mix soy milk, water, broth powder, tamari, flour and salt with a whisk, until well combined.
3.  Pour gravy over the veggies.  Simmer and stir until sauce thickens slightly.
4. Transfer entire mixture to a casserole dish or an 8 x 13 x 2 inch baking pan.
5. **Biscuit topping:** Combine the 2 C. whole wheat pastry flour with the salt, baking powder, and sweetener.  Stir together well.  With a fork stir in vegetable oil.  Add soymilk and form mixture into a smooth ball.  Add more flour if mixture is too sticky.  Pat the dough on a lightly floured board.  Cut dough with a small round cookie cutter.  Lay these round shapes over the vegetable mixture in the casserole or baking pan.
6. Bake in pre-heated oven for 20-30 minutes or until the veggies are cooked through, the biscuits are lightly browned and the filling is bubbly.  If the biscuits brown too quickly, lay a piece of parchment paper and foil over the casserole.  Serves 4-6

* **Note:**  *Other veggies can be substituted, such as sliced zucchini, broccoli etc.*

"Vegetarians always ask about getting enough protein.  But, I don't know any nutrition expert that can plan a diet of natural foods resulting in a protein deficiency, so long as you're not deficient in calories.  You need only six percent of total calories in protein...and it's practically impossible to get below nine percent in ordinary diets." - Nathan Pritikin

# SHEPHERD'S PIE

**Topping:**
3 medium size potatoes, cubed
1 TB. olive oil
1/4 C. <u>unsweetened</u> soy milk
Salt and pepper to taste

**Filling:**
1 TB. oil
1 clove garlic, minced
1 medium size onion, sliced
1 C. shitake or other mushrooms, sliced
1 C. zucchini, cubed
1 stalk celery, chopped or sliced
1 ½ C. broccoli florets
1 C. green cabbage, chopped or shredded
1 C. tomatoes, diced
1/4 tsp. each dried thyme, dill, and basil
1 tsp. fresh, minced hot pepper, or use equivalent of dry (optional)
1/4 tsp. each salt and black pepper
1 C. water
1 TB. broth powder
1/2 TB. cornstarch
1 TB. soy margarine
Paprika

Preheat oven 350°
1. Steam potatoes until soft. Mash with 1 TB. olive oil and 1/4 C. soymilk. Salt and pepper to taste and set aside.
2. In a large skillet or wok, brown onion and garlic in 1 TB. oil. Add mushrooms and cook until tender.
3. Add zucchini, celery, broccoli, cabbage, tomatoes, thyme, dill, basil, hot pepper, salt and black pepper. Stir veggies and spices together well. Cover pan and simmer slowly until veggies are only partly cooked.
4. Whisk together water, broth powder and cornstarch in a small bowl. Add mixture to veggies in skillet and simmer 1 minute longer.
5. Lightly oil a 1¾ qt. casserole dish. Pour veggie and broth mixture into bottom of casserole. Pat potato mixture evenly over the veggies and to the sides of the dish. Dot potatoes with 1 TB. soy margarine, and sprinkle lightly with paprika. Bake 20-30 minutes.
Serves 3-4

**VARIATIONS:** *This casserole lends itself to much creativity. Experiment with different combinations of vegetables and spices, and use any combination of veggies that are in season, or that you have on hand. Garlic and herbs can be added to the potato topping.*

## RICE STUFFED GREEN PEPPERS

*Serve these with a green salad for a delicious and hearty meal.*

6 large green peppers
2 TB. oil
1 small onion, chopped
1 C. celery, diced
1/2 C. sliced mushrooms

1/2 C. walnuts, chopped fine
1/2 C. soy cheddar, shredded
3 C. cooked brown rice
salt and pepper to taste
4 TB. vegan parmesan

1. Sauté onion, celery, and mushrooms in the oil. Turn off heat and stir in walnuts, soy cheddar, rice, salt and pepper.
2. Cut top off of each pepper and take out and dispose of seeds.
3. Fill each pepper with rice mixture. Sprinkle with parmesan. Set peppers upright in an oiled baking dish containing about 1/2 inch of water.
4. Preheat oven to 350° and bake 35-45 minutes, or until peppers are tender. Cover loosely if top of peppers brown too quickly. Makes 6 servings.

**VARIATIONS**: Tempeh Stuffed Green Peppers: *Fill peppers with a mixture of 12 oz mashed or finely chopped tempeh, 1/2 C. water, 2 TB. soy sauce, 3 cloves garlic, minced, and 1 tsp. dried basil. Sprinkle top of filling with breadcrumbs and drizzle with olive oil. Bake the same as rice stuffed green peppers.*

## STUFFED SQUASH

1 butternut, acorn or other squash
2 C. cooked brown rice
1/3 C. chopped onion
2 garlic cloves, minced
1 TB. oil
1/2 C. celery, chopped
1/4 C. sliced black olives

1/2 tsp. dried thyme
1/8 tsp. each of salt and pepper (or to taste)
1 TB. dry parsley
1 TB. broth powder mixed with 1/3 C. water

Preheat oven 450°
Cut squash in half lengthwise and scoop out the seeds and pulp. Place in a baking pan containing 1/4 inch of water. Cover pan tightly and bake for 30 minutes.
While squash bakes, sauté onion and garlic in oil, until soft. Stir onion and garlic into cooked rice along with remaining ingredients. After squash has cooked for thirty minutes, take out of oven. Empty any water in cavity of squash and fill each cavity with rice filling. Cover and bake an additional 30 minutes, or until squash is tender. Serve with a lettuce and sprout salad. Serves 2-4, depending on size of squash.

**VARIATIONS**: *Include chopped nuts in stuffing mix. Experiment with different spice combinations. Add 1/4 tsp. of turmeric to rice before cooking, for a pretty yellow stuffing.*

## STUFFED ZUCCHINI

1 oversized or 4 regular zucchini
 (about 2 lbs.)
2 TB. oil
2 scallions, chopped (substitute onion)
1/2 lb. mushrooms, chopped
1/2 C. walnuts, chopped

1 C. fresh breadcrumbs
2 TB. parsley, chopped,  (l tsp dried)
1 TB. dried basil
 salt and pepper to taste
1/2 C. vegan cheddar cheese, grated

Preheat oven 350°

1.  Scrub squash and cut in half lengthwise.  Scoop out reserve pulp and set aside.
Leave at least a 1/4-inch shell.   Steam or partially bake shells for approximately 5 minutes.
2.  Chop zucchini pulp, minus the seeds.  Sauté pulp in oil with scallions and mushrooms,
for 5 minutes.
3.  Remove from heat and add walnuts, breadcrumbs, parsley, basil and salt and pepper to
taste.  Add just enough water, if necessary, to make a moist mixture.
4.  Fill zucchini shells.  Sprinkle with grated vegan cheddar.  Bake in a lightly oiled,
uncovered pan, containing about 1/2 inch of water, for approximately 30 minutes, or until
shells are tender and stuffing is hot.  Serves 2-4

## STUFFED CABBAGE ROLLS  **A traditional Polish dish**

8 cabbage leaves
2 C. cooked brown rice
1 medium size onion, chopped
1 clove garlic, minced
1 C. mushrooms, chopped
1/2 C. celery, and green pepper, chopped
l C. meatless sausage, * (optional)

1/4 C. fresh parsley, chopped (2 tsp. dried)
2 TB. fresh dill weed (1 tsp. dried)
1 TB. tamari
3-4 C. tomato sauce

Preheat oven 350°
1. Steam cabbage leaves until limp but still bright green.  Set aside to cool slightly.
2. In lightly oiled pan sauté onion, garlic, mushrooms, celery and green pepper until soft.
3. Crumble the meatless sausage and add to the veggie mixture.  Stir and fry until
ingredients are well combined.
4. Turn heat off and add cooked brown rice, parsley, dill and soy tamari, mixing well.
5. Divide filling into 8 portions.  Spoon each portion into the center of cabbage leaves. Roll
leaves, folding in sides.  Arrange rolls in a lightly oiled baking dish, seams down.
6. Pour tomato sauce evenly over cabbage rolls.  Cover dish and bake at 350° for
approximately 45 minutes.  Serves 4
**VARIATION:**   * *Reconstituted TVP can be substituted for the meatless sausage.  Substitute cooked
barley for the rice.*

# Side Dishes

# STUFFED MUSHROOMS

12 large mushrooms
1/4 C. breadcrumbs
1 TB. egg replacer mixed with ¼ cup warm water
1/2 tsp. each: salt, dried basil and oregano
1 red pepper, chopped fine
1/4 C. almonds, ground
1 medium size onion, minced
1 tsp. lemon juice

1. Mix all ingredients together, except mushrooms.
2. Brush mushrooms with oil and fill <u>un</u>cooked mushrooms with stuffing.
3. Place mushrooms in a shallow, lightly oiled pan.
4. Broil for 5 minutes, or bake at 400 degrees, until browned on top and mushrooms are tender.

# BATTER FRIED MUSHROOMS AND VEGGIES

*Batter fried mushrooms and veggies are so delicious. My sister Marina and I came up with this vegan batter recipe, and her husband Denis deep-fried them at their French River cottage in northern Ontario, Canada. The scenery might not be the same, but I'm sure they'll taste just as good cooked anywhere.*

**The Batter:**
5 TB. whole wheat pastry flour *
1/2 tsp. baking powder
1/2 tsp. chili fiesta blend powder, pg. 102 (optional, replace with salt)
1 TB. egg replacer powder mixed with 6 TB. warm water
4 TB. <u>un</u>sweetened soy milk
* For a wheat free version, use a mixture of bean and tapioca flour.

Mix the flour, baking powder and chili powder together. Add egg replacer mixed with water, and soy milk, and stir together until well combined. Add more liquid or flour to make a consistency thick enough to stick to the veggies.

**The Veggies:** Have ready any of the following for dipping: button mushrooms, sliced or cubed zucchini, onion rings. Dip veggies in batter and deep fry in hot oil, until batter is light brown and veggies are cooked, but still firm. Drain <u>really well</u> to remove excess oil. *Serve with peanut sauce, page 162.*

"It's not what you do some of the time, but what you do most of the time, that can cause problems."

## BOSTON STYLE BAKED BEANS

4 C. cooked kidney beans  
1 ½ C. water  
1 medium size onion, chopped  
1/2 green pepper, chopped  
1 TB. molasses  
1/2 C. ketchup or tomato sauce  

1/2 tsp. dry mustard  
1/4 tsp. dried parsley  
1/8 tsp. cayenne pepper (optional)  
1 tsp. chili fiesta blend powder (see pg. 102)  
1 clove garlic, minced  
1 tsp. spike seasoning  

Combine all ingredients in a casserole dish. Bake covered in a 350° oven for 1 hour. Remove lid and continue cooking until thickened.

**SERVING SUGGESTIONS:** *Serve these beans with your favourite soy or gluten sausage. Or cut them up in bite size pieces and cook along with the beans.*

## ITALIAN BEAN CASSEROLE

2 C. cooked great northern or navy beans  
2 TB. olive oil  
2 cloves garlic, minced  
4 C. tomatoes, diced or ground  
1 tsp. dried oregano  
2 tsp. dried parsley  
fresh basil for garnishing  

Heat oil in a large skillet or pot. Add garlic and sauté until soft. Add tomatoes, oregano and parsley to skillet. Simmer over medium heat, approximately 30 minutes, or until liquid is slightly thickened. Add beans and simmer an additional 10 minutes. Salt and pepper to taste. Garnish with fresh basil and serve.

"In choosing a diet, we must think of the real requirements of the body and find the natural foods which contain all the enzymes, the vitamins and minerals which the body needs. Merely satisfying the appetite and old habits or customs is not enough when we want to get well and have started out on a Health-Building Program. It is like building a house; we must have good material."
Dr. Randolph Stone, D.O., D.C. –
Health Building, the Conscious Art of Living Well.

## FUL MEDAMES    Egyptian Bean Casserole

1 C. dried fava beans
2 tsp. cumin powder
4 cloves garlic, minced or pressed
2 TB. lemon juice
2 TB. fresh parsley, chopped (1 tsp. dried)
2 TB. olive oil
Salt and pepper to taste
Paprika
1 tomato, medium size, chopped

Soak beans overnight in 3 cups water.  In morning drain off water and discard.  Cook beans in 3 cups of water, until soft.  (25 minutes in a pressure cooker)  Remove from heat and set aside 1 cup of the cooking liquid, before draining the beans.  In a small skillet or pan, simmer beans with the cooking liquid, cumin and garlic.  Simmer until the liquid has reduced by about half.  Remove from heat and add the lemon juice, 1 TB. parsley, and olive oil.  Salt and pepper to taste.  Serve immediately, sprinkled with remaining 1TB. parsley, a little paprika and the chopped tomato.  Serves 4

**Note:** *Fava beans come in both large flat and small rounded. The large bean is preferred for this recipe, or use any bean of similar quality.*

## CREAMY MASHED POTATOES

*These are great served with the brown gravy recipe on page 158.*

6 peeled or unpeeled, washed potatoes
1 clove garlic, minced
1/2 C. onion, chopped fine
1/2 C. soy sour cream
4 TB. soy margarine or olive oil
2 TB. prepared horseradish
salt and pepper to taste

1. Cut potatoes into quarters and steam with minced garlic until potatoes are tender.
2. Mash potatoes and garlic by hand, or with an electric mixer.
3. When potatoes are mashed to your preference, add onion, sour cream, margarine and horseradish, mixing all until well combined.  Salt and pepper to taste.

**Tip:** *When using unpeeled potatoes, watch for small stones that sometimes lodge in the eyes of potatoes.*

## POTATO CAKES

*My version of Aaron's specialty. Serve these any time of day.*

1 ½ C. (approx. ¾ lb.) grated potatoes
1/3 C. minced onion
1 clove garlic, minced
1 tsp. spike
1/4 tsp. black pepper
1/16 tsp. cayenne pepper (optional)
1 TB. cornmeal

1. Grate potatoes.
2. Mix potatoes with all other ingredients.
3. Drop by large spoonfuls onto hot, oiled griddle. Fry 5 minutes on each side or until potatoes are browned & crisp on the outside and tender on the inside. Serves 2-4

**Tip:** <u>Mashed Potato Cakes:</u> *Use leftover or freshly mashed potatoes instead of the fresh grated.*

## POTATO AUGRATIN

4 medium size potatoes, grated (about 4 Cups)
1 C. mushrooms, chopped
1/2 C. minced onion
2 tsp. oil
2 C. <u>un</u>sweetened soy milk
1 clove garlic, minced
1 TB. cornstarch
2 TB. vegan parmesan (or grated cheddar)
1/2 tsp. each of salt, black pepper and spike

Preheat oven 350°
1. Sautee the mushrooms and onion in the oil, until mushrooms are soft.
2. Whisk milk with garlic, cornstarch and vegan parmesan and simmer until mixture is slightly thickened. Add salt, pepper and spike. Adjust seasonings if necessary.
3. Combine grated potatoes, sautéed veggies, and thickened milk mixture, in a 1½ quart lightly oiled casserole dish. Cover dish and bake 35-45 minutes, or until the dish is bubbly and the potatoes are tender.

## OVEN FRIED POTATOES

*Or as they're called in Canada & the British Isles—Chips.*

4 large baking potatoes
1/4 C. vegetable oil
1/4 C. vegan parmesan (optional)
1 tsp. paprika
1/4 tsp. black pepper
salt to taste

Preheat oven 475°
1. Slice potatoes lengthwise into thin sticks.
2. Toss potatoes in a bowl with oil until well coated.
3. Sprinkle parmesan, paprika and pepper on potatoes and mix to coat all slices. Place potatoes in a single layer, on a baking sheet.
4. Bake 20-30 minutes, or until crisp and tender. Turn once during baking for uniform colour. Serve sprinkle with desired amount of salt, and for authentic "chips"- a dash or two of malt vinegar. **VARIATION:** *Sprinkle baked chips with dried, granulated or fresh minced garlic.* Sweet Potato Chips: *Substitute sweet potatoes for the regular potatoes.*


## SCALLOPED POTATOES

**Creamy sliced potato casserole**

4-5 thinly sliced potatoes
1 medium size onion, sliced
1 garlic clove, minced
1/2 C. fresh chopped parsley, (2 tsp. dried) (optional)
1 ½ C. unsweetened soy milk
2 TB. vegetable broth powder
½-1 tsp. salt (depending on saltiness of broth powder)
3 TB. unbleached white flour
vegan parmesan
paprika

Preheat oven 350°
1. Put potatoes, onion, garlic and parsley in a lightly oiled 1½ qt. baking dish.
2. Mix together soymilk, broth powder, salt and flour with a wire whisk.
3. Cover veggies with soymilk mixture, and bake covered at 350° for 30-45 minutes, or until potatoes are tender.
4. Remove cover and sprinkle with vegan parmesan and paprika, and bake an additional 5-10 minutes uncovered.

## ROSEMARY ROASTED POTATOES

3-4 garlic cloves, minced
1/4 C. olive oil
1/3 C. fresh rosemary leaves, finely chopped (2-3 tsp. dried)
1/2 tsp. salt
1/8 tsp. cayenne pepper (optional)
4-5 large potatoes scrubbed and cubed
1 tsp. paprika (optional)

Preheat oven 425°
1. Combine garlic, oil, rosemary, salt and cayenne pepper.
2. Toss the potatoes with the oil mixture and set aside for 5-10 minutes.
3. Sprinkle potatoes lightly with optional paprika and place them on a cookie sheet.
4. Bake 20-30 minutes or until the potatoes are done, turning once during baking for uniform browning.

**VARIATION:** Roasted Herbal Wedges — *Cut potatoes into wedges and sprinkle with a mixture of ¼ C. oil, 2-3 tsp. crushed Italian seasoning (or a mixture of dried oregano, basil and thyme) and ½ tsp. each of salt and garlic granules.*

## STEAMED YELLOW RICE

2 C. long grain brown rice
4 ½ C. water
Dash of salt
1/8 - 1/4 tsp. turmeric powder

In a medium size saucepan with a lid, bring all ingredients to a boil. Turn heat down and simmer for about 45 minutes, or until rice is tender and the liquid has been absorbed Makes 4-6 servings. **Reminder:** *Below 3000 ft. altitude - use 4 cups water to 2 cups rice.*

**VARIATION:** Steamed Brown Rice - *Eliminate the turmeric.*

"Health depends not alone upon food and drink. Sunshine, fresh air, pure water and exercise are equally important elements in health. Balanced healthful living requires at oneness with all aspects of nature."
Helen & Scott Nearing, - Living the Good Life

# EASY SPANISH RICE

1 C. long grained brown rice
2 ½ C. water
1/4 tsp. each coriander powder, garlic granules and salt
1 tsp. onion powder
1/8 tsp. cumin powder
1 heaping tsp. veggie broth powder
1 tsp. dry parsley (1 TB. fresh)
3-4 large tomatoes, chopped fine (or substitute canned )
1 TB. fresh cilantro, chopped (optional)
salt & pepper to taste

Cook rice in 2-2 ½ cups water with a dash of salt. Bring the water to a boil and then lower heat and simmer for approximately 45 minutes, or until the rice is tender and the water has been absorbed. Stir in all of the remaining ingredients, transferring to a larger pot if necessary. Simmer approximately 10-15 minutes or until ingredients are well combined and hot. Salt and pepper to taste. Makes 4 servings.

**VARIATION:** *This dish is also delicious without the tomatoes.*

# RICE PILAF

| | |
|---|---|
| 1 C. brown rice | 1/2 green pepper, chopped |
| 2 ½ C. water | 1/2 red pepper, chopped |
| 1 TB. oil | 1/2 C. green peas or chopped spinach |
| 1 clove garlic, minced | 1 TB. dried parsley |
| 1 small onion, chopped | 1/2 tsp. dried basil |
| 1/2 C. raw cashews | 1/4 tsp. salt and pepper |

Cook rice in 2-2 ½ C. water, and a dash of salt, for 45 minutes, or until rice is tender, and water has been absorbed. In 1 TB. oil sauté the garlic, onion, peppers and cashews until veggies are soft. Add peas or spinach, parsley, basil, salt, pepper and cooked rice. Stir and sauté until mixture is well combined and hot. Adjust seasonings if necessary.
Serves 2-4

**VARIATION:** <u>Wild Rice Pilaf:</u> *Substitute ¼ C. of the brown rice with wild rice.*
<u>Quinoa or Millet Pilaf:</u> *Use cooked millet or quinoa instead of the cooked brown rice.*

## INDIAN COUSCOUS

2 TB. oil
1 tsp. brown or yellow mustard seed
2 cloves garlic minced
1 green pepper, chopped
1 large onion (1 C.) chopped
2 C. couscous (uncooked)
3-4 C. water

3 TB. veggie broth powder
1/2 tsp. turmeric
1/2 tsp. salt
1 TB. ginger, minced
1/2 C. cashew pieces
1/2–1 C. fresh or frozen peas
juice of one lemon (2 TB.)

1.  In a wok or large skillet sauté mustard seed in oil.  Add garlic, pepper and onion and cook until tender.
2.  Add couscous, 3 C. water and the rest of ingredients, except lemon.
3.  Simmer on low heat, 5-10 minutes or until couscous is soft. Stir occasionally adding more water if needed.  Add lemon last five minutes of cooking, when water has been absorbed and couscous is soft.  Adjust seasoning, adding more salt and pepper if desired. Serve with a green salad and steamed veggies. Serves 4-6
**VARIATION:** _Indian Millet or Quinoa:_ _Substitute uncooked millet or quinoa for the couscous. Allow an additional 10-20 minutes cooking time._


## SEASONED GREENS

3 C. chopped chard, kale, spinach or other greens
    (or a combination of all)
1 clove garlic, minced
2 TB. margarine or olive oil
salt and pepper to taste
1 lemon cut in wedges

1.  Steam greens briefly until tender but not limp.
2.  Toss in pan with margarine or oil and garlic.
3.  Season with salt, and pepper and serve with a slice of lemon.

"I would like to emphasize that the calcium losing effect of protein on the human body is not an area of controversy in scientific circles.  The many studies performed during the past fifty five years consistently show that the most important dietary change that we can make, if we want to create a positive calcium balance that will keep our bones solid, is to decrease the amount of proteins we eat each day.  The important change is not to increase the amount of calcium we take in."  Dr. John McDougall  - The McDougall Plan

## CORN FRITTERS   *These fritters bring back fond memories of living in Toronto, Canada. This is my version of Gramma Lilian's specialty.*

1-15 oz. can or 2 C. fresh corn kernels
2 TB. egg replacer mixed w/ 4 TB. hot water
1/8 C. green pepper, chopped fine (optional)
1/8 C. black olives, chopped (optional)
1/4 tsp. each: salt, spike and pepper

1/8 tsp. nutmeg
1/2 tsp. dried parsley
6 TB. whole-wheat pastry flour
2 TB. quick oatmeal

1. Whiz half of whole corn in a blender, with liquid from can, or a little water, before starting.
2. Mix corn and remaining ingredients together until well-blended, and let sit for a few minutes before dropping by spoonfuls onto a hot, lightly oiled skillet.  Fry 5-10 minutes on each side, until lightly browned and crisp.

## MID-EASTERN ZUCCHINI CAKES

1 zucchini, (approximately ¾ lb. or 2 C.)  grated *
1 carrot  (¾ C. grated)
1/2 C. minced scallions or onion
1 tsp. dried dill weed
1/2 tsp. each of dried oregano, basil, salt & pepper
1/2 C. crumbled vegan feta (pg. 153) (optional)
1/2 C. walnuts, chopped
1/3 C. cornmeal or flour
oil for sautéing

Combine the zucchini, carrots, onions, herbs and salt and pepper. Set aside for 5-10 minutes.  Gently stir in the vegan feta, walnuts and flour.  Form into patties or drop batter by large spoonfuls onto a hot oiled skillet. Fry each cake until golden brown, about 3-5 minutes on each side.   Makes 9-3inch cakes. * *Vegetables can be ground in an electric food chopper.*

> "All the good food that may be eaten cannot do the body any good until you have eliminated and cleansed the body of excess acids and mucus. The intestines retain these poisons and they are one of the main causes of disease and old age. By eating an abundance of alkaline or base forming foods, one can rid themselves of poisons and acids."
>
> Jethro Kloss,  - Back to Eden

## SPICY FRENCH RATATOUILLE

*A summer-time veggie medley.*

1 small eggplant, peeled and cubed
2 large onions, sliced
1/4 C. olive oil
3 small zucchini, sliced
4 medium size tomatoes, chopped

2 green peppers, chopped
2 cloves garlic, minced
1 TB. fresh parsley, minced (½ tsp. dried)
1 tsp. salt
1/2 tsp. each, dried thyme and oregano

Preheat oven 350°
Sauté eggplant and onion in olive oil until eggplant is browned but not soggy. Remove to an ovenproof casserole along with remaining ingredients. Bake covered at 350° for approximately 45- 60 minutes. Serve with brown rice and a salad.

## CREAMY HOT BEETS

6-8 medium size beets
1 C. soy sour cream
2 TB. prepared horseradish sauce
1 tsp. dried dill weed,
2 TB. lemon juice
salt and pepper to taste

Steam beets until tender. While beets are steaming, mix remaining ingredients together to make a creamy sauce. When beets are tender, remove skins. Cut into cubes or slices and immediately toss beets with creamy sauce, or just serve beets with a dollop of sauce.

**VARIATION:** *Try this recipe without the sour cream and horseradish. Toss hot beets with remaining ingredients plus some soy margarine or olive oil, or just sprinkle hot cooked beets with ume plum vinegar and serve.* <u>Creamed Cauliflower or Peas:</u> *Substitute cooked cauliflower or peas for the beets.*

---

"It isn't what you do once in a while that counts. It's what you do most of the time."

Bernard Jensen, Ph.D. - The Healing Mind of Man

---

## EASY ROASTED GARLIC

3-4 heads of garlic (not just the cloves-- the entire heads)
olive oil

Preheat oven 350°
Cut across the top of the head of garlic, so that the cloves are exposed.  Set the garlic in an ovenproof dish.  Drizzle olive oil over the tops of garlic.  Seal the dish with foil or a cover.  Set in a 350° oven and bake 45-60 minutes, or until garlic cloves are soft.  These are great just popped out of the skin and eaten as is, or spread on rolls or other breads.

*GROWING GARLIC IS EASY AND FUN:  Just when you thought that gardening had come to a grand finale, with the harvesting of late fall crops, along comes pungent and hardy garlic.  It's the last crop to be planted in the year and one of the first plants to greet you in the spring, and not often bothered by insects or other pests.  The colder your climate is, the spicier your garlic will be.  Garlic likes a soil which is acid, around pH of 6.5.  Plant the peeled garlic cloves approximately 3 inches deep in rows 5-6 inches apart.  Cover them with a blanket of mulch (leaves, straw, pine needles) to protect them from any freeze and thaw conditions.  Mid October is the optimum time for planting garlic and the bulbs should be ready to harvest by the end of June.  The clue for when to harvest the garlic is when the leaves start to turn brown.  When this happens, stop watering the garlic and hope for a week or so of dry weather, so that the skins dry out some before harvesting.  Pull the bulbs gently from the soil and brush off any soil.  Hang them in bundles and cure the bulbs out of direct sunlight, in a cool, dry area.  They will keep through the winter, if stored in a dry, airy room.  Set aside the biggest garlic for next years crop.*

"The power foods are foods from plants.  Vegetarians have a much better menu for the heart.  Lacto-ovo vegetarians (those who shun meats, poultry and fish, but consume dairy products and eggs) do much better than those on lean meat diets, while pure vegetarians who steer clear of all animal products do best of all."
Neal Barnard, M.D. - Food For Life

# Burgers
# Loaves
# Barbequing
# Sandwiches
# & Snacks

# BURGERS & LOAVES

## LENTIL SLOPPY JOES

2 C. lentils
5 C. water
2 medium size onions, chopped
3 cloves garlic, minced
1/4 tsp. each of dried thyme, summer savory, paprika, salt
1/8 tsp.+ cayenne pepper (optional)
1 tsp. chili blend powder (pg. 102)
1/2 C. barbeque sauce, ketchup or tomato sauce

1. Cook lentils in 5 C. water for approximately 1 hour, or until very soft.
2. Sauté onion and garlic in a lightly oiled skillet.
3. Add all remaining ingredients, plus cooked drained lentils, stirring and heating thoroughly.
4. Adjust spices if necessary.  Serve between burger buns or pita bread.

## BAKED TVP BURGERS

2 C. TVP granules soaked in 3 C. hot water
1 tsp. each: onion powder & garlic granules
1 ½ tsp. dried oregano
2 TB. Tamari

1/2 C. quick or regular oatmeal
1/2 tsp. salt
1/4 tsp. black pepper
1/3 C. flour

Preheat oven 350°
Soak TVP until soft and water is absorbed.  Add all remaining ingredients to softened TVP and mix together well.  Form into patties with wet hands. Place on lightly oiled cookie sheet.  Bake for approximately 15-20 minutes.  Flip over and bake 15 minutes more, or until browned.  Serve these with brown gravy, pg. 158, or between buns.

---

*A long life lived is not always good enough; but a good life lived is always long enough.*

---

## TOFU BALLS

1 lb. firm tofu, pressed and squeezed of water*
1/2 C. chopped onion
1-2 cloves garlic, minced
1 small carrot, grated
1 green pepper, chopped

1/2 tsp. each salt & pepper
2 TB water or broth
1/4 C. walnuts, chopped
2 TB. fresh parsley, chopped
   (2 tsp. dried)

1. Sauté onions and garlic in a lightly oiled skillet. Stir in carrot and green pepper and continue frying until veggies are soft. Remove from heat to cool slightly.
2. Mash tofu in a bowl. Stir water or broth into tofu along with salt and pepper. Add slightly cooled veggies, walnuts and parsley and combine well.
3. Preheat oven to 350°. Form tofu mixture into 1-inch balls. Arrange on lightly oiled cookie sheet and bake 30 minutes, or until lightly browned. Turn balls half way through baking for uniform browning. Makes 12-18 balls.

**TIP:** * **To press tofu**: *Lay block of tofu in a colander. Cover tofu with a light cloth and put a heavy weight like a brick or jug of water on top of the cloth, for 20-30 minutes.*

## LENTIL PATTIES

1 ½ C. dry lentils
1/2 C. brown rice
4 ½ C. water
1/2 C. walnuts or other nuts, chopped
1 medium size onion, chopped
1 tsp. each garlic powder, dried thyme
1/2 C. flour
2 TB. dried parsley
1 C. grated vegan cheddar
2 TB. egg replacer powder dissolved in 1/4 C. warm water

1. Cook lentils and rice together in 4 ½ C. water for approximately 45 minutes, or until tender.
2. Add all remaining ingredients to cooled rice and lentils. Salt and pepper to taste.
3. Mold into patties or drop by spoonfuls onto hot griddle. Cook on both sides until crisp.

---

*"It takes a hundred times more water to produce a pound of meat as it does to produce a pound of wheat"*    John Robbins - Diet For A New America

---

## OAT BURGERS or LOAF

1 C. chopped onion
1-2 tsp. garlic granules or 1 clove, minced
2 TB. oil
1 C. TVP granules
1/2 C. couscous
1 C. quick oatmeal
1 tsp. each of dried basil, oregano and dill weed
1/4 C. nutritional yeast flakes
1/3 C. chopped walnuts, or other nut
1/2 tsp. each of salt and black pepper
1/4 C. tamari
2 C. warm water
ketchup or tomato sauce, optional

1. Sauté onion and garlic with oil in a pot or deep-sided skillet, until onion is soft.
2. In a bowl mix the TVP, couscous, oatmeal, spices, yeast, walnuts and salt and pepper, stirring to combine. Add tamari and water and mix well.
3. Pour grain mixture into skillet containing the garlic and onion.
4. Stir to combine and cook on low heat for about 2 minutes stirring and combining continuously.
5. Form into patties with wet hands, or press into an 8 x 8 inch lightly oiled baking pan, and drizzle with ketchup or tomato sauce.
6. Place patties on lightly oiled cookie sheet and bake in preheated 350° oven, 15-20 minutes, then flip patties over and continue to back an additional 15 minutes or until browned on both sides. Bake loaf uncovered at 350° for 30 minutes.

**VARIATION:** Oat Burger Balls-*for spaghetti sauce, form into small balls and either bake or fry until browned.*

---

"The shopper should always keep in mind several principles. Food should be as natural as possible. It should be as whole and pure as possible---uncooked, unpreserved, unpolished and un-devitalized. Insist upon foods raised in nature's garden, not made or manhandled by man."
Bernard Jensen, Ph.D. - Food Healing For Man

---

## SPROUTED LENTIL PATTIES

*Lentils are very easy to sprout. See pg. 268 on how to sprout. Allow 4-7 days for mature sprouts, depending on sprouting method.*

1 C. sprouted lentils, (approximately 1/2" in length) chopped coarse
1/2-1 C. kernel corn (drain liquid if canned)
1 C. dry burger mix  (or substitute a mixture of flour and oatmeal)
1/4 C. flour
1/2 TB. dried parsley
1 small onion, chopped
1 clove of garlic, minced
1/2 tsp. each of dried thyme, oregano, salt and pepper
1 TB. egg replacer powder mixed with 3/4 C. hot water

Mix all ingredients together until well combined. Let mixture sit for at least 20 minutes before dropping by spoonfuls onto a hot lightly oiled griddle.  Fry both sides until browned.


## FALAFELS

*This is a delicious Middle Eastern bean patty.  Serve as a side dish along with tabooli salad, or inside pita bread with sesame tahini sauce or hummus.*

3 C. cooked garbanzo beans,
1 small onion, chopped
2-4 cloves garlic, minced
1 tsp.  oil
1/2 C. mashed potatoes

1/4 C. fresh parsley or cilantro, minced
1 TB. lemon juice
1/2 tsp. each of turmeric, cumin, salt & pepper
3 TB. flour

Sauté onion and garlic in oil until soft.  In a blender or food processor grind the cooked garbanzo beans.  Combine onion, garlic, beans and remaining ingredients.  The mixture will look dry, but should easily form into balls using your hands.   Flatten balls slightly and sauté them in an oiled skillet, until browned on both sides.   Serve with sesame tahini sauce or hummus. Makes approximately 20 - 1 ½ inch patties.

---

*"For kindness, common sense, economy, simplicity, aesthetics, and health reasons, we eat nothing that walks or wiggles."*
*Helen & Scott Nearing  - Living the Good Life, 1970*

---

## TOFU PATTIES

1 lb. firm tofu
1/2 medium size onion, minced
1 stalk celery, minced
1/2 green pepper, minced
2 TB. oil
2 TB. flour
2 TB. tamari
1/2 C. vegan cheddar
salt and pepper to taste
2 TB. egg replacer powder mixed with 1/4 C. warm water
cornmeal

1. Sauté onion, celery and green pepper in oil until soft.
2. Crumble tofu in a medium size bowl.
3. Add Sautéed veggies and all remaining ingredients except cornmeal. Mix together well.
4. With wet hands form into patties and roll in cornmeal. Fry on oiled griddle, or bake in 350° oven for approximately 30 minutes, or until browned, flipping over half way through baking.

## WALNUT VEGGIE LOAF

1 C. walnuts, chopped
1 C. cooked brown rice
1/2 C. wheat germ or flour
1 medium size onion, chopped
1/2 green pepper, chopped
1 C. vegan cheddar, grated
2 TB. egg replacer powder mixed with 1/2 C. water
1 TB. dried parsley
1 tsp. Italian seasoning or oregano
1/2 C. flour
1/2 tsp. salt & pepper
1/2 - 1 C. more water

Mix all ingredients except water, stirring together well. Add only enough water to make a moist but firm mixture. Press mixture into an oiled loaf pan. Bake in a preheated 350° oven approximately 45 minutes, or until browned and firm. Let cool 10-15 minutes before removing from pan. Slice and serve.

**Serving suggestion:** *Serve with mashed potatoes, steamed veggies and brown gravy pg. 158.*

## PAULA'S TOFU DINNER LOAF

*This recipe brings back fond memories of good food and fine company in northern Michigan.*

1 C. fresh whole wheat breadcrumbs
1/3 C. water
2 C. onion, minced
2 cloves garlic, minced
1 ½ lb. firm tofu, pressed and squeezed of water,
1/4 C. tamari
1/2 tsp each of dried basil, sage and oregano
1/4 tsp. each dried thyme and savory
1 TB. ketchup
1/4 C. wheat gluten (or whole wheat flour)
tomato sauce or ketchup
Preheat oven 350°

1. In a large bowl mix breadcrumbs and water.
2. In a large skillet steam fry the onion and garlic, using a little water instead of oil. When onions are soft and slightly browned, add to the breadcrumbs.
3. Crumble the tofu and add to the breadcrumb mixture, along with all remaining ingredients, mixing until well combined.
4. Pat mixture into a lightly oiled 9-inch pie pan. Spread with a thin layer of tomato sauce or ketchup. Bake 30 minutes. Sit 10-15 minutes before cutting into wedges.

**Serving Suggestions:** *Serve loaf with creamy mashed potatoes, brown gravy, steamed veggies and a salad.*

**Other Ideas:** <u>Wheat Free Tofu Dinner Loaf:</u> *Use wheat free breadcrumbs and bean or rice flour instead of wheat gluten.*

> "Every time you make a choice that expresses respect for life, you bring a little more love into your body, into your family, into your society, and into a world that is calling out for this blessing."
> John Robbins - May All Be Fed, Diet for a New World

# SUMMERTIME BARBEQUING

*A complete vegan meal can easily be cooked on an outside grill.*

**IDEAS**:

Marinated Veggies: Make a simple marinade with tamari and herbs, such as basil, oregano or dill. Marinate your choice of portabellas, chunks of green pepper, onions, or sweet potatoes, regular or pressed tofu or tempeh, for 2-6 hours or overnight, before cooking on a hot grill. Try a splash of hot or regular toasted sesame oil or salty Ume plum vinegar in the marinade. See marinades on page 163 for other ideas.

Veggie Tofu Kebabs: Place on skewers: small tomatoes, chunks of firm, regular or pressed tofu, thick slices of green pepper, mushrooms and zucchini, and any other vegetables on hand, then cook until lightly browned and tender. Tofu and vegetables can be marinated before putting on the skewers.

Corn on the Cob: Peel cornhusk back to 2 layers. Soak corn in cool water, at least 1 hour or longer. After draining corn, brush outside of husks with vegetable oil and place on a hot grill, turning occasionally until tender, or approximately 30 minutes. Brush with oil one or more times during cooking.

**Tip:** *To press tofu for a firmer texture, lay block of tofu in a colander. Cover the tofu with a light cloth. Set a heavy weight, such as a brick or jug of water on top of the cloth. Set aside for 20-30 minutes.*

**OTHER GRILLING IDEAS:** *Oat burgers pg. 138, vegan sausages or dogs, slabs of tempeh or pressed tofu. (Partially bake the oat burgers before putting on the grill, so that they don't fall apart.)*

"Numerous medical studies have shown that the intake of calcium on a vegan diet is entirely adequate, and that true calcium deficiency on a vegan diet has never been reported."

Michael Klaper M.D. - Vegan Nutrition; Pure & Simple

# WRAPS & SANDWICHES

## AVOCADO VEGGIE WRAP

*Assemble the following ingredients, and lay along the center of a tortilla and roll up. Fold in ends if desired.*

Avocado slices, tomato chunks, sautéed and sliced mushroom, fresh sprouts or lettuce, vegan mayonnaise.

Sprinkle with spike, salt and pepper to taste. **Other ideas:** *Instead of a wrap, stuff the filling into pita bread or between two pieces of whole grain bread or toast.*

## EGGPLANT HUMMUS WRAPS

4 large whole wheat tortillas *
1 small eggplant (3½ C. peeled and cubed)
3 TB. olive oil
1 TB. balsamic vinegar
2 tsp. lemon juice
1/4 tsp. salt
1/8 tsp. black pepper
1 C. hummus (pg. 150)
sprouts or lettuce

* substitute warm pita/pocket bread

Cut eggplant into bite size cubes and salt lightly. Heat skillet and add 3 TB. Olive oil. Fry eggplant until browned on both sides and soft, but not mushy. Remove from heat. Immediately toss with vinegar, lemon juice, salt and pepper. Heat tortillas briefly in a warm oven and then slather with hummus. Divide eggplant mixture evenly between the four tortillas, spreading it down the center of each tortilla. Top with sprouts or lettuce. Roll up into a tube shape. The sides don't get tucked in. Serves 4.

## MIDDLE EASTERN WRAP or POCKET

large whole wheat tortilla or pita/pocket bread
hummus  (pg.150)
falafel patties, baked or fried  (pg. 139)
cucumber or dill pickle, chopped
chopped tomatoes
sprouts or lettuce (optional)

Warm the tortilla or pita bread.  Place a layer of hummus on tortilla or inside pita.  Add 2-3
falafel patties and the remaining ingredients.  If using tortilla, fold or roll before serving.

## THE B*L*T

whole wheat bread or toast
vegan mayonnaise
meatless bacon (fried until crisp) or use dry soy bacun bits
tomato slices
spike, salt and pepper
lettuce or sprouts

Slather one side of bread or toast with mayonnaise.  If using dry bacun bits, sprinkle those
on the mayonnaise.  If using meatless bacon, proceed with laying tomatoes on the
mayonnaise, then the cooked bacon. Sprinkle with spike, salt and pepper and top with a
handful of lettuce greens or sprouts.  Place second piece of bread or toast on top and serve.

"Seeds and sprouts are the survival foods of the future and for today.  They are
the most perfect foods because they contain everything necessary to foster a new
life.  They are "live" foods."
Bernard Jensen, Ph.D.   - The Healing Mind of Man

## TOFU OF THE SEA SANDWICH

1/2 lb. firm tofu
1/2 C. celery, chopped
1/4 C. minced onion
1/4 C. vegan mayonnaise
1 TB. tamari
2 tsp. lemon juice
1/2 tsp. kelp powder
sprouts or lettuce
sandwich bread or pita

Place tofu in a colander. Cover with a clean cloth and a heavy weight. Leave for 30 minutes, to allow liquid to drain. Crumble tofu into small pieces. Add celery, onion, mayonnaise, tamari, lemon juice and kelp powder. Stir together well. Spread mixture between bread or inside a pita, and top with sprouts or lettuce. Serves 4

## THE VEGAN RUBEN

8 oz. tempeh cut in thin slices
1 ½ - 2 C. sauerkraut
1 small red onion, sliced thin
4 slices vegan cheese (optional)
prepared mustard
8 slices Rye or Pumpernickel bread

Fry tempeh in a lightly oiled skillet. Layer tempeh, and kraut that has been squeezed of excess water, onion and vegan cheese on one piece of bread. Slather remaining slice of bread with mustard, and lay over the other piece. Serve. Makes 4 sandwiches.

**VARIATION:** *Substitute sliced avocado, and tomato, for the tempeh. Sliced and sautéed mushrooms can also be included. For a traditional style Ruben, spread vegan margarine on the outer sides of bread, and fry in a dry skillet, until browned on both sides and vegan cheese is soft.*

"Cancer of the prostate is strongly linked to what men eat. Again, animal products are consistently indicted. Milk, meat, eggs, cheese, cream, butter and fats are found in one research after another, to be linked to prostate cancer."
Neal Barnard, M.D. - Food For Life

## GRILLED PORTOBELLO ON A BUN

Grill a large Portobello mushroom, which has been marinated for 30-60 minutes in tamari and a splash of olive oil, or your favourite marinade. Serve it in a toasted whole wheat bun with sliced tomato and lettuce or sprouts.

## GRILLED VEGAN CHEESE SANDWICH

Place one or two slices of vegan cheddar between two pieces of whole grain bread. Slip in a few slices of onion, dill pickle, and a dab or two of mustard, if you like. Slather margarine on the outside of bread. Fry in an un-oiled skillet until browned on both sides and cheese is softened.

## QUESADILLAS   Mexican Cheese Sandwich

6 corn or wheat tortillas
4-6 oz. vegan cheese
Your choice of garnishes such as: cilantro, avocado, onion, and salsa sauce

Tortillas can be used whole or cut into 4 triangles before grilling. Lay cheese and any of your chosen garnishes on one tortilla or triangle. Lay other side or triangle on top. Cook on hot griddle until the cheese softens and tortilla is golden on both sides. Serve
**Note:** *Garnishes such as salsa and avocado can be served on the side, rather than being put in the sandwich.*

"Some people insist that dairy products are necessary for calcium. We're led to believe that milk is a major source of calcium and if we don't drink milk our teeth will fall out and our bones will collapse. First of all, the calcium in cows milk is much coarser than in human's milk and is tied up with casein. This prevents the calcium from being absorbable."
Harvey & Marilyn Diamond - Fit For Life

## THE P*B*J

*The old and faithful standby. What would we do without it? It's so easy to make and packs well in lunch bags. Use natural, organic, non-pasteurized peanut butter and whole grain bread.*

Assemble bread, peanut butter, jam or jelly and optional sliced bananas. Serve.

## THE PEANUT BUTTER BANANA

*Try this when you're out of bread, or for a quick and different snack. The peanut butter provides a nutritious and chewy filling; and can be substituted with cashew or almond butter.*

Take a peeled banana and slit it lengthwise. Smear crunchy peanut butter along the one half and top with the other. The stickiness of the peanut butter holds the banana together.

## OTHER SANDWICH IDEAS

See the **Breakfast Section:** for Bean Burritos, pg.45 and Veggie Wraps, pg.44
The **Burger Section:** for burger on bun ideas, pg. 136-141
The **Yeasted Bread Section:** for Veggie Stuff Bagels, pg. 32
The **Salad Section:** for the following: Spring Rolls, pg. 56
Wheat Gluten or Tempeh Salad, pg.61 and Tofu "egg" salad. pg. 60

> "To be a vegetarian is to disagree----to disagree with the course of
> things today...starvation, world hunger, cruelty, waste, wars----
> We must make a statement against these things.
> Vegetarianism is my statement. And I think it's a strong one."
> Isaac Bashevis Singer - writer

# SNACKS

## TOMAS'S POPCORN

*What other snack is there? Tomas says that it's the freshness of the popcorn and the weight of the pot, that makes the best popcorn. I think the popcorn maker should also get some credit. Store popcorn in a cool pantry. The pot should have a thick bottom.*

Pour into a heavy 6-quart pot: 4 TB. vegetable oil, 1-cup organic popcorn kernels and 4 pressed or finely minced cloves of garlic. Turn the burner on. When the popcorn begins to pop, shake the pot from side to side until it stops popping. Immediately take off of heat. Pour popcorn into two or more large bowls. Season liberally, or to taste, with nutritional yeast and spike. Popcorn made this way is so good, with the nutritional yeast adding a buttery flavour. **Note:** *Your favourite veggie oil can also be sprinkled on the popped kernels.*

## TRAIL MIX

*Mix any of the following ingredients in equal amounts or whatever proportions you fancy. Cut the dried fruit into bite size pieces. Trail mix is great to have on hand when hiking, camping or on long road trips.*

| | |
|---|---|
| raw cashews | raisins |
| whole almonds | dried pineapple and papaya chunks |
| raw sunflower seeds | dry coconut in large flakes |
| peanuts | dried peaches, apples, and apricots |
| walnuts | |

**Note:** *If preferred, the nuts can be lightly roasted in the oven before mixing with the fruit.*

"Fundamentally I came up against an intellectual argument that I simply wasn't able to refute---nor has anyone I've ever mentioned it to ever been able to refute it. The core of that argument is that eating animals or animal products causes pain and suffering to the animals. Second, it isn't necessary to eat animals or animal products to optimize one's health. Quite the opposite; a well balanced vegan diet is the healthiest diet a person can eat. Third, the only reasons to eat animals or animal products are simple cultural habit and the pleasure of one's own palate. And finally, is the trivial pleasure of one's palate sufficient reason to cause pain and suffering to animals? I think the answer is obvious. No it isn't.
  John Mackey, CEO of Whole Foods Market  - in Veg/News, Mar/Apr. 2004

# Dips, Soy "Dairy", Sauces & Marinades

## HUMMUS

1 C. garbanzo beans, cooked
1-3 cloves of garlic, minced
1/4 C. tahini
1/4 tsp. sea salt
juice of l lime or lemon
3 TB. olive oil
1-4 TB. water

Place all ingredients except water in a blender and whiz until smooth and creamy, adding water if needed to give desired consistency. Salt and pepper to taste. Serve with raw veggies or warm chapati bread.

## SPROUTED BEAN DIP

2 C. sprouted lentils
1 C. celery, minced
1 TB. ginger, minced
1-2 TB. white miso
1 TB. garlic, finely minced
3 TB. nutritional yeast flakes
1/2 C. raw cashews, ground

1/2 tsp. cumin
1 tsp. dried  basil
2 TB. tahini
salt & pepper to taste
water or lemon juice

Blend all ingredients except salt, pepper and water or lemon juice in a food processor or blender until creamy smooth. Thin with water or lemon juice, if necessary, and salt and pepper to taste. Serve with raw veggies.

"Pure vegetarians from many populations of the world have maintained excellent health"
    - The Food and Nutrition Board of the National Academy of Sciences

## BABA GHANNOUJ
***A great Middle Eastern eggplant dip for veggies or warm chapati***

3 eggplants (approx. 4 lbs)
1/2 C tahini
3-6 cloves garlic
3 TB. olive oil
juice of 2 lemons
dash cayenne pepper

1/2 tsp. each of spike & coriander powder
1 TB. dried parsley
salt and pepper to taste
Paprika

Preheat oven 350°
1. Wash eggplants, and remove stems. Prick skins liberally with a fork. Set eggplants in a baking pan with a little water and bake in the oven for 45-60 minutes, or until soft and deflated. Replace the water in the bottom of pan, if necessary, to keep eggplant from sticking.
2. Remove from oven and allow to cool before scooping the flesh out. Discard the skins.
3. Combine cooled eggplant with all remaining ingredients, except salt, pepper and paprika, and puree in a blender until very creamy smooth. Salt and pepper to taste and serve in a large bowl sprinkled lightly with paprika.


## SOY/GREEN ONION VEGGIE DIP

1/2 C. soft tofu
1/2 tsp. ginger powder
1 TB. tamari
2 TB. nuts, chopped fine
2 TB. soy mayo
1 C. plain soy yogurt or sour cream
1/2 C. green onions, finely chopped
1/4 C. fresh parsley, chopped

Combine everything in a blender, except yogurt, onions and parsley. Whiz until mixture is smooth and creamy. Stir in yogurt and onions and sprinkle with parsley. Serve with raw veggies.

> "Any time we eat it's holy. We should have ritual and ceremony, not just gobbling down some food to keep alive."   - M.F.K.Fisher

## GUACAMOLE

2 ripe avocados
1 clove of garlic, minced
1/4 C. onion or scallions, chopped
1/4 –1/2 C. tomatoes, diced (optional)
2 TB. lime juice
1/4 tsp. each of salt and black pepper
cilantro leaves, chopped (optional)

Mash or finely chop the avocado flesh. Mix with garlic, onion, optional tomatoes, lime juice, salt and pepper. Taste and adjust seasonings if necessary. Garnish with cilantro leaves. Serve with warm pita bread or crackers.


## PECAN YOGURT DIP

1/4 C. finely chopped pecans
1-2 cloves garlic, pressed or minced
1 TB. olive oil
3/4 C. plain soy yogurt
1/2 C. cucumber, peeled and diced fine
1 tsp. lemon juice

Combine all ingredients, blending well with a wire whisk. Chill and serve with crisp raw veggies.

> "When I was 88 years old, I gave up meat entirely and switched to a plant –foods diet following a slight stroke. During the following months, I not only lost 50 pounds but gained strength in my legs and picked up stamina. Now, at age 93, I'm on the same plant-based diet, and still don't eat any meat or dairy products. I either swim, walk or paddle a canoe daily and feel the best I've felt since my heart problems began."
> - Dr. Benjamin Spock M.D. (1903-1998)

## SOY FETA

8 oz. firm tofu (drained and weighted to compress)*
3 TB. Ume plum vinegar
(or use rice vinegar with 1/2 tsp. salt) **
2 TB. olive oil
1/4 tsp. dried oregano
1/4 tsp. black pepper

*This recipe works best if the tofu has been weighted to remove some of the water. Place tofu in a colander. Cover tofu with a light cloth and lay a heavy weight such as a brick or heavy jug, on top of the cloth for at least 20 minutes, or until tofu has been flattened slightly. ** Salt can be eliminated by using all rice vinegar and a salt-less herbal seasoning.*

Crumble tofu and gently stir in remaining ingredients. Adjust seasonings, adding more salt if necessary. Place in a covered container and marinade for at least 1 hour before using. Makes 1¼ cups.


## SOY RICOTTA

1 pound firm tofu
1/3 C. olive oil
1/2 tsp. ground nutmeg
1/2 tsp. sea salt

Crumble tofu. Add remaining ingredients and mix together with a fork until well blended. Makes 2½-3 cups.

**VARIATION**: Herbal Ricotta: *Eliminate the nutmeg and add 1 tsp. each of garlic granules, onion powder, basil and oregano, or any combination of your favourite herbs.*


## SOY SOUR CREAM

1 C. firm style tofu                 2 tsp. brown rice vinegar
2 TB. lemon juice                    1/4 tsp. sea salt
2 TB. vegetable oil

Mix all in a blender until very smooth. Thin with a little water if necessary. Store in airtight container in fridge. Makes approximately 1½ cups.

## SIMPLE BASIC WHITE SAUCE
*Serve over cooked veggies*

2 C. <u>un</u>sweetened soy milk
2 TB. each of cornstarch and flour
1 TB. veggie broth powder
2 TB. olive oil
salt and pepper to taste

Combine all ingredients and mix well with a wire whisk.  Simmer over medium heat until thick.  Thin sauce with more soy milk to desired thickness. .
**Note:**  This makes a thick sauce. For a thinner sauce use less cornstarch and flour, or add more soy milk.
**VARIATION:**  <u>Herbal White Sauce</u>:  *Add to the above mixture before cooking: 1 tsp. each of onion powder, dried thyme, and dried basil, or any combination of your favourite herbs.*


## TOFU SAUCE
*Pour over cooked veggies, then if desired, brown topping in broiler or oven.*

1 lb. soft tofu
1 TB. oil
2 cloves garlic
1 TB. fresh minced ginger
2 TB. tahini
1 TB. tamari
1/2 tsp. salt
2-6 TB. water, for thinning.

Combine all ingredients and only 2 TB. water in a blender, and mix until very smooth.  Add more water if needed, to bring sauce to desired thickness.

---

"It takes less water to produce a year's food for a pure vegetarian than to produce a month's food for a meat eater."   John Robbins  - Diet for a New America

---

## CASHEW GINGER SAUCE
*Pour this sauce over a shallow pan of veggies and bake.*

2 C. lightly roasted cashews
2 TB. fresh ginger (minced)
1 C. water
1 TB. tamari
1 TB. cornstarch

1 TB. sweetener
2 ½ TB. cider vinegar
1/2 tsp. sea salt
black or cayenne pepper to taste

Put everything except salt and pepper in a blender and mix until smooth. Season with salt and pepper to taste. Pour sauce over a shallow pan containing sliced veggies; such as eggplant or zucchini slices, and bake until vegetables are done and sauce is browned.

## SWEET N' SOUR SAUCE   *For stir fry's*

3/4 C. water
2 TB. veggie broth powder
1 TB. tamari
2 TB. ketchup or tomato sauce
1 TB. rice or other vinegar
1 TB. sweetener
2 tsp. arrowroot or cornstarch
   dissolved in 3 TB. water
1/4 C. dried parsley

Blend all together until smooth. Add to pan containing cooked veggies and stir until sauce thickens. Add more water to thin sauce, if necessary.

## SESAME TAHINI SAUCE
*This is good served with falafel balls.*

3/4 C. sesame tahini
2 cloves garlic, minced very fine
1/3 C. lemon juice
salt and pepper to taste
up to 1/4 C. water, if needed for thinning.

Mix everything together until creamy.

# PESTO SAUCE

*One of the many good reasons to grow a patch of basil in the garden, or potted and placed in a sunny window. Placed by the door, basil is supposed to ward off flies. Pesto stirred into pasta noodles is great served hot or cold. This recipe makes 1 cup of finished pesto sauce, enough for a pound or more of pasta.*

4 C. fresh basil (loose pack)
1/2 C. olive oil
2 TB. water
2-3 cloves garlic
1/2 tsp. sea salt
1/2 tsp. black pepper (or to taste)
1/2 C. pine nuts or other nuts (optional)
1/2 C. vegan parmesan (optional)

In blender or food processor mix all ingredients until smooth and well combined. This is great mixed with hot or cold pasta and sprinkled with vegan parmesan.

**Note:** *Sautéed veggies; such as mushrooms, onions and broccoli can be served on the side, or on top of the pasta. Nuts & vegan parmesan can be left out of the blender, and sprinkled directly on the pasta.*

**Suggestions:** *Some blenders work better when a double batch is made and the parmesan is added after processing.*

## PESTO VARIATIONS:

Lemon Pesto: *Add 1/4 C. lemon juice to the above recipe and eliminate the 2 TB. water.*
Parsley Pesto: *Use half parsley and half basil.*
Spicy Italian Pesto: *Use half fresh oregano and half basil.*
Spinach Basil Pesto: *Use part spinach and part basil, or mix some spinach with any of the above variations.*

**OTHER PESTO USES:** Pesto Bread: *1/3 C. pesto, 1 C. grated vegan Jack cheese, and 1 loaf of French bread. Mix pesto and cheese together. Slice loaf of bread lengthwise. Spread bread with pesto mixture. Place each side of loaf under a broiler until bubbly and well toasted. Cut into serving size pieces.*
Pesto Pizza: *Instead of tomato sauce use pesto.*

---

**TIPS FOR STORING BASIL or PESTO, FOR LATER USE:** *Dry basil by tying stalks together with string and hanging in a dark pantry or corner of the kitchen, or place sprigs of basil in a paper bag and hang or place paper bag in a cool place. You can hang the bag from the limb of a shady tree. If you have freezer space and don't have the time to make pesto, but have an abundance of basil, just wash and dry the basil and fill a freezer bag or container and freeze for later use. (Cilantro and parsley which loses much of their potency when dried, can be frozen in this manner). There's no need to thaw frozen basil when making pesto or using in any cooked dish. To store pre-made pesto for later use: Process in half or pint jars, or freeze in ice cube trays. When solid, remove cubes and place in a freezer bag.*

---

## CREAMY PESTO BASIL SAUCE

*A delightful variation of traditional pesto. This is delicious mixed with hot pasta, or smoothed between layers of lasagna noodles, instead of tomato sauce.*

3 TB. soy margarine
1-2 cloves garlic (minced)
3 TB. flour
2 ½ C. <u>unsweetened</u> soy milk
   (or 4 TB. soy milk powder mixed with 2 ½ C. water)
1 C. finely ground fresh basil leaves (about 2 C. before grinding)
1/2 C. vegan parmesan cheese (optional, can be sprinkled directly on pasta )

1. Melt margarine on low heat in saucepan.
2. Add minced garlic and cook until garlic is soft.
3. Stir in flour and add milk in a slow stream using a wire whisk to blend mixture together.
4. Simmer until thickened. (5-10 minutes)
5. Add basil leaves and optional vegan parmesan. Stir and simmer until all ingredients are combined.

**Quick n' easy variation:** *Instead of fresh basil, use 1/4-1/2 C. frozen or canned, prepared pesto.*


## CASSEROLE SAUCE MIX

*Have this tasty powdered mix on hand, for simple and easy preparation.*

2 C. <u>unsweetened</u> soy milk powder
3/4 C. cornstarch
1/4 C. broth powder
4 tsp. onion powder
1½ tsp. dried thyme
1½ tsp. dried basil
1/2 tsp. black pepper

Mix all ingredients together and store in an airtight container. **TO USE:** *Add 3/4 C. dry mix with 2 C. water and 2 TB soy margarine or oil in a saucepan, and whisk together well. Simmer until sauce is desired thickness. Thin with more water if necessary. Salt and Pepper to taste and use as a base for your favourite casserole dish.*

> *"There is a great deal of truth in the saying that man becomes what he eats."*
> *- Mahatma Gandhi*

## BROWN GRAVY

*This is the best and only gravy recipe you will ever need. It's rich and brown coloured, and can be made thicker or thinner depending on amount of water used. Great on mashed potatoes and your favourite loaf or patties.*

2- 2 ½ C. water
3 TB. whole wheat pastry flour
1 TB. cornstarch
2 TB. olive oil
1 TB. onion powder
1/2 tsp. garlic powder

1/4-1/2 tsp. sea salt
3 TB. tamari
1 TB. nutritional yeast flakes

Combine 2 cups of water and all remaining ingredients in a saucepan, and mix together well with a wire whisk. Cook and stir until thick. Add additional ½ cup of water, if thinner gravy is desired.


## HORSERADISH SAUCE

*This is easy to prepare and keeps for a long time in the fridge. Make sure you grind it in a well-ventilated room, as it's quite pungent.*

1 (6-8 oz) horseradish root; cleaned, peeled and cut into small pieces
1/2 C. apple cider vinegar
1/4 tsp. sea salt

1. Grind horseradish in a blender or electric nut grinder, until very fine.
2. In a saucepan combine 1/2 C. apple cider vinegar and 1/4 tsp. salt to each cup of grated horseradish.
3. Heat the mixture until warmed through, but do not boil. Store in a covered container in the fridge, or pour into canning jars and process in canning kettle to seal jar lids. Store in pantry or cupboard for future enjoyment. See index for canning directions.

**To serve**: *Horseradish sauce is delicious eaten right off a spoon, or as a side dish with vegan brats, burgers or other main meals. Try it between sandwiches and mixed in salad dressings.*

"Numerous studies have shown that vegetarians have lower blood pressures than non-vegetarians. It is not just that vegetarians tend to have healthier life-styles overall. There's something about the vegetarian diet that lowers blood pressure."
Neal Barnard, M.D. - Food For Life

## MUSHROOM TOMATO SAUCE

*Great for pasta or pizza.*

1 lb. mushrooms (sliced)
1 clove garlic (minced)
1 medium size onion (chopped)
1 stalk celery or ½ C. green pepper (chopped)
1/4 C. olive oil
1 tsp. sea salt
1/2 tsp. dried basil
1/4 tsp. paprika
1/4 tsp. black pepper
1-28 oz. can crushed or tomato sauce (or 3 C. fresh diced)

1. Cook mushrooms, garlic, onion and celery in olive oil for approximately 10 minutes, or until veggies are soft.
2. Add remaining ingredients and simmer uncovered for 45- 60 minutes, or until sauce is thick. Makes enough sauce for approximately one pound of spaghetti.


## QUICK PIZZA OR SPAGHETTI SAUCE

4 TB. olive oil
1 C. chopped onions
2 cloves garlic (minced)
2 green peppers (diced)
4 C. chunky or regular tomato sauce
1 TB. dried oregano
1 TB. dried basil
2 tsp. sea salt

Sauté onions, garlic and peppers in olive oil. Add all remaining ingredients and simmer 10-15 minutes, or until desired thickness is reached.

> "The doctor of the future will give no medicine, but will interest his patients in the care of the human frame and the cause of and prevention of disease."
> - Thomas A. Edison

## LIGHT PRIMAVERA SAUCE  *This is a nice change from tomato sauce.*

3 C. unsweetened soy milk
4 TB. cornstarch
1 clove garlic (minced fine) or 1 tsp. garlic powder
1/4 C. vegan parmesan
Salt and pepper to taste

In a small saucepan whisk all ingredients together, except salt and pepper. Cook and stir until sauce is thick and creamy. Salt and pepper to taste. Stir into cooked spaghetti or noodles.


## CRANBERRY SAUCE

2 C. fresh cranberries
1/2 C. apple juice or water
1/4-1/2 C. sweetener
1/2 -1 tsp. grated orange rind (optional)

Combine cranberries, juice and sweetener in saucepan and simmer 5-10 minutes, or until berries pop. Remove from heat and stir in the orange rind. Cool to room temperature. Store in the fridge. This is a traditional wintertime sauce. Serve it with your favourite holiday meal.


## MUSTARD SAUCE

1/4 C. prepared mustard
2 tsp. Chinese mustard powder
1-2 tsp. prepared horseradish
1/2-1 tsp. sweetener (optional)

Mix all ingredients together and store in the refrigerator. Serve with spring rolls, sandwiches or as a hot n' spicy veggie dip.

"Our health depends on how nearly we live in harmony with nature's laws.........Wrong habits of eating and the use of refined and adulterated foods are largely responsible for the intemperance and crime, and sickness that curse this world."

Jethro Kloss - Back to Eden

## EASY SOUR CREAM SAUCE

*This is an un-cooked sauce. It's delicious poured over hot or cold veggies.*

1 C. soy sour cream
2 TB. prepared horseradish sauce
1 tsp. dried dill weed

2 TB. lemon juice
salt and pepper to taste

Mix all ingredients with a wire whisk.


## SOY MAYONAISSE

1 C. soft style tofu
2 TB. lemon juice or vinegar
3 TB. vegetable oil
salt and pepper to taste

Process tofu, lemon juice and oil in a blender until smooth. Salt and pepper to taste. Thin with water if necessary.


## SOY DIPPING SAUCE

*A great dip for nori rolls or fresh spring rolls.*

3 TB. tamari
3 TB. rice vinegar
1-3 TB. lime juice
1/2 tsp. toasted sesame oil
1/2 tsp. toasted hot sesame oil (optional)
1/2 tsp. ginger powder
2 scallions, finely minced (optional)

Shake all ingredients together in a jar and adjust seasonings to your taste. Serve.

---

"It is virtually impossible not to get enough protein, provided you have enough to eat of natural unrefined foods." Paavo Airola, - Nutritionist and author

---

## BARBEQUE SAUCE

*This sauce is great with grilled tofu or tempeh.*

1/2 C. ketchup
1/4 C. cider vinegar
1/4 C. molasses
1/2 medium onion, diced
1/4 tsp. chili fiesta blend (pg. 102)
1/4 tsp. each salt & pepper
cayenne pepper, to taste (if you like it hot)

Blend all ingredients together until well combined.  Store in the fridge.


## PEANUT SAUCE

*This is a delicious sauce for dipping deep fried veggies.*

2 TB. rice vinegar
¼-1/2 tsp. sea salt *
1 TB. sweetener (optional)
3 TB. smooth peanut butter

1/2 tsp. chili fiesta blend (pg. 102)
3 TB. Barbeque sauce

Combine all ingredients in a small saucepan.  Stir with a wire whisk.  Bring to boil and then simmer slowly for about 2 minutes, or until ingredients are well combined.  Serve at room temperature.
* Addition of salt depends on whether you use a salted or unsalted peanut butter.

"Medical studies clearly show that the higher the consumption of meat and dairy products in any nation, the more its people suffer from heart attacks, strokes, diabetes, and cancer of bowels, breast and prostate gland.  Conversely, nations whose dietary patterns are based upon fruits, vegetables and grains, inevitably have low incidences of these diseases."
Michael Klaper M.D. - Vegan Nutrition: Pure & Simple

## ORIENTAL MARINADE

*For tofu, tempeh and veggies.*

1/2 C. toasted sesame oil
1/4 C. rice vinegar
1 TB. tamari
1 clove garlic, minced (½ tsp. powder)
1 tsp. ginger, grated  (¼ tsp. powder)

Shake all ingredients together in a lidded jar.  Pour marinade over veggies and set aside for 2-8 hours before cooking.


## SPICY ITALIAN MARINADE

1/2 C. olive oil
1/4 C. mixture of Ume plum and rice vinegar
1-2 cloves garlic, minced
1 tsp. each of dried oregano, basil and dill weed
Salt and pepper to taste

Mix all ingredients together and use to marinade tofu, tempeh or veggies for 2-8 hours or overnight, before cooking.


"therefore, if one eats grains and vegetables, which contain much potassium, the blood will oxidize well and allow better physiological functioning.  On the other hand, if one eats a lot of meats, poultry, fish and eggs, which contain high amounts of sodium, blood oxidation is not so good and leaves much poisonous acid.  Therefore, vegetarians live longer and eaters of animal food live a shorter life. "   Herman Aihara, - Acid & Alkaline

# Desserts

# COOKIES, BARS & CRISPS

**EFFECTS OF ALTITUDE ON INGREDIENTS FOR BAKING**: These desserts were developed at 6700 feet. At sea level to 3,000 feet, the increased air pressure makes it necessary to make ingredient changes. Increase baking powder or soda by 25-50%. Increase each cup of sweetener by 2-3 tablespoons. Decrease flour by 10%, or increase liquid. The best way to determine which changes are necessary is to follow the recipe first, then experiment by increasing some ingredients and decreasing others, as it is difficult to give the amounts accurately for all altitudes.

**Tips and suggestions:**
*\* If the batter is too thin—the dough could spread out too much during baking, producing an overly thin and possibly burnt cookie.*
*\* Unless stated in the recipe, there is no need to flatten the dough before baking.*
*\* Where dry sweetener is listed, organic, unbleached sugar was used.*
*\* When substituting with a liquid sweetener, decrease sweetener and liquid in recipe.*
*\* Make delicious wheat free desserts by replacing the whole wheat flour, with a combination of two or three of the following flours: oat, barley, bean, tapioca or rice and ¼ tsp. xantham gum powder per cup of flour.*


## OATMEAL COOKIES

2 ½ C. whole wheat pastry flour
2 C. quick or regular oatmeal
1 tsp. baking soda
1 ½ C. dry sweetener
1/2 tsp. salt
1 tsp. each of cinnamon, ginger
   and nutmeg

1 C. vegetable oil
2/3 C. soy milk
2 tsp. vanilla or almond extract
1 C. raisins
1/2 C. walnuts, chopped

Preheat oven 375°
1. Mix first row of ingredients together with a spoon.
2. Add oil, milk and extract to dry ingredients and mix until well combined.
3. Stir in raisins and chopped nuts.
4. Drop by rounded spoonfuls, 2 inches apart on a lightly oiled baking sheet, and bake 10 to 12 minutes, or until lightly browned. Makes 3-4 dozen cookies.

**Suggestions:** *Replace raisins with other chopped, dried fruit, such as dates, figs, or apricots.*
**VARIATIONS:** <u>Chocolate Chip Cookies:</u> *Replace raisins with chocolate chips, and eliminate the cinnamon, ginger and nutmeg.* <u>Minty Chocolate Chip Cookies:</u> *Add 3 drops of peppermint extract along with the chocolate chips.*

## NUT BUTTER COOKIES

1/2 C. soy margarine, softened
1 C. peanut or almond butter
3/4 C. dry sweetener
1 tsp. vanilla extract
1/2 tsp. salt
1/2 tsp. baking soda
1 C. whole wheat pastry flour

Preheat oven 350°
1. In medium size bowl mix the softened margarine and peanut butter until well combined.
2. Beat in the dry sweetener.
3. Add all of the remaining ingredients until well combined and thick enough to hold shape on a spoon.
4. Drop spoonfuls 2 inches apart on a lightly oiled baking sheet, and score each one with the back of a fork.
5. Bake approximately 12-15 minutes, or until lightly browned.

## CRISPY ALMOND COCONUT COOKIES

1 ½ C. dry sweetener
3/4 C. vegetable oil
1/2 tsp. salt
1 TB. almond extract
2 ¼ C. whole wheat pastry flour

1 C. quick or regular oatmeal
1 tsp. baking soda
1 tsp. baking powder
3/4 C. unsweetened dry shredded coconut
2/3 C. soy milk

Preheat oven 350°
1. Combine sweetener, oil, salt and almond extract and whisk together well.
2. Stir together flour, oatmeal, baking soda, baking powder and coconut and add to wet ingredients, along with soymilk, mixing well.
3. Drop by rounded teaspoonfuls, 2 ½ inches apart on lightly oiled baking sheets. The dough will spread during baking. Bake 10-12 minutes, or until golden brown. Makes 3 dozen cookies.

"The best medical technology in the world cannot save the health of nations and people who choose to eat wrong foods."
Bernard Jensen, PhD.- The Chemistry of Man

## GINGERSNAPS

1/2 C. blackstrap molasses
1/2 C. maple syrup or other liquid sweetener
1/2 C. vegetable oil
1/2 tsp. baking soda
1 TB. ground ginger
1 tsp. salt
3-3½ C. whole wheat pastry flour

Preheat oven 350°
1. Mix molasses and sweetener together.
2. Stir in the oil, soda, ginger powder and salt.
3. Add the flour one cupful at a time, until the mixture is firm enough to be rolled out on a floured surface. Add more flour if necessary, and cut with a small round cookie cutter.
4. Bake on a lightly oiled cookie sheet 8-10 minutes, or until done.


## GINGERBREAD COOKIES

5 C. whole wheat pastry flour
1 ½ C. sweetener
2 tsp. baking powder
4 tsp. cinnamon
1 tsp. ground cloves
3 tsp. ground ginger
1 tsp. salt
1/2 C. blackstrap molasses
1/2 C. vegetable oil
1/3 C. soy milk or water

Preheat oven 350°
1. Stir together dry ingredients.
2. Add molasses, oil and soy milk and blend together well.
3. Add more flour if necessary to make the dough firm enough to roll.
4. Roll dough about 1/4 inch thick, on a floured surface.
5. Cut dough into desired shapes and place on lightly oiled cookie sheet.
6. Bake in a preheated oven for 12-15 minutes, or until done.

# TRADITIONAL CHOCOLATE CHIP COOKIES

2 C. whole wheat pastry flour
1/2 tsp. baking soda
3/4 C. dry sweetener
1/4 tsp. salt
1/2 C. vegetable oil
1/3 C. soy milk
1 tsp. vanilla extract
1 C. chocolate chips
1/4 C. chopped walnuts

Preheat oven 375°
1. Mix flour, soda, sweetener and salt together until well combined.
2. Add vegetable oil, soy milk and vanilla and stir together well.
3. Mix in the chocolate chips and nuts. The batter will be very thick.
Drop rounded spoonfuls 2 inches apart onto lightly oiled cookie sheets. Bake 10-12 minutes, and until cookies are lightly browned. Cool well before storing.
Makes 2 dozen cookies.
**VARIATION**: <u>Minty Chocolate Chip Cookies</u>: *Add 2 drops of mint oil to the batter.*


# PEANUT BUTTER BALLS

*For a quick sweet, this is a yummy treat that's fun to make, and requires no baking.*

| | |
|---|---|
| 1/2 C. carob or cocoa powder | 1/2 C. sesame seeds |
| 1/2 C. liquid sweetener | 1/2 C. raisins |
| 1/2 C. peanut butter * | soy milk powder |
| 1/2 C. raw sunflower seeds | unsweetened shredded coconut |

1. In a medium size bowl mix everything except the milk powder and coconut.
2. Add enough soy milk powder to produce a mixture that can be easily formed into balls about one inch in size.
3. Roll balls into shredded coconut.

**Suggestions:**
* *The peanut butter can be substituted with almond butter.*
* *These will be firmer if refrigerated a few hours or overnight before serving*
* *Coconut can be mixed in with the main ingredients, eliminating the need for the soy milk powder.*
* *Variations can be made using other chopped, dried fruit, such as apricots, dates, figs, etc.*

# CHOCOLATE PEANUT BUTTER CUPS

*This is an old time favourite that requires no baking.*

1/2 C. soy margarine
3/4 C. peanut butter
3/4 C. crushed graham crackers
1/4 C. dry sweetener

1 C. chocolate chips
1/4 C. soy milk
1/2 C. walnuts, chopped
12 paper cupcake liners

1. In a small saucepan melt the margarine over medium heat. Stir in the peanut butter, cracker crumbs and sweetener, until mixed together well.
2. Spoon the mixture, dividing evenly between 12 paper cupcake liners, set inside muffin tins, (approximately 1 ½ TB. for each liner.) Press mixture into liners.
3. In another saucepan melt the chocolate chips with the soy milk, stirring often.
4. Spoon the slightly cooled chocolate mixture over the peanut butter layer in the liners.
5. Garnish with chopped walnuts, and set in the fridge for at least 6 hrs. before serving. Makes 12 cups.

**Suggestions & Variations:** <u>Minty Peanut Butter Cups</u>: *Add a drop or two of mint oil to the chocolate.* <u>Carob Peanut Butter Cups</u>: *Use carob instead of chocolate chips. Experiment with other nut butters, such as almond or cashew.*

# SCOTTISH COCONUT SHORTBREAD COOKIES

*These are very simple to make. Traditionally the original version was served around the winter holiday season, but, these are good any time of the year.*

1/2 C. soy margarine
3/4 C. maple syrup
1/2 tsp. each of vanilla & almond extract

1-1¾ C. whole wheat pastry flour
1-1¾ C. quick oatmeal (not instant)
1-1¾ C. unsweetened, dry shredded
coconut

Preheat Oven 350°
1. With an electric mixer, beat margarine, syrup and extracts together in a large bowl, until well combined. Add 1 cup each of flour, oatmeal and coconut. Continue beating until batter becomes smooth. Add up to an additional ¾ cup of flour, oatmeal and coconut, adding in quarter cup portions, just until batter can be handled easily without being too sticky.
2. Press into a lightly oiled 9 x 13 inch cookie sheet. Pat the mixture with floured hands to a thickness of about 1/2 inch. Prick with a fork every 2 inches.
3. Bake 20-25 minutes, or until the shortbread is lightly browned and darker around the edges. Cut into squares while still warm, but don't remove from the pan until cookies are cool.

**VARIATION:** *Finely chopped walnuts or pecans can replace some or all of the coconut.*

# LEMON BARS

**Bottom Crust:**
1/3 C. soy margarine
1/4 C. dry sweetener
1 C. soft wheat pastry flour
1-2 TB. water

**Lemon Filling:**
2 TB. egg replacer powder
1/8 C. warm water
2/3 C. dry sweetener
4 TB. pastry flour
2 tsp. lemon peel, finely grated (optional)
6 TB. lemon juice
1/4 tsp. baking powder

**To make bottom crust:**
Preheat oven 350°

1. In a medium size bowl beat margarine and sweetener together until well combined.
2. Beat in the 1 C. of flour until mixture is crumbly. Add 1-2 TB. water and mix well.
3. With lightly floured hands, press mixture into bottom of an 8 x 8 x 2 inch, lightly oiled cake pan. Bake 15–20 minutes, or until lightly browned.

**To make filling:**

1. Combine in a small bowl: egg replacer and warm water. Mix well with wire whisk or beater.
2. Add 2/3 C. sweetener, 4 TB. flour, lemon peel, juice and baking powder. Beat all until well combined.
3. Pour filling into slightly cooled baked crust. Put back in the oven and bake another 20 minutes at 350° or until lightly browned around the edges. The top may look soft, but don't be tempted to over bake it. Cool on a rack before cutting into bars

---

"People often say that humans have always eaten animals, as if this is a justification for continuing the practice. According to this logic, we should not try to prevent people from murdering other people, since this has also been done since the earliest of times."
Isaac Bashevis Singer (1904-1991) - writer & 1978 Nobel Prize recipient

---

# CHOCOLATE BROWNIES

**Note:** *The batter should be very thick. If the batter is too thin, the brownies will end up being cake like, rather than chewy.* **Reminder:** *When baking at sea level or below 3,000 feet altitude, refer to the "Effects of Altitude on Ingredients for Baking" on pg. 166, and make the necessary adjustments.*

| | |
|---|---|
| 1 C. whole wheat pastry flour | 2 tsp. egg replacer powder mixed with |
| 1/2 C. cocoa powder | 1/2 C. warm water |
| 1/2 tsp. baking powder | 1/4 C. vegetable oil |
| 1/2 tsp. salt | 2 tsp. vanilla extract |
| 1 C. dry sweetener | 1/2 C. walnuts or pecans, coarsely chopped |

Preheat oven 350°

1. Mix in medium size bowl: flour, cocoa, baking powder, salt and dry sweetener.
2. In a small bowl mix egg replacer mixed with the 1/2 C. warm water, vegetable oil, and vanilla. Stir until well blended, and mix into the dry ingredients.
3. Gently fold in the walnuts or pecans.
4. Spoon batter into a lightly oiled 8-inch square pan and bake 25-30 minutes. For a fudgy texture, don't over bake. For a classic brownie texture, the toothpick tester when inserted in the center of pan should have only a few moist crumbs attached.
5. Cool before cutting into squares.

**Suggestions:** *To make a 9 x 13 inch pan of brownies; simply double all the ingredients, except the salt and baking powder. Brownies will have a better texture if they are mixed gently with a spoon rather than an electric mixer.*

**Substitutions:** *Approximately 3 squares or ounces of baking chocolate can replace the ½ C. cocoa. Add ½ C. semi-sweet chocolate chips for a fudgy texture. Don't use them if you want the quality of a classic brownie.*

**VARIATIONS:** *Carob Brownies: Replace all of the cocoa powder and chips with carob.*

*Wheat Free Brownies: Substitute the following for the wheat flour: 1/2 C. Garbanzo or garbfava flour, 1/4 C. tapioca flour, 1/4 C. potato starch (not flour) and 1/4 tsp. xanthan gum powder.*

*Nancy's Variations: Almondies: Omit cocoa and replace with shredded coconut. Replace vanilla with almond extract, and walnuts with chopped almonds. Sunnies: Omit cocoa and replace with quick oatmeal. Use sunflower seeds instead of walnuts. (maple flavouring could replace vanilla)*

*Peanut Butter: Replace the oil with peanut butter, and the walnuts with chopped peanuts.*

---

"To avoid causing terror to living beings, let the disciple refrain from eating meat."

The BUDDHA (circa 563-483 B.C.)

---

# FRUIT BARS

*These are very easy to make and have many variations.*

**Top and bottom Crust:**
3/4 C. vegetable oil
1/2 C. maple syrup
   (or dry sweetener &  1/2  C. water)
2 C. whole wheat pastry flour
2 C. quick oatmeal (not instant)
1 tsp. salt
1 tsp. baking powder

**Fruit Filling:**  3-5 C. fresh, frozen or canned fruit  (see following variations)

Preheat oven 400°
1. Cream oil and sweetener together until well combined.
2. In another bowl, mix flour, oatmeal, salt and baking powder together.
3. Add the dry ingredients to the creamed ingredients and mix together well.
4. Press less than half of the mixture into an un-oiled 9 x 13 inch cake pan. This is easiest to accomplish with wet or floured fingertips.
5. Spread with any of the following filling variations.
6. Sprinkle remaining topping mixture over the filling, pressing lightly with fingertips.
7. Bake 25-30 minutes, or until the top is lightly browned and the filling bubbly.

**APPLE:**  4 C. (3-3 ½ lb.) sliced apples, 1/2 C. water, and 1/4-1/2 C. sweetener.
If apples are very juicy add 1-2 TB. flour or decrease water.
**BLUEBERRY:**  5 C. fresh or canned berries, 1/4-1/2 C. sweetener,
3-4 TB. flour (note:  the sweetener will vary depending on the sweetness of fruit, and the flour for thickening varies depending on the fruits juiciness.)
**BLUEBERRY/PEACH***:*  4 C. fresh or canned blueberries and 1 C. sliced peaches. (Or all peaches)  1/4-1/2 C. sweetener, and 3-4 TB. flour.
**CHERRY**:  3-5 C. pitted uncooked cherries mixed with 1/4-3/4 C. sweetener, (depending on sweetness of cherries used) and 2-4 TB. flour.
**DATE:**  3-4 C. pitted dates, simmered in 1/2 - 1 C. water, until soft.  Add sweetener if desired.  Dates tend to be naturally very sweet.
**PINEAPPLE:**  1-20 oz. can drained pineapple chunks, plus 1-20 oz. can drained crushed pineapple,  (or use equivalent amount of fresh diced pineapple), 1 C. of the drained pineapple juice, 3 TB. flour and 1/4-1/2 C.  sweetener.

**Suggestion:**  *Experiment with your favourite combinations of fruits.*

## APPLE CRISP

**Topping:**

1 C. whole wheat pastry flour
1/2 C. quick (not instant) oatmeal
1/2 C. dry sweetener
1 tsp. cinnamon

1/4 tsp. nutmeg
1/2 C. soy margarine
1-2 TB. water

**Filling:**

6 C. apples, sliced or cut in chunks
1/4 - 1/2 C. maple syrup or other sweetener
1/4 C. raisins (optional)
1/4 C. water
Sprinkling of cinnamon

Preheat oven 350°

1. Mix flour, oatmeal, sweetener and spices together.
2. With fingers blend margarine into flour mixture until well combined. Add just enough water, if needed, so that mixture is crumbly but slightly moist.
3. Spread apple mixture in the bottom of a lightly oiled 9 x 13 inch cake pan.
4. Sprinkle topping over apple filling and bake 30-40 minutes, or until browned on top and fruit is soft.

**VARIATION:** Rhubarb Berry Crisp: *Replace apples and raisins with 7 C. chopped rhubarb, and 1 C. fresh or canned strawberries or raspberries. Use 3/4 C. sweetener and 1-2 TB. flour.*

**Suggestions:** *Almost any fruit can be used in this recipe; such as sliced peaches, blueberries, blackberries, and mulberries. The sweetener and flour may need adjusting, depending on sweetness and juiciness of fruit and desired thickness of sauce. Replace all or part of margarine with coconut oil.*

---

"If we form the habit of daily eating and drinking only for health--physical, mental and spiritual--we will find a growing sense of well-being, accompanied by the energy and happiness that come when one is no longer bound by cravings and appetites. We should not merely live to eat, blindly obeying our sense of taste, regardless of the consequences to ourselves and others; but we must strive to eat to live, in order to find peace within ourselves and be a source of love and happiness for all beings around us."

Dr. Randolph Stone, D.O., D.C. - Health Building

---

# CAKES & FROSTINGS

**TIPS FOR CAKE BAKING:** *(See pg. 20 for more tips on altitude adjustments)*
- At altitudes 3,000 ft. and lower: decrease flour by 10-20% or increase liquid. Increase sweetener by at least 3 TB. for each cup listed. Increase baking powder by 25-50%.
- Use whole wheat pastry flour, not bread flour.
- Organic, unbleached cane sugar was used where dry sweetener is listed.
- Decrease liquids in recipes if substituting a liquid sweetener.
- Use 2/3-3/4 cup liquid sweetener for each cup of dry sugar.
- Use 1¼ cup dry sweetener for every cup of liquid sweetener listed in recipe, and adjust other liquids.
- For layered cakes and ease in removing them from pans, use spring form pans with removable sides.
- For wheat free cakes, use a combination of barley, oat, bean, rice, tapioca flour and potato starch, along with ¼ tsp. xantham gum powder per cup of flour.
- To make cupcakes: Spoon any of the cake recipes into paper cupcake liners. Bake 15-20 minutes, or until done. Cool and frost with your favourite frosting.

**General Directions for Baking:** Divide the baking time in quarters. In the first quarter when the cake begins to rise and brown in spots, the cake may be moved. In the second and third quarter; when the cake continues to rise and brown, it must *not* be moved. In the fourth quarter when the cake finishes browning and shrinks slightly, it may be moved.

**BAKING TESTS:** Various tests to determine whether a cake is done may be applied. The simplest one consists of touching the cake lightly in the center, with the tip of a finger. If a depression remains, the cake is not done. If the surface springs back, leaving no depression, the cake is done. Another good test is to insert a toothpick into the center of the cake. If it comes out clean, the cake is done. If cake mixture sticks to it, the cake needs more baking.

**BAKING TIME & TEMPERATURES FOR CAKES:**

| | | |
|---|---|---|
| Layer cake (1 inch) | 20-30 min. | 325-350° |
| Sheet cake (2 inch) | 35-45 min. | 300-350° |
| Small loaf cakes | 1 hour | 250-350° |

**CAUSES OF POOR RESULTS:**

- Insufficient oil and sugar can cause a coarse, heavy cake.
- Too much oil can cause cake to fall and be soggy.
- Too much sweetener can make a cake hard and produces a hard top crust.
- Too much flour can cause cake to rise high in the center and the surface to crack, and make it dry.
- Too much liquid can cause cake to fall.
- Too little flour can cause cake to fall.
- Too much baking powder can make cake coarse and dry.
- Uneven spreading in pan causes cake to be thick on one side and thin on the other.
- Insufficient creaming, beating or lack of thoroughness in mixing, can cause a cake of poor texture.
- Too cool an oven can cause a coarse texture.
- Too hot of an oven can cause cake to form a hard crust too soon, and to crack in rising.
- Insufficient baking can cause the cake to fall.
- If all precautions are observed and the cake falls, it will be due to wrong proportion of ingredients and not a draft, the slamming of a door or jumping on the floor.
- In altitudes higher than 5,000 feet, it may be necessary to increase the oven temperature by 15-25 degrees, especially if your cakes have a tendency to fall in the middle, even when all other precautions have been taken.

# FUDGY CHOCOLATE CAKE
*A rich and deeply chocolate cake*

**Some suggestions before starting**: *To make pureeing the tofu easier, try putting it in the blender with just enough maple syrup or liquid to get the blender whizzing.*

1-12.3 oz. silken tofu, pureed in blender  (approximately 1 cup ) *
1 C. maple syrup *
1/2 C. soy milk, or grain beverage, leftover coffee or water
2 tsp. vanilla extract
1 ¼ C. whole wheat pastry flour
1 C. cocoa powder (or substitute carob powder)
1 tsp. each of baking powder and baking soda
1/2 tsp. salt

* **Note**: *Substitute regular soft tofu and increase liquid by approximately ¼ cup. Vegan mayonnaise or sour cream can also be used instead of the pureed tofu. * If replacing maple syrup with a dry sweetener, adjust the amount of liquid used in recipe.*

Preheat oven 350°
1. Lightly oil and flour a 8 inch square cake pan or 2-8 inch round layer pans.
2. In a bowl mix together the pureed tofu, syrup, soy milk and vanilla.
3. In another bowl mix all the remaining ingredients.
4. Add flour mixture to tofu mixture and beat together until well blended. Batter will be quite thick.
5. Pour into prepared pan(s) and bake until done, approximately 25-30 minutes, or 20-25 minutes for layer pans.
6. Cool on rack for 10 minutes, before removing from layer pans.
7. Cover with your favourite frosting. See Frostings on pg. 192-193

**Suggestion**: *If you are going to remove the cake from pan(s), do so when the cakes have cooled at least 10 minutes. Loosen around the sides with a knife, before inverting the pan over a wire rack. Tapping gently on the bottom of pan will help release the cake from the pan. Spring form pans or pans with removable bottoms are highly recommended for layer cakes.*

## CHOCOLATE CAKE

3 C. whole wheat pastry flour
1 ¾ C. dry sweetener
2/3 C. cocoa powder (or substitute carob powder)
1 tsp. each of baking powder & baking soda
1 tsp. salt
1/2 C. vegetable oil
1 ½ C. lukewarm water
2 TB. apple cider vinegar
2 tsp. vanilla extract

Preheat oven 350°
1. In medium size bowl mix flour, sweetener, cocoa, baking powder, soda, and salt.
2. In large bowl mix vegetable oil, water, vinegar and vanilla.
3. Add dry ingredients to wet ingredients and beat. Pour into a lightly oiled 9 x 13 inch cake pan or two 8 inch round layer pans. Bake approximately 25-30 minutes, (20-25 minutes for layers) or until cake tests done. Cover with frosting. See pg. 192-193

**VARIATIONS**: <u>Chocolate Spice Cake</u>: *Add 1 tsp. cinnamon and 1/2 tsp. each of ground cloves, ginger and nutmeg to the above recipe.*


## CARROT PINEAPPLE CAKE

1½ C. whole wheat pastry flour
3/4 C. dry sweetener
1 tsp. cinnamon
1 tsp. baking powder
1 tsp. baking soda
1/2 tsp. salt

1/3 C. vegetable oil
1 C. finely grated carrots
1/2 C. crushed pineapple with juice
1 tsp. vanilla extract
1/3 C. water
1/2 C. chopped walnuts (or other nuts)

Preheat oven 350°
1. Lightly oil an 8-9-inch square cake pan.
2. Stir together dry ingredients. Add all remaining ingredients to dry ingredients and blend together well. Pour into prepared cake pan.
3. Bake 25-30 minutes, or until cake tests done. Cool on rack before frosting. This cake is delicious with Vanilla Cream Frosting, pg. 192

**VARIATIONS**: <u>Banana Coconut Pineapple Cake</u>: *Substitute bananas for the carrots. Replace water with coconut milk. Sprinkle top of frosting with shredded coconut.*

## ZUCCHINI CAKE

3 C. whole wheat flour
1 ½ C. dry sweetener
1 tsp. baking powder
1 tsp. baking soda
1/2 tsp. salt

1/2 C. vegetable oil
2 C. grated zucchini
2 tsp. vanilla extract
2 C. crushed pineapple with juice
1 C. walnuts, chopped

Preheat oven 350°
1. Lightly oil a 9 x 13 inch cake pan.
2. In medium size bowl mix first row of dry ingredients.
3. In another bowl mix together second row of ingredients except the walnuts.
4. Mix liquid ingredients into dry ingredients until well blended. Fold in the walnuts.
5. Pour batter into prepared pan and bake 30-40 minutes, or until cake tests done. Cool before frosting.

## GRAMMA'S BOILED CAKE

*This is my version of a recipe which originated in Ireland. It was traditionally served without frosting.*

2 C. raisins (about 1 lb.)
1 ½ C. dry sweetener (or 1 C. liquid)
2 C. water
3/4 C. vegetable oil
1 TB. cinnamon
1 tsp. each of cloves and nutmeg

1 tsp. salt
2 tsp. baking soda
1/2 C. boiling water
3 C. whole wheat pastry flour
1/2-1 C. walnuts, chopped

Preheat oven 350°
1. Lightly oil a 9 x 13 inch cake pan.
2. Put raisins, sweetener, water, oil, cinnamon, cloves and nutmeg into a saucepan and bring to a boil.
3. Take pan from heat and let ingredients cool to room temperature.
4. In a mixing bowl pour cooled ingredients, along with soda dissolved in the 1/2 C. boiling water, and the salt.
5. Add the flour one cup at a time, mixing well after each addition. Fold in the nuts.
6. Pour batter into prepared pan and bake 30-40 minutes, or until cake tests done.

# GINGERBREAD CAKE
## With warm lemon sauce

2 C. whole wheat pastry flour
1/2 C. dry sweetener
1 TB. ginger, ground
1 tsp. cinnamon
1/4 tsp. cloves
1 tsp. baking powder
1/2 tsp. salt

1/8 C. blackstrap molasses
1/2 C. maple syrup
2 tsp. egg replacer powder mixed with
1/3 C. warm water
3/4 C. soy milk

Preheat oven 350°

1. Lightly oil an 8-inch square cake pan.
2. Thoroughly mix all dry ingredients in first row.
3. Mix all remaining wet ingredients of second row into the dry mixture. Combine well.
4. Pour batter into prepared pan and bake 25-30 minutes, or until cake tests done.
5. While cake bakes, prepare the lemon sauce.
6. Cool cake on wire rack before cutting. Serve with warm lemon sauce.

## LEMON SAUCE:

1/4 C. lemon juice
1/2 C. dry sweetener
3/4 C. water
1 tsp. lemon peel, grated (optional)
1 ½ TB. cornstarch

Combine all above ingredients and bring to a boil over medium heat. Lower heat and simmer, stirring constantly until thickened. Best served warm. Serves 4-6

## SPICED APPLESAUCE CAKE

2 C. whole wheat pastry flour
1 tsp. baking soda
1 tsp. baking powder
1 tsp. cinnamon
1/2 tsp. nutmeg
1/4 tsp. salt

3/4 C. maple syrup
1/4 C. vegetable oil
1 C. unsweetened applesauce
1 tsp. vanilla extract
1/2 C. walnuts, chopped
1/2 C. raisins (optional)

Preheat oven 350°
1. Stir first row of dry ingredients together well.
2. Add all remaining ingredients and beat until thoroughly combined.
3. Pour mixture into lightly oiled 8-9 inch square cake pan and bake 30-40 minutes, or until cake tests done. Cover with Vanilla Cream Frosting pg. 192

## APPLE JOEBEAR

*This dessert is made in a similar fashion as apple crisp, but it has a cake topping. It's named after one of its biggest fans.*

1/4 C + 2 TB. vegetable oil
1/2 C. maple syrup (or liquid sweetener)
2 TB. egg replacer powder
   mixed with 1/4 C. warm water
1 ½ C. whole wheat pastry flour
2 tsp. baking powder
1 tsp. salt
1/2 C. soy milk
1 tsp. vanilla extract

7-9 medium size apples, cored & peeled
1/2 C. sweetener
1/4 - 1/2 C. walnuts, chopped
2-4 TB. water (if apples are dry)
cinnamon powder

Preheat oven 350°
1. With mixer or whisk, blend oil and syrup together.
2. Beat in egg replacer mixed with water, flour, baking powder, salt, milk and vanilla.
3. Slice or cube apples and spread in the bottom of a lightly oiled 9 x 13 inch cake pan. Pour sweetener, walnuts and water over the apples. Sprinkle with cinnamon powder.
4. Pour cake batter evenly over the apple mixture, and bake 30-35 minutes, or until cake is browned on top and apples are soft.

**Suggestions:** *Any fruit can be used for the filling. Just adjust the sweetener and be sure to add some flour for thickening, if needed. (1-4 TB.- depending on the fruits juiciness). Try blueberries, peaches or wild blackberries.*

# CHOCOLATE PUDDING CAKE
**Cake with a pudding bottom.**

1 C. whole wheat pastry flour
2 tsp. baking powder
1/4 C. cocoa powder
1/4 tsp. salt
1/2 C. dry sweetener
1/4 C. vegetable oil
1/2 C. soymilk
1/2 C. chopped nuts (optional)

**Topping:**
3/4 C. dry sweetener
1/4 C. cocoa powder
1 ¾ C. boiling water

Preheat oven 350°

1. Blend the first row of ingredients together in a medium size bowl, and spoon into a lightly oiled 8-inch square cake pan. Batter will be quite thick.
2. In a small bowl mix together the 3/4 C. dry sweetener and 1/4 C. cocoa powder and sprinkle on top of the cake batter.
3. Very carefully pour 1 ¾ cup boiling water over top of the batter.
4. Bake in preheated oven for 25 minutes, or until cake tests done.
5. Cool slightly. This is best when served warm.

**VARIATION:** <u>Carob Pudding Cake:</u> *Replace cocoa powder with same amount of carob powder. Since carob is naturally sweet, addition of sweeteners may need adjusting.*

# TANGY LEMON PUDDING CAKE

1 C. whole wheat pastry flour
2 tsp. baking powder
1/4 tsp. salt
1/2 C. dry sweetener

1/4 C. water
1/4 C. lemon juice
1 tsp. grated lemon rind
1/4 C. vegetable oil

**Topping:**
3/4 C. dry sweetener
2 tsp. grated lemon rind (optional)

1 ¾ C. boiling water
1/4 C. lemon juice

Preheat oven 350°

1. Mix flour, baking powder, salt and 1/2 C. sweetener together.
2. Add ¼ cup of water, lemon juice, grated lemon rind and oil and beat until well combined.
3. Pour mixture into a lightly oiled 8-inch square cake pan.
4. Combine the topping ingredients of sweetener and optional lemon rind and sprinkle over the cake batter. Mix together the lemon juice with the boiling water and very carefully and slowly pour this over the entire top of the cake batter.
5. Bake in preheated oven for 25-30 minutes. This is delicious served warm or cold.


# CINNAMON PUDDING CAKE

1 C. whole wheat pastry flour
1/2 dry sweetener
2 tsp. baking powder
1 tsp. cinnamon powder
1/2 tsp. ground ginger
1/4 tsp. salt
1/2 C. walnuts, chopped

1/2 C. soy milk
2 TB. vegetable oil

**Topping:**
3/4 C. dry sweetener
1 tsp. each of cinnamon and vanilla extract
1 ¾ C. boiling water

Preheat oven 350°

1. Mix first row of ingredients together.
2. Beat in soy milk and oil until well combined. Batter will be slightly thick.
3. Pour into a lightly oiled 8-inch square cake pan.
4. Combine topping of dry sweetener, and cinnamon and sprinkle over the cake batter.
5. Mix boiling water and vanilla extract together and very carefully and slowly pour this evenly over the entire cake.
6. Bake in preheated oven for 25-30 minutes.

# ENGLISH PLUM PUDDING CAKE

*This very sweet cake is typically served around the winter holidays. Like many old-fashioned fruit type cakes, it takes time in preparation and in baking. It can be made 2 weeks in advance and stored in the refrigerator or freezer. It's served warm with a sweet sauce. Traditionally a coin was hidden in the batter, and the one to find it would remain lucky throughout the year. This is my version of Gramma Wilda's cake that she brought to our home every December. It's very sweet, so serve small portions.*

**Before you start:** You will need two large mixing bowls and two to four 1– 2 quart stainless steel bowls or molds to steam the cakes, and 1-2 pots with lids for steaming, that are large enough to hold the molds. A canning kettle works nicely.

| | |
|---|---|
| 1 C. currants | 1/4 C. lemon juice |
| 4 C. raisins | 1/4 C. orange juice |
| 4 C. mixed dried fruit, chopped fine, | 4 C. soft whole wheat bread crumbs |
| (Figs, apricots, dates, pineapple & papaya) | 2 C. whole wheat pastry flour |
| 2 apples, grated | 2/3 C. dry sweetener |
| 1 carrot, grated | 1 ½ tsp. each of allspice, cinnamon, nutmeg |
| 3 TB. orange rind, grated | 1 tsp. sea salt |
| 1 TB. lemon rind, grated | 1/2 lb. soy margarine, cut in small pieces |
| 1 C. almonds, chopped | 3 TB. egg replacer powder mixed |
| 1 C. apple juice | with 3/4 C. warm water |

1. In a large bowl combine currants, raisins and mixed dried fruit, apple, carrot, rind of orange and lemon, chopped almonds, apple juice, lemon and orange juices.
2. In another bowl: combine breadcrumbs, flour, sweetener, spices, salt and margarine. Mix together well.
3. Add egg replacer mixed with water and combine with the fruit mixture. Stir well.
4. Add the flour mixture to the fruit mixture and mix well with a spoon or your hands.
5. Cover the bowl with a towel, and sit overnight, or at least 10-12 hours in a cool part of the kitchen.
6. Fill two-2 quart or four-1 quart oiled bowls or molds, 2 inches from the top with cake mixture. Cover each with parchment paper or an oiled cloth. (A thin piece of muslin will do) and tie securely around the mold, with a piece of string. Place a piece of foil securely over the top.
7. Place molds in large pots or canning kettles, with water three fourths of the way up the sides of molds. Cover pots and steam on low heat for 4-6 hours. Don't let the water boil away. Add more hot water when needed.
8. Remove molds from pot after desired time. Size of molds will determine length of time. Cool puddings in the molds. You can either refrigerate them in the molds or remove them from the molds now. Refrigerate for at least 1 week before serving.

9. <u>To prepare for serving:</u> Place bowl back in pot, to steam as done previously, or wrap cake which was removed from mold, in a piece of parchment then foil, and steam on a wire rack with a little water in the bottom of pot, for 1-2 hours, or until the cake is hot.  The larger the mold, the longer it will take to heat through.
10. When removing the cake from the bowls or molds, first loosen carefully around outside with a rubber spatula or knife, and invert on a serving platter.  Serve small, warm pieces of pudding cake drizzled with warm sweet sauce.


*Warm Sweet Sauce*

1/2 C. dry or liquid sweetener
1 ½ TB. flour
dash of salt
3/4-1 C. boiling water
1 TB. soy margarine
1 tsp. vanilla extract

Mix sweetener, flour and salt together in a saucepan.  Slowly add 3/4 cup of the boiling water and heat and stir until the mixture is smooth and slightly thickened.  Simmer another 5 minutes, adding additional 1/4 cup water if necessary.  Remove from heat and add margarine and vanilla extract, combining well with a wire whisk.  Drizzle sauce over individual pieces of warm Plum Pudding Cake.  Serves 4-6

"With advancing civilization, the American diet pattern, like everything else, has undergone a thorough-going change.  The business of procuring the necessities of life has been shifted from the wood lot, the garden, the kitchen and the family to the factory and the large-scale enterprises.  In our case, we moved our center back to the land.  There we raised the food we ate. We found it sufficient, delicious and nourishing.  On this diet we maintained a rugged health and patronized no doctors.  Our apothecary shop was the woods and fields.

Helen and Scott Nearing, - Living the Good Life

# SCOTTISH FRUITCAKE

*This is my version of a fruitcake made by Mary Willis of the Melvin family, who turned the recipe into tiered wedding cakes for family members. She would wrap the finished cakes in brandy cloth and store them in a cool place for at least one month or longer. This is a dark, rich and delicious fruitcake. My version has a few healthier substitutions: dried rather than candied fruit, whole wheat flour, soy margarine, powdered vegan egg replacer and apple cider instead of brandy. The original recipe is four times larger in quantity. If you're interested in making the original size, for gifts, a crowd or a wedding cake, simply increase the ingredients by four. This recipe makes 2 - 7" or 8" round cakes. Bake the cakes in spring form pans for ease in removing.*

1½ C. currants
3/4 C. dark raisins
3/4 C. dates
3/4 C. figs
3/4 C. dried pineapple
3/4 C. dried cherries or cranberries
3/4 C. dried mixed fruit
 (such as apples, papaya & apricots)
1/2 C. orange peel, grated
1/4 C. lemon peel, grated
1/2 C. + 2 TB. vegan margarine
1 ¼ C. dry sweetener
3 TB. egg replacer powder, mixed
  with 1 C. warm water

1/3 C. semi-sweet chocolate chips
3/4 C. walnuts, chopped coarse
2 ½ C. whole wheat pastry flour
3/4 tsp. baking powder
3/4 tsp. cinnamon
1/4 tsp. each of allspice, mace, nutmeg
  and cloves
1/2 tsp. salt
1/4 C. soy milk
1/2 C. crushed pineapple
1 TB. each of vanilla,
  and almond extracts
2 TB. lemon juice
1/2 C. apple cider or other juice

1. Cut dates, figs, dried pineapple, cherries and mixed fruit into small pieces. In a large bowl add currants, dark raisins, the orange and lemon peel and the cut up fruit. Flour fruit with 1/2 cup of the whole wheat pastry flour, mixing in by hand or a large spoon.

2. With a mixer, beat margarine and sweetener together until creamy. Add the egg replacer mixed with the warm water.

3. Melt the chocolate chips over hot water in a double boiler. Add the chocolate to the creamed margarine mixture.

4. In a separate bowl mix the remaining 2 C. whole wheat flour with the walnuts, baking powder, cinnamon, allspice, mace, nutmeg, cloves and salt.

5. In another bowl mix the soy milk, crushed pineapple, vanilla and almond extracts, lemon juice and apple cider.

6. Combine the margarine chocolate mixture with the fruit and alternately add some of the flour mixture and some of the milk mixture, until everything is combined and the mixture is well blended. It should be very thick and drop in clumps from a spoon.

7. Pour batter into 1-2 lightly oiled 8-inch cake pans. Round spring form pans with removable sides are ideal. **Bake at a low temperature of 250-275°** for 2-4 hours, depending on the size of pans. Check for doneness at 1-1 ½ hours. When done, set aside on a rack to cool before carefully removing from pans. Wrap in parchment paper and then foil, and store in the refrigerator for at least one week before serving.

1

2

3

# THE ORIGINAL NEW YORK CHEESECAKE

*This recipe was invented long before packaged soy sour cream and soy cream cheese were available. For a lighter version, see the Traditional Cheesecake recipe on page 188.*

**Cookie Crust:** (or substitute a graham cracker crust)

1+1/8 C. soft wheat flour
1 tsp. lemon rind, grated (optional)
1/4 C. dry sweetener
1/3 C. vegetable oil
1 tsp. egg replacer mixed with 1/8 C. warm water
1/4 tsp. vanilla extract

Preheat oven 400°
Combine flour, rind and sweetener and mix to combine. Mix in the oil, egg replacer mixed with water and vanilla. Stir and gather into a ball. Press dough into an un-greased, 8-inch spring form pan and ½ inch up the sides. Bake 15-20 minutes or until lightly browned. Set aside to cool.

**Filling:**

1 lb. soft or firm tofu
3/4 C. dry sweetener
2 TB. lemon juice
2 TB. cornstarch
1 TB. almond butter (optional)
1/2 tsp. salt
1/2 tsp. almond extract

Preheat oven 350°
Blend all filling ingredients in a blender until smooth and creamy.
Pour filling mixture into the cooled crust. Bake 35-40 minutes, or until filling is lightly browned around the edges. Cool on rack, and then refrigerate 4-6 hours, preferably overnight, before serving. Top with crushed fresh berries or preserves.

**VARIATION:** _Chocolate or Carob Cheesecake:_ *Eliminate lemon juice and add 1/2 C. cocoa or carob powder, and 3 TB. soy milk to the mixture. Use less sweetener if using carob, as it's naturally sweet.*

---

A study conducted at Loma Linda University in California, in 1975, and involving 24,000 people, and reported in the American Journal of Clinical Nutrition, found that pure vegetarians (vegans) had only one-tenth the heart disease death rate of meat eaters.

---

# TRADITIONAL CHEESECAKE

*Often called Italian style, this is a lighter version than the "Original Cheesecake" recipe.*

**Crust:** 1 C. graham crackers (crushed)
       1/2 C. almonds, ground fine
       3 TB. dry sweetener
       2 TB. soy margarine
       1-2 TB. Water

In a medium size bowl mix the cracker crumbs, almonds and sweetener. With fingertips work in the margarine, until mixture is crumbly. Stir in just enough water to moisten mixture. Press into the bottom and 1/2 inch up the sides of a lightly oiled 8-inch spring form pan. Bake in preheated 350° oven for 12-15 minutes or until lightly browned. Prepare filling while crust bakes.

**Filling:**

1 lb. firm tofu (cut in small pieces)
8 oz. soy cream cheese (1 C.)
1/2 C. soy sour cream
3/4 C. dry sweetener
1 tsp. almond extract
1/2 tsp. salt
2 TB egg replacer powder, mixed with 1/4 C. warm water

Preheat oven 350°
1. Combine all of filling ingredients in blender or vita mixer. Blend until smooth and creamy.
2. Pour filling into cooled, prepared crust.
3. Bake at 350° for 20 minutes. Reduce heat to 325° and continue baking another 35-40 minutes, or until filling is set in the middle.
4. Cool on a rack. When completely cool, refrigerate 4-6 hours, preferably overnight before serving. Serve topped with fresh sliced fruit or preserves.

**VARIATIONS:** <u>Chocolate Cheesecake;</u> *Add 1/2 C. cocoa to filling mixture.*

**TIP:** *The easiest way to crush crackers is inside a zip lock bag with a rolling pin or bottle.*

"I believe if the viewing of slaughter was required to eat meat, most folks would become vegetarians."
       Howard Lyman, - ex-cattle rancher & author of Mad Cowboy.

# HAWAIIAN CHEESECAKE with Pineapple and Chocolate

*This tropical lemon & lime cheesecake has a yummy, chocolate bottom layer.*

Preheat oven 350°

**Crust:**      1 C. graham crackers (crushed)
                1/2 C. unsweetened shredded coconut
                3 TB. dry sweetener
                2 TB. soy margarine
                1-2 TB. water

Combine crackers, coconut and sweetener in medium size bowl. With fingertips work in the margarine until mixture is crumbly. Add just enough of the water (if necessary) to moisten mixture. Press into the bottom and approximately 1/2 inch up the sides of a lightly oiled 8-inch spring form pan. Bake in 350° oven 12-15 minutes, or until lightly browned. Prepare the chocolate layer and filling while crust bakes.

**Chocolate Layer:**

| | |
|---|---|
| 1 C. semi-sweet chocolate chips | 2 TB. margarine |
| 1/3 C. soy milk | 1/2 tsp. vanilla extract |

In a double boiler or saucepan, heat all of the chocolate layer ingredients until the chips are melted. Stir well to combine ingredients. Set aside while preparing the filling.

**Filling:**

| | |
|---|---|
| 1 lb. firm tofu, cut into small pieces | 1 TB. egg replacer powder |
| 1/2 tsp. salt | 1 TB. cornstarch |
| 8 oz. soy cream cheese | 1/8 C. lemon juice |
| 1/2 C. soy sour cream | 1/8 C. lime juice |
| 3/4 C. dry sweetener | 1 tsp. lemon extract |

1. Blend filling ingredients in a blender until very smooth and creamy.
2. Pour slightly cooled chocolate mixture into bottom of baked crust.
3. Carefully pour filling over the chocolate layer.
4. Bake at 350° for 20 minutes. Reduce heat to 325° and bake another 35-40 minutes, or until filling is set and raised slightly. Cool on wire rack. Refrigerate 6-8 hours, preferably overnight, before serving. When ready to serve, spread cake with pineapple/coconut topping.

**PINEAPPLE TOPPING:** Combine in saucepan: 1 ½ C. crushed, un-drained, pineapple and 2 tsp. cornstarch. Stir and cook briefly, until thickened. Or eliminate the cornstarch and cooking and simply use well-drained or fresh crushed pineapple. Carefully spread topping over cheesecake. Sprinkle lightly with 2 TB. unsweetened shredded coconut.

# PUMPKIN CHEESECAKE

**Crust:** Use same graham cracker crust as the Traditional Cheesecake recipe, and one 8 inch, lightly oiled spring form pan.

Preheat oven 350°

**Filling:**

1 lb. firm tofu
1 C. pureed pumpkin
1/2 C. soy cream cheese
1/2 C. soy sour cream
2 TB. egg replacer powder
2 TB. water
1 TB. cornstarch
3/4 C. dry sweetener
1 tsp. vanilla extract
1/2 tsp. salt
1 ½ tsp. cinnamon
1 tsp. nutmeg
1/2 tsp. allspice
1/2 tsp. ginger

1. Blend all above ingredients in a blender until smooth and creamy.
2. Pour into the baked graham cracker crust.
3. Bake 20 minutes at 350°. Reduce heat to 325° and continue baking 35-40 minutes, or until filling is set in the middle. Cool on wire rack. Refrigerate over night, or until very well chilled, before serving.

" Various philosophers and religious leaders tried to convince their disciples and followers that animals are nothing more than machines without a soul, without feelings. However, anyone who has ever lived with an animal, ---be it a dog, a bird, or even a mouse, ---knows that this theory is a brazen lie, invented to justify cruelty."

Issac Bashevis Singer (1904-1991) - Author & 1978 Nobel Prize recipient.

# STRAWBERRY SHORTCAKE
**A sweet whole wheat biscuit topped with fresh sliced berries and soy whip cream.**

2 C. whole wheat pastry flour
4-5 TB. dry sweetener
2 tsp. baking powder
1/2 tsp. salt
3/8 C. vegetable oil
2 tsp. egg replacer powder
1/3-1/2 C. soy milk

3 C. sliced strawberries & 1 C. mashed
1/4 C. sweetener
Soy whip cream

Preheat oven 425°
1. Mix together in a medium size bowl, the flour, sweetener, baking powder, and salt.
2. With a fork, stir in the oil, until mixture is crumbly.
3. Add egg replacer mixed with 1/3 cup soy milk. Add just enough of the additional milk, if necessary, to form a smooth ball.
4. Roll or press the dough on floured surface to ¾ inch thick, and cut into six 3-4 inch circles. Bake about 8-10 minutes, or until golden brown. Cool on rack.
5. Combine sliced and mashed berries with the sweetener.
6. **To serve:** Slice biscuits in half. Pile berries on top of one half. Top with a dollop of soy whip cream. **VARIATIONS:** *Many kinds of fruit can be used in this recipe. Try peaches, blackberries, or blueberries.*

# RHUBERRY COBBLER

**Filling:**
4 C. rhubarb, cut in ½" pieces
1 ½ C. fresh raspberries, strawberries or canned preserves
1/2 C. dry sweetener
2 TB. cornstarch
1 TB. lemon juice
**Topping:**
1 C. whole wheat pastry flour
1 tsp. baking powder
1/4 tsp. salt
1/4 C. soy milk

2 TB. dry sweetener
3 TB. vegetable oil
1 TB. egg replacer flour & 1/2 C. warm water

Preheat oven 400° Mix fruit, ½ C. sweetener, cornstarch and lemon juice in a 2 qt. casserole dish. In a medium size bowl mix flour, baking powder and salt together. Add soy milk, sweetener, oil, and egg replacer mixed with water. Mix together to combine well. Drop by spoonfuls on top of filling. Bake for 20-25 minutes, or until fruit is soft, filling is bubbly and topping is lightly browned. **VARIATIONS:** *Use 4-6 cups of your favourite fruit, in place of rhubarb and raspberries.*

# FROSTINGS & TOPPINGS

## CREAMY CHOCOLATE FROSTING

1 pkg. (12.3 oz.) soft or firm silken tofu
1 tsp. vanilla extract
6 oz. (1 cup) chocolate chips (melted and cooled slightly)
3 TB. maple syrup (or other sweetener)

Combine all ingredients in blender and mix until well combined and creamy. Chill in fridge to thicken. <u>Creamy Carob Frosting</u>: *Use carob chips instead of chocolate.*


## VANILLA CREAM FROSTING

1/4 C. soy margarine
1/4 C. dry sweetener
3 oz. (1/4 C.) plain soy cream cheese
1/2 - 1 tsp. almond or vanilla extract
Powdered soy milk

Blend margarine, sweetener and cream cheese until smooth. Stir in extract and enough soy milk powder to make desired consistency. Frosts an 8 x 8 inch cake. Double ingredients for a 9 x 13 inch cake, and triple ingredients for a layered cake.

**VARIATION:** <u>Chocolate or Carob frosting</u>: *Eliminate the soy milk powder and add 1/4 C. cocoa or carob powder.*


## EASY CHOCOLATE MINT FROSTING

1 C. chocolate chips (or substitute carob chips)
1/3 C. soy milk or soy creamer
2 TB. soy margarine
1/2 tsp. mint extract

In a double boiler or saucepan, melt and stir all ingredients together until smooth and thick. The frosting thickens more as it cools. Frosts an 8 x 8 inch cake.

## MOCK WHIP CREAM TOPPING

*This is especially good with shortcake or single crust pies, such as pumpkin or chocolate. Also, look for the delicious store bought version, by Ceres Organics, called Soy Whip.*

1/2 lb. soft tofu, cubed
2 tsp. vanilla extract

3 TB. maple syrup or other sweetener
soy milk or creamer

Blend tofu, vanilla and maple syrup in blender or food processor, until light and fluffy. Add soy milk or creamer, if topping seems too thick. Continue whipping until desired lightness is reached. Taste for sweetness, adding more if necessary. Refrigerate at least an hour, to chill and thicken further. **Suggestion:** *Add a little cornstarch or flour for a thicker version.*

## COCONUT CAKE FILLING

*This version of coconut cake filling is traditionally spread between two or more layers of Chocolate Cake, and referred to as German Chocolate Cake.*

3/4 C. soy milk
1/2 C. dry sweetener
1/2 C. soy margarine
1+1/3 C. unsweetened dry shredded coconut
1 C. pecans or walnuts, chopped

Simmer soy milk, sweetener and margarine in saucepan. When well combined add remaining ingredients. Simmer and stir until mixture thickens. Cool to room temperature before using.

In no mammal and species, except for humans, is milk consumption continued after the weaning period, and calves thrive on cows milk. Cows milk is for calves.

# PUDDINGS & GELS

**Tips**: *Serve puddings like the vanilla or tofu puddings by themselves, or on top of crushed or chopped fruit; or try some poured over slightly dry cake. The dry sweetener used in recipes is organic, unbleached cane sugar. Adjust amount used to satisfy your sweet preference. Don't be tempted to over cook puddings, as they thicken more as they cool. Cooling the pudding <u>before</u> covering them prevents condensation from forming, which could thin the pudding.*

## TAPIOCA PUDDING

1/2 C. small pearl tapioca
3 C. soy milk
1/4 tsp. salt

1/2 C. dry sweetener
1 TB. cornstarch mixed with 1/2 C. soymilk
1 tsp. vanilla extract

1. In a saucepan soak the tapioca in 3 cups of soy milk for 30 minutes. Add salt and sweetener and bring mixture to a boil. Turn heat down and simmer and stir for approximately 8 minutes.
2. Add cornstarch/milk mixture and stir well, bringing to a boil. Turn heat down and simmer for 5-8 minutes, or until thick and tapioca pearls are soft. Remove from stove and cool <u>un</u>covered for 10-15 minutes before adding the vanilla. It thickens more as it cools. Let mixture cool completely before refrigerating. Serve warm or cold.
**VARIATIONS:** <u>Chocolate Tapioca:</u> *Add 1/4 cocoa along with an additional 1/4-1/2 C. soy milk.*

## INDIAN RICE PUDDING

1 C. long grain brown rice & 2 C. water
1 ¾ quarts soy milk
8 cardamom pods (crushing the seeds within)
3/4-1 C. dry sweetener or maple syrup

3 TB. soy margarine
1/2 C. raisins
1/8-1/4 tsp. crushed saffron threads
1/2 C pistachio nuts (chopped).

1. Partially cook rice for 30 minutes, in the 2 C. water. Add soymilk and crushed cardamom seeds.
2. On medium heat simmer without lid, for about 1 hour, or until the mixture thickens. stirring every 5 minutes or so.
3. Add sweetener, margarine, raisins and saffron and continue to cook and stir 5-15 minutes longer.
4. Test for sweetness, adding more if needed. Remove from heat and pour pudding into a 1 ¾ qt. serving dish. Sprinkle pudding with chopped nuts. Cool without a lid and then refrigerate with a lid for at least 2 hours or overnight, before serving.

## TRADITIONAL CREAMY RICE PUDDING

2 C. cooked short or long grain brown rice
1 ½ C. soy milk (or part soy creamer)
3/4 C. raisins
1/3-1/2 dry sweetener
2 tsp. cornstarch mixed with 1/2 C. soy milk
2 tsp. vanilla extract
cinnamon

1.  In medium size saucepan, combine rice, 1 ½ C. soy milk, raisins and sweetener.  Cook and stir 15-20 minutes.
2.  Add cornstarch mixed with 1/2 C. soy milk and vanilla extract to rice mixture and continue to cook and stir an additional 5-10 minutes, or until thickened.  The pudding will thicken more as it cools.  Serve at room temperature or cold, sprinkled with cinnamon powder.

## OLD FASHIONED VANILLA PUDDING

1/2 C. dry sweetener
4 TB. cornstarch
1/2 tsp. salt
3 C. soy milk
2 tsp. vanilla

1.  In saucepan whisk together all of the above ingredients, except vanilla.  Bring to a boil.
2.  Reduce heat and whisk constantly on low heat, cooking an additional 2-5 minutes, until thick.
3.  Take pan off of heat; stir in vanilla and cool before serving.

**VARIATION:**  <u>Chocolate or Carob Pudding</u>:  *Add 1/4 C. unsweetened cocoa or carob powder to mixture before cooking.*

---

" One farmer says to me:  You cannot live on vegetable food solely, for it furnishes nothing to make bones with, walking all the while he talks behind his oxen, who with vegetable made bones, jerk him and his lumbering plow along in spite of every obstacle."

Henry David Thoreau   (1817-1862) - Poet, Naturalist & author of Walden

## CHOCOLATE TOFU PUDDING

1 lb. soft or firm tofu
1/2 -3/4 C. maple syrup or other sweetener
1/2 C. cocoa powder
2 tsp. vanilla extract

Mix all ingredients in a blender until smooth and creamy.  Refrigerate to chill and thicken.
**VARIATION:** _Carob Tofu Pudding_:  *Use carob powder instead of cocoa and reduce the sweetener.*
**Note:**  *If replacing maple syrup with a dry sweetener, add a little soy milk to the ingredients.*


## LEMON TOFU COCONUT PUDDING

1 C. soft or firm tofu
4 TB. lemon juice
1/4-1/2 C. shredded coconut (optional)
1/3 C. sweetener

Blend all ingredients in blender until smooth and creamy. Sprinkle individual servings with shredded coconut or crushed nuts.  Refrigerate to chill and thicken.


## ORANGE TOFU PUDDING

1 C. soft or firm tofu
4 TB. orange juice
1/3 C. maple syrup or other sweetener
1 tsp. vanilla
1/8 C. vegetable oil

Blend all ingredients until smooth and creamy.  Chill in fridge before serving.

**VARIATIONS:**  _Mango, Pineapple or Cherry Pudding_: *Use mango, pineapple or cherry juice instead of orange.  Serve pudding on top of crushed or chopped fruit.*

---

If there's no love in the kitchen, there's no life in the food.

---

## CHOCOLATE BANANA PUDDING

1 ½ C. bananas
4 TB. cocoa powder
1 C. soft or firm tofu
1 TB. vanilla extract
1/2 C. sweetener, or to taste

Blend all ingredients in blender or processor until smooth and creamy.  Refrigerate to chill and thicken further.
**VARIATION:** _Carob Banana Pudding_: _Use carob powder instead of cocoa, and since carob is naturally sweet, adjust any added sweetener._


## EASY FRUIT GEL

2 C. juice (apple, pineapple, mango or a combination)
2 tsp. agar powder or flakes
1 C. fruit, cut up.  (Pineapples, oranges, cherries, raspberries, strawberries or a combination of fruit)

1.  Put juice and agar in a small saucepan.  Let mixture sit for 5 minutes.
2.  Bring juice and agar to boil, stirring to combine with a wire whisk.  When it comes to a boil, turn heat down and simmer and stir for 5 minutes.
3. Transfer mixture to a bowl or mold and set in the refrigerator.  When it just begins to set up, about 15-30 minutes, fold in the cut up fruit.  Chill in the refrigerator to set completely.

**Suggestion:** _For a larger mold, simply double or triple quantity of ingredients._

"Vegetarians have the best diet.  They have the lowest rates of coronary disease of any group in the country...some people scoff at vegetarians, but they have a fraction of our heart attack rate and they have only 40% of our cancer rate.  They outlive us.  On the average they outlive other men by about six years now."
William Castelli M.D. - Director of the Farmington Heart Study

# PIES, TARTS & TURNOVERS

## TIPS FOR MAKING PERFECT PIES

1.  If you are baking at sea level to 3,000 ft., decrease liquid in crust recipes, or increase flour, and increase sweetener in filling. Refer to page 20 for specifics on altitude adjustments.
2.  A flaky and nutritious piecrust can be made with whole wheat pastry flour. Whole wheat <u>bread</u> flour is too coarsely ground to bring successful results. A wheat free crust can be made with barley or oat flour. Also see wheat free guidelines on page 274.
3.  Add only enough water to stick the dough together, rather than add all of the water in the recipe, and then have to add more flour. It is overworking of the dough that causes tough pastry. Handle it as little as possible.
4. To prevent the thinner outside edge of crust from burning, cover with strips of aluminum foil or a metal piecrust shield, available at most kitchen supply stores.
5.  Always use flour to thicken acid type fruit fillings, such as: blueberries and rhubarb. The amount of thickener depends on the juiciness of the fruit. Cornstarch works better with non-acid fruits.
6.  Protect the bottom of your oven from any over flows from juicy fruit filling, with a piece of aluminum foil or a cookie sheet.
7.  The amount of sweetener used in any pie filling depends not only on your taste preference, but also on the sweetness of the fruit used.
8. For single crust pies that are pre-baked before filling, prick the unbaked crust liberally with a fork, before putting in the oven.
9. Always make a couple of small slits in the top crust of the pie, before baking. This allows steam to escape.
10. Don't cover cream type pies until they cool, as condensation can cause filling to thin.

## SINGLE CRUST PIE

*For those cream type pies, that don't require a top crust.*

2 C. whole wheat pastry flour    1/3 C. plus 1 TB. vegetable oil
dash of salt    1/3 C. cold water
1/2 tsp. ground nutmeg (optional)

1. Mix flour, salt and nutmeg together with a fork. Stir in the vegetable oil until mixture is crumbly.
2. Add up to 1/3 C. water until dough can be rolled into a ball, adding more flour or water if needed.
3. Roll out between two pieces of waxed paper or simply press with your fingertips into the bottom of an un-oiled 9-inch pie pan. If pre-baking a bottom crust, prick dough with a fork before baking in 375° oven for 10-15 minutes, or until golden brown. Remember to protect the fluted edges with a metal pie protector ring.

## DOUBLE CRUST PIE

*Use for one double or two small, single crust pies*

3 C. whole wheat pastry flour    1/2 C. vegetable oil
1/2 tsp. salt    1/2 C. water

1. Mix the flour and salt with a fork. Stir in the vegetable oil until mixture is crumbly.
2. Add enough water to make dough that is pliable and forms into a smooth ball.
3. With fingertips press half of the ball into a 9-inch pie pan.
4. Fill with desired filling.
5. Roll out the second ball between two pieces of wax paper, to a size that will cover the pie. Carefully peel back the top layer of paper and flip the dough over on top of the filling, then peel off the other piece of wax paper.
6. Use a fork to press around the edge of the pie dough, securing the top and bottom crusts together. Make a couple of small slits in the center of the pie for the steam to escape. Use any extra dough to make leaf, flower and other shapes, to decorate the piecrust. Bake as per individual recipe.

## GRAHAM CRACKER CRUST

1 C. crushed graham crackers
1/2 C. finely ground almonds (or other nuts)
3 TB. sweetener
3 TB. soy margarine
1-2 TB. water

Combine crackers, almonds and sweetener in a bowl. Blend margarine in with fingertips, until well combined. Stir in just enough water to moisten the mixture, if necessary. Press mixture into an 8-9 inch pie pan. Bake in a preheated 350° oven for 12-15 minutes, or until golden brown.
**VARIATION:** *Use unsweetened shredded coconut instead of the almonds.*
**TIP:** *The easiest way to crush graham crackers is in a zip lock bag, with a rolling pin or bottle.*


## COOKIE CRUST

*This is especially good with unbaked pies or for a different cheesecake crust.*

1+1/8 C. whole wheat pastry flour
1 tsp. lemon rind, grated (optional)
1/4 C. dry sweetener

1/3 C. vegetable oil
1 tsp. egg replacer mixed
with 1/8 C. warm water
1/4 tsp. vanilla extract

Mix together flour, rind and dry sweetener. With a fork, stir oil, egg replacer and vanilla into the flour mixture until well combined, and can be gathered into a ball. Press dough into an un-oiled 8-inch pan. Bake in a preheated 400° oven for 15-20 minutes; or until lightly browned. Cool before filling.


## CRUMB CRUST or TOPPING

*This is a yummy topping for fruit pies, where a lighter crust is desired. It's similar to the topping for apple crisp.*

3/4 C. whole wheat pastry flour
1/3 C. dry sweetener
1/3 C. ground or finely chopped walnuts

1 tsp. cinnamon powder
¼ tsp. salt
5 TB. soy margarine

Mix dry ingredients together. Add margarine and combine with finger tips until a crumbly texture is reached. Sprinkle on top of any of the fruit pies instead of the rolled pie crust. Bake pies with a crumb crust at 375° for 30-60 minutes or until fruit is soft and crust is lightly browned. If crust browns too quickly, cover lightly with parchment paper and foil.
**VARIATION:** *Replace wheat flour with barley or oat flour for a wheat free version.*

## OLD FASHIONED APPLE PIE

One 9 inch double crust pie recipe
4-5 C. sliced tart or semi tart apples
1/4 –3/4 C. dry sweetener
Dash of salt
2-3 tsp. cinnamon powder

Mix apples, sweetener, and salt in bowl. Pour into an unbaked pie shell. Sprinkle with cinnamon powder. Cover with top crust. Make two or three slits in crust. Bake in preheated 450° oven for 20 minutes. Lower heat to 350° and continue baking 30-40 minutes, or until apples are tender, but not mushy.

**SUGGESTIONS:** *Add 1/3 C. water to apple mixture if apples are dry. Try using a combination of sweet and tart apples. Amount of sweetener is totally dependent on sweetness of apples and your preference. To test for doneness of apples, stick the tip of a sharp knife between one of the slits in the top crust. Apples should be cooked, but still slightly firm…not mushy.*

# RHUBERRY PIE

*A scrumptious combination of rhubarb and strawberries*

One  9 inch double crust pie recipe
5-6 C. rhubarb, cut into 1-1 ½ inch pieces
1 C. sliced strawberries (or substitute raspberries)
3/4 C. dry sweetener
2-4 TB. flour (depending on juiciness of fruit)

Mix rhubarb, strawberries, sweetener and flour together in a large bowl.  Pour into unbaked pastry shell.  Cover with top crust and crust edge protector.  Bake at 450° for 15 minutes. Turn heat down to 350° and bake another 30-45 minutes longer, or until the rhubarb is soft.

**VARIATIONS:** *Although this is a delicious combination of fruit, you can make all rhubarb or all strawberry pie.  Adjust the sweetener and flour for thickening when doing so.  Crushed pineapple can replace the berries.*

# PEACH PIE

One 9 inch double crust pie recipe
4 C. sliced, peeled peaches
1/2- 3/4 C. dry sweetener
pinch of salt
3 TB.  flour

Mix peaches, sweetener, salt and flour together in a large bowl.  Pour into an unbaked pie shell and cover with top crust.  Bake at 450° oven for 15 minutes.  Lower the heat to 350° and bake an additional 30-35 minutes, or until filling is bubbly .

**Note:** *The amount of sweetener always depends on your taste preference, as well as the sweetness of the fruit.*

## CHERRY PIE

One 9 inch double crust pie recipe
4 C. pitted sweet or sour cherries
3/4-1 C. dry sweetener (depending on sweetness of cherries)
3-4 TB. flour
pinch of salt

Mix cherries, sweetener, flour and pinch of salt together in a bowl. Pour into the unbaked pie shell. Cover with top crust. Bake at 450° for 15 minutes. Lower heat to 350° and bake 30-40 minutes longer.

## BERRY PIES    *Includes: blueberry, mulberry, blackberries etc.*

One 9 inch double crust pie recipe
4 C. berries
1/2 C. dry sweetener
2-4 TB. flour (depending on juiciness of fruit)

Mix berries, sweetener and flour in a bowl. Pour into an unbaked pie shell. Cover with top crust. Make a couple of slits in the top crust with a sharp knife, and seal and flute edges. Bake at 450° for 15 minutes. Lower heat to 350° and bake 30-40 minutes longer.

Nobel-prize winning author, Issac Bashevis Singer became a vegetarian in 1962 at age fifty-eight. He said, "naturally I am sorry now that I waited so long, but it is better later than never."

# FALL MINCEMEAT PIE

*Also see pg. 231 in the canning section, for making a large batch of mincemeat.*
*Have a 9" pie pan and a double crust pie recipe ready.*

1 ½ C. green tomatoes, chopped fine*    4 tsp. apple cider vinegar
1 ½ C. apples, chopped fine    1/8 C. orange juice
1/2 C. raisins    3/4 C. dry sweetener
1/4 C. walnuts, chopped    1/2 tsp. each cinnamon and nutmeg
1/8 C. vegetable oil    1/4 tsp. allspice
1/4 TB. lemon rind    1/8 tsp. ground cloves
4 tsp. lemon juice    1/8 tsp. salt

Mix all ingredients together in a kettle and bring to a boil. Lower heat and simmer for 1 hour, or until the mixture is thick. Let the mixture cool down before filling a 9 inch unbaked, whole wheat pie crust. Cover with top crust, cutting a couple of slits in the center of the crust, for the steam to escape. Bake at 450° for 10 minutes. Protect fluted edge of crust with a pie protector ring. Lower heat to 350° and continue baking for 40-50 minutes, or until pie is golden brown and filling is bubbly.

**VARIATION:** * *If you don't have any green tomatoes, increase raisins to 1½ cups and walnuts to 1/2-3/4 cups.*

"A vegetarian diet, and especially a low protein vegetarian diet, improves the general health of the body and is superior for one's health in almost every way, as compared to a flesh centered diet. A vegetarian diet is a way of loving yourself and your body.

Gabriel Cousens, M.D. – Conscious Eating

# SINGLE CRUST PIES

## APPLE PIE WITH CRUMB CRUST

*My version of Mina "Buckets" pie, served at the end of a beautiful Northern Ontario summer.*

You will need one 9 inch <u>un</u>baked, single crust pie shell
Use same filling as Old Fashioned Apple Pie, pg. 201
Cover filling with following crumb crust recipe.

**Crumb Crust**

| | |
|---|---|
| 3/4 C. whole wheat pastry flour | 1 tsp. cinnamon powder |
| 1/3 C. dry sweetener | 1/4 tsp. salt |
| 1/3 C. ground or finely chopped walnuts | 5 TB. soy margarine |

Mix the dry ingredients together. Add margarine and combine with finger tips until a crumbly consistency is reached. Sprinkle and press lightly on top of pie filling. Bake in a preheated 375° oven for 50-60 minutes, or until top is lightly browned and apples are soft, but not mushy. Check pie at 20-30 minutes and cover lightly with a piece of parchment paper and foil, if crumbs are darkening too quickly.
**SUGGESTION:** *Add 1/3 C. water to filling, if apples are dry. Don't forget to protect the fluted edge of the pastry with a metal protector ring.*

## SOUTHERN PECAN PIE

| | |
|---|---|
| One 9 inch <u>un</u>baked, single crust, whole wheat pie shell. | 1/2 C. maple syrup |
| | 1 tsp. vanilla extract |
| 1/2 C. margarine | 1/4 tsp. salt |
| 1 TB. egg replacer powder | 1½ C. whole or broken pecans |
| 1 TB. cornstarch | |
| 1/2 C. warm water | |
| 1/2 C. dry sweetener | |

Melt margarine over low heat or in a double boiler. With a wire whisk blend egg replacer powder and cornstarch with warm water. Add sweetener, syrup, vanilla, salt and pecans, along with margarine, and beat until smooth. Pour into a 9 inch unbaked pie shell. Bake at 450° for 10 minutes. Lower heat to 350°. Bake 25-30 minutes longer, until filling is set.

# TRADITIONAL PUMPKIN PIE

*This pie is best made the day before serving, so that the filling can cool and set well.*

One 9 inch <u>un</u>baked single crust pie shell
2¼ C. canned or home cooked pumpkin*
1 C. soymilk or all or part soy creamer
3/4 C. raw sugar
1/4 C. cornstarch
1 tsp. blackstrap molasses

1/2 tsp. vanilla extract
1 tsp. cinnamon
1/2 tsp. each: nutmeg & allspice
1/4 tsp. ginger
1/2 tsp. salt

Have one 9 inch unbaked pie shell ready. Combine all remaining ingredients in a blender, until very smooth and creamy. Pour mixture into pie shell. Bake at 425° for 10 minutes. Reduce heat to 350° and continue baking an additional 45-50 minutes, or until filling sets. Cool on a wire rack and then refrigerate covered overnight. Serve with or without soy whip cream.

**VARIATION:** <u>Squash or Sweet Potato Pie:</u> *Substitute well mashed squash or sweet potatoes for the pumpkin. Sweeten to taste depending on sweetness of ingredients used.*

# TOFU PUMPKIN PIE

*This pie is great with or without a whipped topping.*

Have a 9 inch <u>un</u>baked single crust pie shell ready for this yummy filling. (pg. 199)

1¼ lb. firm tofu
3/4 C. dry sweetener
1¾ C. pureed pumpkin*
2 tsp. cinnamon
1 tsp. nutmeg
1/2 tsp. each of allspice, ginger
1/4 tsp. salt

Mix all ingredients in a blender until smooth and creamy. Pour into unbaked pie shell. Bake at 400° for 15 minutes. Turn oven down to 350° and continue baking an additional 40 minutes, or until filling is set. Cool on a rack, and then refrigerate covered for 8-10 hours, or overnight, before serving.

**VARIATION:** <u>Tofu Squash or Sweet Potato Pie:</u> *Substitute either for the pureed pumpkin.*

## BANANA CREAM PIE

*An old time favourite, with substitutions of soymilk and egg replacer powder.*

2 C. soy milk
1/2 C dry sweetener
1/2 C. unbleached white flour
1/8 tsp. salt

1 TB. egg replacer powder
1/2 C. warm water
1 tsp. vanilla extract
3 large bananas, thinly sliced
unsweetened shredded coconut (optional)

Have ready a *baked* and cooled 9-inch single crust pie shell, (pg. 199) before proceeding with filling.

Heat milk with sweetener, flour, salt and egg replacer mixed with hot water, and whisk it together well. Cook over medium/hot heat, stirring constantly with a wire whisk for 10-15 minutes, or until the filling is creamy and thick. Take off of heat and whisk in the vanilla extract. When the filling has cooled to room temperature, slice bananas and spread evenly in the bottom of the cooled pie shell, and pour the filling over the bananas, smoothing it evenly towards the crimped pie shell edge. Sprinkle the top with shredded, dry, unsweetened coconut. Chill overnight before serving.

**Note:** *The filling stiffens up more after being refrigerated. Bake one day and serve the next.*
**VARIATION:** Pineapple Cream Pie: *Eliminate the bananas. When the filling has cooled to room temperature, gently stir in 1C. crushed and well drained pineapple.*
Coconut Cream Pie: *Eliminate bananas and stir in 1/2 -1 C. dry shredded coconut, when adding vanilla.*

## CREAMY LEMON PIE

1 baked and cooled 9" graham cracker crust
2 C. plain soy milk
3/4 C. dry sweetener
1/4 tsp. salt

1/2 C. unbleached white flour
1 TB. egg replacer powder
1/2 C. soy milk
1/2 C. lemon juice

Mix in a medium size saucepan: soy milk, sweetener, salt, flour and egg replacer mixed with the 1/2 C. soy milk. Beat together well, with a wire whisk. Cook over medium heat, stirring constantly for 8-10 minutes, or until the mixture is very thick and creamy. Slowly beat in the lemon juice and immediately remove from heat. Let mixture cool slightly before pouring into the graham cracker crust. Cool completely before covering and putting in the refrigerator. The filling stiffens up more after being refrigerated. Refrigerate overnight before serving.
**VARIATION:** "Key" Lime Pie: *Use lime juice instead of lemon.* Cherry Lemon: *Sprinkle baked crust with 1 C. cooked, and cooled, sliced sweet cherries, before adding lemon mixture.*

## EASY UNBAKED CHOCOLATE CREAM PIE

One baked and cooled graham cracker crust
  in a 8-9 inch spring form or pie pan
1½ C. semi-sweet chocolate chips
1 lb. soft tofu
2 tsp. vanilla extract
4 TB. maple syrup
1/4 C. soy milk
1/4 C. finely chopped walnuts, or unsweetened shredded coconut

Melt chocolate chips in a double boiler, or in a saucepan over very low heat. Break tofu into small pieces and combine in a blender with vanilla, maple syrup, soy milk, and cooled chocolate. Blend until very smooth and creamy. Pour mixture into pre-baked pie shell. Sprinkle top with chopped walnuts or shredded coconut. Chill in fridge at least 6-8 hours, or overnight before serving.

**VARIATIONS:**   <u>Carob Cream Pie:</u> *Use carob chips instead of chocolate*
                      <u>Out of chocolate or carob chips?</u> *Use 1/2 C. cocoa or carob powder and adjust the sweetener.*
                      <u>Out of regular tofu?</u> *Use two pkgs. of firm silken tofu, and eliminate the soy milk.*


## OLD FASHIONED CHOCOLATE PIE

2 C. soy milk
1/2 C. dry sweetener
1/3 C. unbleached white flour
1/8 tsp. salt
1/2 C. cocoa
1 TB. egg replacer mixed with 1/2 C. warm water
1/2 tsp. vanilla extract

Have ready a baked and cooled 9-inch single crust pie shell, before proceeding with the filling.
Mix all ingredients together in a saucepan. Beat with a wire whisk and cook over medium heat, stirring constantly for 8-10 minutes, or until mixture is thick and creamy. Let mixture cool slightly before pouring into the pie shell. Cool before refrigerating. The filling will stiffen up more after refrigeration. Refrigerate 6-8 hrs. or overnight before serving.

---

> *The most important ingredient in any kitchen, in any recipe, is love.*

## FRUIT TURNOVERS

*Turnovers pack better than a slice of pie, in lunch boxes or on camping/ hiking trips.*

**To make:** Use a double crust whole wheat pie recipe, pg. 199. Roll dough out as thin as possible. Cut into 5-inch rounds or squares. Fill one half of the round with any of the fruit fillings for pies, leaving at least a half-inch around the edge empty. Fold turnover in half producing a half moon or triangle shape. Cut a couple small slits in the crust or poke two or three times with a regular fork. Bake on a cookie sheet at 350° for 15-20 minutes, or until fruit is soft and pastry is lightly browned.

**NOTE**: *If you're concerned about the crust browning quicker than the fruit will get soft, such as apples, precook or partially cook the fruit before filling turnover dough.*

**Tips:** *The single piecrust recipe on page 199 will make about 12 medium size tarts. When the recipe requires baked shells, press dough into muffin tins, and prick shells well with a fork before baking at 375° for 8-12 minutes, or until lightly browned. Remove from muffin tins when cooled and fill with desired filling. All the single crust pie fillings and tofu puddings can also be used for tart filling.*

" All our ecologic, political and social problems are multiplied in magnitude by devoting huge amounts of land, water and energy, to create an animal-based diet. Fortunately, so many ecologic problems are improved or remedied as we evolve our food choices, as individuals and nations, towards plant-based nutrition."
Michael Klaper M.D. - Vegan Nutrition; Pure & Simple.

## BUTTER TARTS
*A less sweet version of the much-loved Canadian Butter Tart*

You will need one single crust pie dough recipe, to make 12 medium or 18-2 inch miniature tarts.
Break the dough into pieces to fill the muffin tins you are using. Press into the tins with your fingers.

**Filling:**

1/2 C. raisins
1/4 C. soy margarine
1/4 C. dry sweetener
1/4 C. maple syrup (or other liquid sweetener)
1/2 tsp. vanilla
1/4 C. chopped walnuts
1/4 tsp. salt
1 TB. egg replacer mixed with 1/4 C. hot water

Preheat oven 450°

Soak raisins in enough boiling water to cover, for 10 minutes, then drain. Mix hot raisins with rest of ingredients until well blended and creamy. Fill unbaked pastry shells 2/3 full. Don't overfill, or some of the filling will be lost as it bubbles and seeps over the sides of tarts while baking. Bake at 450° for 10 minutes. Turn oven down to 350° and bake an additional 10-20 minutes, or until filling is bubbly and crusts are lightly browned.


## RAISIN TARTS

One single crust whole wheat pie recipe
1½ C. raisins
2 C. water
1/2 C. sweetener
4 TB. cornstarch
1/2 tsp. cinnamon
1/4 tsp. cloves
1/4 tsp. salt

Bake tart shells for 8-12 minutes at 375° or until lightly browned. Cook all remaining ingredients until thick. Fill baked and cooled tart shells. Cool tarts before serving.

## BERRY TARTS

One single crust whole wheat pie recipe
1 C. of your favourite berry (such as strawberries, raspberries, blueberries, boysenberries)
1/4 C. sweetener
2 tsp. cornstarch mixed with 1/4 C. water

Bake tart shells for 8-12 minutes at 375°. Simmer sliced or whole berries with sweetener and cornstarch mixture, just until liquid is thickened. Cool mixture slightly and fill baked and cooled tart shells. These can be eaten as is, or served with your favourite topping. Try topping with any of the tofu puddings.

## LEMON TARTS

One single crust whole wheat pie recipe          1/3-1/2 C. sweetener
1 lb. firm tofu                                  6 TB. lemon juice

Bake tart shells for 8-12 minutes at 375°. Mix tofu, sweetener and lemon juice in a blender until smooth and creamy. Fill cooled, baked tart shells. Sprinkle with unsweetened shredded coconut. To firm up the filling some, cool and then store in a covered container in the fridge, until ready to serve.
**VARIATIONS:** Lime Tarts: *Use lime juice instead of lemon. Or try a mixture of lemon and lime.*

## FRESH FRUIT CUSTARD TARTS

Fill baked tart shells with fresh, uncooked, sliced or chopped berries, peaches, cherries, mangoes, or your favourite fruit. Cover fruit with the lemon tart filling from above recipe, or with your favourite pudding, or whipped soy topping. Sprinkle with shredded coconut or finely chopped nuts.

# NANCY'S FRESH FRUIT "PIZZA" TART
*Such a light and refreshing treat on a hot summer day.*

**Crust:**

1 C. soy margarine
1 C. dry sweetener
2 C. whole wheat pastry flour
1/2 tsp. baking powder
1 tsp. salt
water

Cream margarine and sweetener together, until fluffy. Add flour, baking powder and salt until crumbly. Add just enough water to hold the mixture together. Roll out onto a lightly oiled round pizza or cookie sheet. Bake at 350° for 20-30 minutes, or until lightly browned. Cool while preparing filling and glaze.

**Filling:**

Place any combination of sliced fresh fruit on the baked and cooled crust, in any creative arrangement. **Suggestions:** strawberries, blackberries, raspberries, cherries, nectarines, peaches, and kiwis. The more variety with the fruit, the more colorful and delicious will be the "pizza" tart. Cover with the following glaze and refrigerate until ready to serve. Cut in pizza shape servings.

**Glaze:**

3/4 –1 C. dry sweetener.
1 TB. cornstarch
1 C. water
juice and grated rind of 1 lemon

Mix sweetener and cornstarch together in a saucepan. Add the water and cook until thick. Add juice and grated rind (zest). Remove from heat and cool before pouring over the fruit.

---

"The standard four food groups are based on American agricultural lobbies. Why do we have a Milk group? Because we have a National Dairy Council. Why do we have a meat group? Because we have an extremely powerful meat lobby."
  Marion Nestle, - Manager of Surgeon Generals landmark report
  on Nutrition and Health, in 1988, and Professor of Nutrition, N.Y.U.

# FROZEN TREATS

## TIPS & DIRECTIONS

*Read these tips before proceeding with recipes*

* Always chill the blended ingredients before processing in an ice cream maker.
Mixture can be chilled quickly for 2-3 hours in the freezer, or for 6-8 hours (or overnight) in the fridge.
* Preserves, canned or fresh mashed or chopped fruit, can be used in recipes.
* Plain soymilk can replace all or part of the soy creamer.
* Soft to firm silken tofu can be used, or replaced with regular soft tofu.
* Where dry sweetener is listed, organic, unbleached cane sugar was used.
* Liquid sweeteners can replace all or part of dry sweetener. Generally ¾ cup of liquid sweetener replaces 1 cup of dry.  Adjust amount of sweetener used, depending on your sweet preference.
* Most of these recipes were processed in a small, one and a half quart electric ice cream maker for 10-20 minutes. (No ice is required) The canister is kept in the freezer until used. Not all of the frozen treats require an ice cream maker.
* Store processed frozen desserts in the freezer, in a covered container.
* Most of these treats can be eaten immediately after processing, or stored in the freezer for a firmer consistency and later enjoyment.  Allow plenty of time after taking it from the freezer, to soften enough for scooping.
* Refer to notes on Fruity Soy Yogurt Ice Cream, pg 215, for substitution idea for pudding mix used in some of the recipes.

## CREAMY FRUIT MEDLEY

*This frozen fruit salad does not require an ice cream maker. It's frozen in a loaf pan.*

1 C. vegan sour cream
8 oz. pkg. vegan cream cheese
1/2 C. maple syrup or other sweetener
1 C. canned or fresh sweet cherries pitted and drained
1 C. canned or fresh-diced pineapple, drained
1/2 C. chopped oranges or other fruit
1/2-3/4 C. chopped walnuts or other nuts

Beat sour cream, cream cheese and sweetener together with an electric mixer, until smooth and creamy. Fold in fruit and nuts and pour mixture into a bread pan. Freeze at least 8 hours or overnight. When ready to serve, briefly put pan in hot water, so that it loosens from the sides. Turn out, slice and serve.

## CHOCOLATE SOY ICE CREAM

2 C. plain soy creamer
1 pkg. (12.3 oz.) silken tofu
1/2 C. cocoa powder
1/2 C. dry sweetener
1 tsp. vanilla extract
1/4 C. vegetable oil

Mix all ingredients in a blender until creamy smooth. Chill the mixture before proceeding. Process in an ice cream maker for 10-20 minutes, or until very thick. Pour into a covered container and freeze until it reaches desired firmness for serving.

**VARIATIONS:**   <u>Mint Chocolate</u>: *Decrease vanilla to 1/2 tsp. and add 1/2 tsp. mint extract.*
<u>Chocolate Chip</u>: *Add 1/2 C. chocolate chips to ice cream, during last few minutes of processing in ice cream maker.*
<u>Chocolate Brownie</u>: *Add 1/2-3/4C. crumbled brownies to the mixture, when it is almost ready to be removed from the ice cream maker.*
<u>Carob</u>: *Substitute the same amount of carob powder for the cocoa powder. The above variations can also be used with carob.*
<u>Creamier & Extra fudgy</u>: *To the original recipe, add an extra ¼ C. Cocoa and 1 pkg. vanilla pudding mix.*

## FRUITY SOYOGURT ICE CREAM

2 C. plain soy creamer
1 TB. vanilla extract
1 C. berry soy yogurt (approx. 2-6 oz containers)
1 pkg. (4 oz.) Mori Nu vanilla pudding mix *
1 ½ C. fruit preserves (raspberry, strawberry or other) *
1/4 C. vegetable oil

Process all ingredients in a blender until smooth and creamy. Chill the mixture before proceeding. Process in an ice cream maker for 10-20 minutes, or until very thick. Pour into a covered container and freeze until it reaches desired firmness for serving.

**Note:** *Pudding mix can be substituted with a mixture of 2 TB. cornstarch, 1/3 C. sweetener, ¼ tsp. sea salt and 1 tsp. dry or liquid lecithin. * Substitute mashed fresh berries instead of preserves, and add 1/4 -1/2 C. sweetener. Experiment by using different yogurt flavours and different types of fruit; such as peaches or mangoes. Raspberries will turn the ice cream a beautiful shade of pink.*

## LEMON GINGER ICE CREAM

1- 6oz. container soy lemon yogurt
2 TB. lemon juice
1/4 C. vegetable oil
1/2 C. dry sweetener
2 TB. maple syrup (or use more dry sweetener)
1 C. plain soy creamer
1 pkg. (12.3 oz.) silken tofu
1/8 tsp. salt
2 tsp. lemon rind, grated (optional)
2 TB. candied ginger, minced

Process all ingredients, except the candied ginger, in a blender until smooth. Chill the mixture before proceeding. Process in an ice cream maker for 10-20 minutes, or until very thick. Add the minced ginger during the last five minutes of processing. Pour into a covered container and freeze until it reaches desired firmness for serving.

**VARIATION:** Lime Ginger; *Replace the lemon juice and rind with lime.*

## CHERRY ALMOND ICE CREAM

2 C. plain soy creamer
1 pkg. (12.3 oz.) silken tofu
1/2 C. dry sweetener
2 TB. maple syrup

1/4 C. vegetable oil
1/8 tsp. salt
2 TB. almond extract
1 C. canned & drained or pitted fresh sweet cherries

Process all ingredients, except the cherries, in a blender until smooth and creamy. Chill the mixture before proceeding. Process in an ice cream maker, for 10-20 minutes, or until the mixture is very thick. Add the cherries and continue to process until the cherries are well mixed in. Pour into a covered container and freeze until it reaches desired firmness for serving. **VARIATION:** _Cherry Almond with Chocolate_: *Add 1/4 C. of a vegan chocolate bar, cut into small pieces, when adding the cherries.*

## PEACHY LEMON FROZEN YOGURT

1 C. soy peach yogurt (2-6 oz. containers)
1/4 C. lemon juice
1/4 C. vegetable oil
1/2 C. dry sweetener

1 C. plain soy creamer
1 pkg. (12.3 oz.) silken tofu
1/8 tsp. salt
1/2 C. peaches, finely chopped or preserves

Process all ingredients in a blender, except the peaches, until smooth and creamy. Chill the mixture before proceeding. Process in an ice cream maker for 10-20 minutes, or until mixture is very thick. Add the peaches during last 5 minutes of processing. Pour into a covered container and freeze until it reaches desired firmness for serving.

## PINEAPPLE ICE CREAM

1 ½ C. plain soy creamer
1 pkg. (12.3oz.) silken tofu
1/2 C. pineapple juice
1/4 C. vegetable oil
1/2 C. dry sweetener

1 TB. liquid sweetener
1/8 tsp. salt
1/4 C. lemon juice
1 C. crushed pineapple

Process all ingredients in a blender, except half of the crushed pineapple. Blend until smooth and creamy. Chill the mixture before proceeding. Process in an ice cream maker for 10-20 minutes, or until mixture is very thick. Add the remaining half-cup of crushed pineapple and process until it is well combined. Pour into a covered container and freeze until it reaches desired firmness for serving.

## MAPLE PECAN ICE CREAM

1 ½ C. plain soy creamer
1/2 C. plain soy yogurt
1 pkg. (12.3 oz.) silken tofu
1/2 C. maple syrup
1/4 C. vegetable oil
2 tsp. maple or vanilla extract
dash of salt
½-3/4 C. chopped pecans
2 TB. maple syrup

Place all ingredients except the pecans and 2 TB. maple syrup, in a blender and process until smooth and creamy. Chill the mixture before proceeding. Process in an ice cream maker for 10-20 minutes, or until very thick. Add the chopped pecans, mixed with the 2 TB. maple syrup, when the mixture is almost done. Pour into a covered container and freeze until it reaches desired firmness for serving.

## OLD FASHIONED VANILLA ICE CREAM

2 C. plain soy creamer
1 pkg. (12.3 oz.) silken tofu
1/2 C. dry sweetener
2 TB. maple syrup
1-1½ TB. vanilla extract *
1/4 C. vegetable oil
1/8 tsp. salt

Mix all ingredients in a blender until smooth and creamy. Chill the mixture before proceeding. Process in an ice cream maker for 10-20 minutes, or until very thick. Pour into a covered container and freeze until it reaches desired firmness for serving.

**VARIATIONS:** *Fruity Vanilla Ice Cream: Add ½ -1 C. of your favourite diced fruit, during the last few minutes of processing in the ice cream maker.*
*\* **Tip:** The amount of vanilla depends on the quality of the vanilla. Extracts in an alcohol solution tend to be stronger than those in an oil base.*

Increased risk of breast cancer for women who eat butter and cheese 3 or more times a week compared to women who eat these foods less than once a week: 3 times higher.
From John Robbins book - Diet For A New America

# BLUEBERRY FROZEN YOGURT

1 C. lemon or lime soy yogurt (approx. 2-6oz containers)
2 C. soy creamer
1 pkg. (4oz.) Mori Nu vanilla pudding mix
1 ½ C. blueberries (if canned, drain liquid)
1/2 C. sweetener
1/4 C. vegetable oil
1 tsp. vanilla extract

Process all ingredients in a blender until smooth and creamy. Chill the mixture before proceeding. Process in a ice cream maker for 10-20 minutes, or until mixture is very thick. Pour into a covered container and freeze until it reaches desired firmness for serving.

# TROPICAL COCONUT ICE CREAM

*Try serving this ice cream with a chilled, crushed pineapple topping.*

1 C. soy creamer
1 C. canned coconut milk
1 pkg. (12.3 oz.) silken tofu
1/4 C. shredded, unsweetened coconut (optional)
1/4 C. vegetable oil
1 tsp. lemon juice
1/2 C. dry sweetener

Mix all ingredients in a blender until smooth and creamy. Chill the mixture before proceeding. Process in an ice cream maker for 10-20 minutes, or until very thick. Pour into a covered container and freeze until it reaches desired firmness for serving.

# ORANGE MANGO SHERBET

2 C. soy milk or creamer
2 C. orange/mango juice
1 pkg. (4 oz.) Mori Nu vanilla pudding mix
1/4 C. vegetable oil
1/2 C. dry sweetener
1/8 tsp. salt

Mix all ingredients in blender until smooth and creamy. Chill mixture before proceeding. Process in an ice cream maker for 10-20 minutes, or until very thick. Pour into a covered container and freeze until it reaches desired firmness for serving.

**VARIATIONS:** *Substitute pineapple, apple or other fruit juices for the orange mango. Fresh or canned diced fruit may also be added during last few minutes of processing.*

## LEMON SHERBET

1 C. lemon juice
3 C. plain soy creamer
1 pkg. (4oz.) Mori Nu vanilla pudding mix
1 tsp. lemon flavour extract
1/2 C. sweetener
1/3 C. vegetable oil

Mix all ingredients in a blender until smooth and creamy. Pour mixture into a covered container and chill in the freezer compartment or fridge before proceeding. Process in an ice cream maker for 10-20 minutes, or until very thick. Store in the freezer until ready to eat.

## CHOCOLATE OR CAROB COVERED FROZEN BANANAS

3-4 large bananas, peeled
1/2 C. semi-sweet chocolate or carob chips
1/8 C. soy milk
1/4 C. walnuts or other nuts, finely chopped
popsicle type sticks or holders

1. Cut bananas across the middle to produce two pieces. Put a popsicle type stick in each flat end.
2. Have the chopped nuts spread on a cookie sheet or plate.
3. Melt the chocolate with soy milk, beating to combine well. Pour the chocolate mixture on another plate, and roll each banana, first in the chocolate and then in the chopped nuts.
4. Lay bananas on a sheet of waxed paper placed on a cookie sheet or tray. Place uncovered sheet in the freezer. Once the bananas have frozen they are ready to eat, or store in a large freezer bag or covered container.

---

"A true diet is not based on calories but on the organic elements that sustain and give life. Our most common and serious diseases are caused by wrong eating and drinking."
    Jethro Kloss - Back to Eden

---

## EASY AND QUICK FROZEN DELIGHT

*This recipe does not require an ice cream maker, but it does require a Champion juicer or similar device. Use the solid plate on the juicer when making this recipe. Freeze the bananas the day before making this treat. When made in this manner, the banana flavour is not strong and the texture is like custard or soft and creamy ice cream. Serve it with or without fresh crushed fruit, or your favourite sauce.*

**Ingredients:** Three or four frozen bananas; for 2-3 servings.
**To freeze bananas:** Peel bananas and cut into 1 inch chunks. Place chunks on a cookie sheet or plate and place in the freezer. In the morning place frozen chunks in a freezer container, or use immediately. "Juice" the frozen chunks in your Champion juicer, using the solid plate. It will come out the small round opening on the front of the juicer, in a creamy solid form. Serve immediately.

## CHOCOLATE ICECREAM TOPPING

1/2 C. semi-sweet chocolate chips
1 C. French vanilla soy creamer
1/4 C. sweetener
2 TB. Soy margarine

In a saucepan combine chocolate chips, creamer and sweetener. Stir and bring the mixture to a boil. Reduce heat and simmer for 5 minutes, or until it is slightly thickened. Remove from heat and stir in 2 TB. soy margarine. Serve immediately or let cool. Do not cover the sauce as it is cooling. The condensation will change its consistency. Makes 1 cup.

**VARIATIONS:** *Replace chocolate with carob. If using plain creamer, add 1-2 tsp. vanilla extract, or try mint instead of vanilla.*

## SIMPLE JUICICLES

fresh or canned fruit juice
popsicle molds

Fill molds with juice and freeze until solid. This is a refreshing treat on a hot summer day.
**VARIATION:** *Include a piece or two of cubed fresh fruit with the juice.*

# Beverages

## "EGG" NOG

1 lb. soft tofu (or 2-10 ½ oz pkgs. silken tofu)
2 C. soy milk
2 TB. sweetener (or to taste)
1/4 tsp. turmeric
nutmeg

Blend all except nutmeg until smooth and creamy. Serve well chilled with nutmeg sprinkled on top. Makes 4 servings.


## HOT COCOA

2 C. soy milk
3 TB. cocoa or carob powder
2 TB. sweetener (or to taste)

pinch of salt
1/2 tsp. vanilla extract

In a medium size pan combine all ingredients. Whisk and stir over low/medium heat until well combined and hot. Makes two servings. * Use part soy creamer for a richer version, or substitute any alternative vegan beverage.

**VARIATIONS:** Cocoa by the cup: *In a mug - mix 1½ TB. cocoa, 2 TB. soy milk powder, and 2-3 tsp. sweetener. Pour 1 cup boiling water into the cup. Whisk until well combined.*
Cold Cocoa: *Dissolve cocoa and sweetener in a small amount of hot water, and add remaining ingredients. Chill before serving.*


## MOCHA SOY BEVERAGE
*A coffee like flavoured drink. Serve hot or cold.*

2 heaping tsp. grain coffee substitute
1 C. heated soy milk
1/4 tsp. cardamom powder (optional)

Mix heated milk with coffee substitute and cardamom. Whisk to blend and foam. Sweeten to taste. Makes one cup.

**VARIATION:** *Use all boiling water instead of soymilk and serve "black" or with just a splash of soymilk or soy creamer.*

## INDIAN STYLE LEMON/LIMEADE

4 C. water
1/4 C. lime juice
1/4 C. lemon juice
1/2 C. maple syrup or other sweetener (or to taste)
1/2-3/4 tsp. ginger powder
pinch of cayenne pepper (optional)

Blend or stir all ingredients together. Chill before serving. It can be put in a blender with ice for a quick, cold and frothy beverage. Adjust sweetener to your preference. Makes 4 servings.
**VARIATION:** _Traditional Lemonade_: _Use all lemon juice and eliminate the ginger and cayenne._


## ICED "CANADIAN" TEA

4 Raspberry Zinger teabags (Celestial seasonings)
2 C. boiling water
1/2 C. raspberry vinegar *
1/8 tsp. stevia powder  (or ½ C. sweetener, or to taste)
6 C. cold water

Steep tea bags in 2 cups boiling water for at least 20 minutes. Remove bags. Add remaining ingredients and the additional 6 cups of cold water. Chill well before serving. Makes 1/2 gal. * _If raspberry vinegar is not available, you can substitute another fruit or cider vinegar, but the raspberry vinegar is what makes this drink so delicious._


## ICED OR HOT THAI TEA

4 C. water
4 black or green tea bags (or 8 tsp. bulk tea leaves)
1-1 ½ tsp. cardamom powder
1/4 -1/2 C. sweetener *
1 C. soy milk

In a small saucepan bring 4 cups of water to a boil. Turn off heat and add the tea bags, and steep for at least 20 minutes. Remove bags and add remaining ingredients, and heat to desired temperature, or add ice and serve cold. Makes 4 servings.
**VARIATION:** _Iced Jasmine Thai:_ _Eliminate the cardamom. Use jasmine tea, and simply add desired sweetener and soy milk or creamer, to steeped and cooled tea. * A few drops of liquid stevia can be substituted for the sweetener._

## CALMING CHAI TEA

2 C. water
1/2 -1 cinnamon stick or 1 tsp. cinnamon powder
1 tsp. cardamom powder
1/2 tsp. whole cloves or 1/4 tsp. ground
1-2 tsp. finely grated ginger root or 1/2 tsp. ginger powder
1/8 tsp. each: ground pepper and nutmeg
1 TB. dried mint leaves (2-4 tea bags or approx. 1/2 C. fresh mint leaves)
2 C. soymilk
1/2 C. sweetener (or to taste)

1. In a saucepan combine water with everything except mint, soy milk and sweetener.
Bring to a boil and simmer at least 10 minutes. Whole spices can be tied in a mesh bag or
put in a tea ball.
2. Add the mint tea bags or loose mint in a tea ball, and remove from heat.
3. Steep 5-10 minutes or longer. Remove the tea bags and whole spices, or strain the
liquid. Add soymilk and sweetener to taste and put back on the stove, heating to desired
temperature. Serve hot or chill and serve cold. Four servings.
**VARIATIONS:** <u>Black or green tea Chai</u>: *Substitute black or green tea for the mint.*
<u>Yerba Mate Chai:</u> *Use all Yerba Mate tea or a blend of Yerba and green or black tea.* <u>Chai Latte:</u>
*Eliminate the soy milk in step 3. Serve Chai in individual cups with or without a topping of frothed soy
milk or creamer. Add more sweetener if desired.*


## PEP-UP DRINK

*This beverage is great for breakfast, or any time of the day that you need a quick pick me up.*

1 C. soymilk or fruit juice
1 tsp. ground flax seed
1 tsp. flax oil
1/2-1 tsp. lecithin granules
1-3 tsp. green powder (such as spirulina, chlorella, alfalfa)
1 ripe banana or other fruit (frozen or fresh)
1-3 tsp. soy protein powder (optional)
1 TB. raw almonds or sunflower seeds
1-3 tsp. nutritional yeast flakes
1 tsp. vitamin C. powder (optional)

Combine all ingredients in a blender and mix until well combined and smooth. Serve at
room temperature or chilled. Frozen fruit will make a thicker and immediately colder
beverage. Makes 1 large serving. **VARIATIONS:** *All ingredients are optional. Any number of
nutritious items can be added, such as: wheat germ, wheat bran, calcium and ginseng powder.*

## ORANGE N' SOY PROTEIN DRINK

*This drink is rich in protein, calcium and vitamin C.*

1/2 C. soymilk
2 TB. soy protein powder
1 TB. calcium/magnesium powder (optional)

1/2 C. fresh or frozen orange juice
1 TB. ground flax or flax oil
2 tsp. lecithin granules

Mix in a blender until smooth and frothy.   Makes 1 serving.   **Suggestions**: *Replace orange juice with your favourite juice.  Add fresh or frozen fruit such as bananas or berries.*


## FRESH FRUIT JUICE SMOOTHIE

2 C. apple juice
1 C. raspberries, or other berries
2 frozen bananas cut in small chunks

Process all ingredients in a blender until thick and smooth.  Makes 2 servings.

**Suggestions:** *Add a scoop of your favourite vegan protein powder and some green powder, such as spirulina or chlorella.  Experiment with different fruit combinations.*

**Tip:  To Freeze bananas:** *Peel bananas and cut into small chunks.  Place bananas on a cookie sheet or plate,  and place in the freezer.  When frozen use immediately, or transfer to a freezer container or bag, for later use.*


## QUICK FRUIT JUICE SPRITZER

*Mix the following ingredients together and pour over ice.  Makes one serving.*

1 C. cold fruit juice (such as grape, cherry, or apple)
1/4 – 1/2 C. sparkling mineral water.

> "The average person does not drink enough pure water.  At least 6 glasses must be taken daily…. more is better depending on the kind of food eaten…When one drinks an abundance of pure, fresh water, the blood and tissues are bathed and purified, thereby being cleansed of all poisons and waste matter."
> Jethro Kloss, - Back to Eden

## SPICY GARDEN VEGGIE JUICE

6 carrots
3 stalks celery
4 large tomatoes
1 C. greens
  (kale, chard, spinach, arugala)
1/4 C. fresh parsley

1/2  small onion
1 garlic clove (optional)
1/8 C. fresh or l tsp. dried basil
1/8 tsp. fresh hot pepper (optional)
1½ tsp. Braggs liquid Aminos or tamari
  salt and pepper to taste

In an electric juicer, process the carrots, celery, tomatoes, greens, parsley, onion and garlic.
Remove from juicer and stir in the remaining ingredients.  Salt and pepper to taste.
Makes 2 servings.


## PINK JUICE DELIGHT

*This fresh juice is high in iron, vitamin A and much more.  The apples give it a sweet taste.  The beets give it a beautiful pink colour.*

4 medium size apples (cored)
3 large carrots
1-2  beets

Cut the apples, carrots and beets into pieces that fit into the juicer opening.  Save the beet
greens to use in a salad.  Juice and enjoy.  Makes one large or two small servings.
**Variation:** *Add some ginger or garlic.*


## IRON BOOSTER TONIC
*Feeling tired and out of sorts?  Try this iron rich tonic.*

1-2 tsp. organic blackstrap molasses
1/4 –1/2 C. warm water

Mix molasses in warm water, and drink.  You can also eat molasses directly from a spoon.
Make sure you rinse your mouth out with water after doing this.

# THE LEMONADE DIET DRINK

*Along with colon cleanse teas and internal salt baths, many people, including myself, have found Stanley Burroughs lemonade fast and his book: "The Master Cleanser, with special needs and Problems," to be life changing. Fasting from food, even for one day, gives the body a chance to rest and rejuvenate. Here's my recipe for a half-gallon. Drink it whenever you feel thirsty or hungry during a fast. The combination of lemon, maple syrup and cayenne pepper acts as a cleanser and a body builder. Hot herbal teas can also be consumed. (If you have health issues or concerns, consult a health care professional before beginning any fast. Stanley Burrough's book gives complete instructions for those with diabetes.)*

Mix in a half-gallon jug:  the juice of 3 fresh lemons, 1/4-3/4 tsp. hot cayenne pepper, (adjust amount depending on the heat of pepper) 1/2 C. maple syrup, (grade B is best, as it contains more minerals and is less expensive) and enough pure or distilled water to fill the jug. (Always use fresh lemons, not bottled.)

**Note: Internal salt baths** *are quite helpful in cases of constipation or for cleaning the colon tract, especially during a fast from food. Plan on being home on the day of an internal salt bath. Refer to a box of Epsom salts for complete directions. Normally 2-4 tsp. Epsom salts is used for adults older than twelve, in an 8 oz. glass of warm water, and consumed on an empty stomach. Limit two doses a day. Lemon juice can be added to enhance flavour. Two alternative solutions are: 2 tsp. sea salt in a quart of warm water. Drink the entire quart on an empty stomach, or drink the sea salt in a 4 oz. glass of water, immediately followed by 3 ½ cups of unsalted water. Or, mix 1 TB. glauber salts (sodium sulphate) with 8 oz. of warm water. The saline solution helps to draw the toxic lymph and body wastes to the intestines and out of the body through bowel elimination. Drink additional water and 4-8 cups of freshly squeezed citrus juice throughout the day, after drinking the salt solution. The juice will have an alkalizing effect on the entire system.*

"Vegetable juices are the builders and regenerators of the body. They contain all the amino acids, minerals, salts, enzymes, and vitamins needed by the human body, provided they are used fresh, raw and without preservatives, and that they have been properly extracted from the vegetables."
N.W. Walker D.Sc., - Fresh Vegetable and Fruit Juices

# KOMBUCHA BEVERAGE

*This is a rejuvenating beverage made with tea, sweetener and a kombucha culture. It is reputed to assist with digestion, metabolism, liver function, immune system, weight control, alkalizing the body, anti-aging, improving condition of skin and hair, and to revitalize, recharge, detoxify and renew the body. Cultures produce "baby" cultures during the brewing process, which can be purchased or received as gifts from kombucha brewing friends. When on the road, checkout GT's organic, raw Kombucha, available at most natural food stores. (Please read Important Notes & Tips before proceeding)*

3-4 Qts. Purified water
1 C. dry sweetener
5 tea bags (black, or green) or a
combination of black or green and herbal

4 oz. reserved kombucha beverage
　　or 1 oz. apple cider vinegar
1 kombucha culture (1/16-1/8 inch thick)

Bring water to a boil in a stainless steel pot. Add sweetener and simmer for 5 minutes. Remove from heat and add the five tea bags. (caffeinated tea sometimes produces a better quality beverage. Bulk tea leaves can also be used. Tie them in a muslin bag or put them in a tea ball.) Steep tea for at least 20 minutes. Remove bags and let mixture cool down. When liquid is cool, pour it into a gallon size glass, stoneware or pyrex jar, or container with a wide mouth top; wide enough for oxygen to enter. Add reserved beverage and place kombucha culture on top of the liquid. (It may sink to the bottom, but it will eventually rise) Place a piece of breathable cloth over the top of container. Secure it with a rubber band or string. (Make sure that the cloth is heavy enough to keep out fruit flies and ants. A piece of cotton muslin is usually adequate.) Place the jar in a dry, dark corner of the kitchen, and protect the jar from any sunlight, by wrapping the sides with a towel. Check the kombucha in 7-10 days by tasting it. The end result should be tart and slightly carbonated in taste. In cooler rooms it may take 10 days or longer. 72 - 80 degrees fahrenheit is the optimal brewing temperature. Remove cultures and store liquid in the refrigerator. Kombucha can be mixed with a little fruit juice for a different flavour. *Lemon and ginger are tasty additions.*

## IMPORTANT NOTES & TIPS:

- *Once the kombucha culture has been added, never allow metal to come in contact with it. Store the kombucha beverage in non-metal containers, such as quart canning jars, and in the refrigerator.*
- *Begin drinking Kombucha in small amounts, 2-4 ounces in the morning, for 7-10 days. If any adverse reactions result; such as excess intestinal gas, itching, rashes, nausea, or a yeast infection, discontinue using until you have consulted a health care practitioner.*
- *Do not drink your Kombucha if it develops an acid or chemical smell similar to that of nail polish remover. This indicates that the beverage lacked oxygen. Another warning signal is the presence of black growths on the culture, indicating mold. These can be extremely dangerous. To avoid this, never grow the culture in a room with potted plants, or near or downwind of a garden compost pile.*
- *Carefully separate the baby culture from the original culture after brewing, and store the cultures for future use in a covered container with a little beverage. Let a little air in the container every 3-4 days. Remember to save 4 oz. of the finished Kombucha beverage for the next batch.*
- *Replace the culture every 5-6 batches. Solar steeped tea also works well for making Kombucha.*

# Home Canning

# PICKLES, JAMS & PRESERVES

**TIPS:**
Most of these recipes can be frozen as well as canned, except for pickles and kraut, which should be canned, stored in the fridge or a very cool pantry.
**For other canning possibilities: Horseradish Sauce pg. 158 & Pesto pg. 156**

## STEP-BY-STEP INSTRUCTIONS FOR HOME CANNING

1. Always select quality ingredients at their peak of freshness.
2. Process acid type foods in a boiling water bath. Acid foods include: jellies, jams, preserves, fruits, tomatoes, pickles and relishes.
3. Process low acid foods, such as squash, carrots, potatoes and beans, in a pressure canner, unless you are pickling them in an acid vinegar mixture.
4. Wash jars, lids and bands in hot soapy water. Rinse well. Keep jars and lids in hot water until ready to use.
5. Fill jars with prepared recipe. Leave a headspace of 1/4-1/2 inch for fruit juices, pickles and soft spreads; 1/2 inch for fruits and tomatoes, 1 inch for vegetables.
6. Wipe rim and threads of jars with a clean, damp cloth. Screw bands down tightly.
7. Place jars in a canner of boiling hot water. Cover with lid and bring water back to rolling boil. Process filled jars as per individual recipe, counting from the time kettle water is bubbling.
8. When processing time is complete, remove jars from canner. Set them upright on a towel to cool. Bands should not be retightened. Let jars cool 12-24 hours before putting them away. After jars are cool, test for a seal by pressing the center of the lid. If the lid does *not* flex up and down, the lid is sealed. The bands can then be removed, if they are needed for canning other jars. Wipe jars and lids with a damp cloth. Label and store jars in a cool, dark place.
9. High acid fruits and vegetables, especially pickles, can be canned without the water bath. Have the jars, lids, preparation or brine boiling hot. Clean rims of jars well. Put lids and rings on the jars. As the jars and ingredients cool down, the lids should naturally seal.

---

*"To forget how to dig the earth and to tend the soil is to forget ourselves."*
*Mahatma Gandhi (1869-1948) - Hindu pacifist & spiritual leader*

---

# GREEN TOMATO MINCEMEAT

*This version combines the best of two old family recipes.*

9 C. (about 5 lb. or 17 medium size) green tomatoes, finely chopped or ground
9 C. finely chopped or ground apples, cored and unpeeled
3/4 C. vegetable oil
2 C. (1 lb.) raisins
1 ½ TB. lemon rind, grated
1/2 C. lemon juice
1/2 C. apple cider vinegar
3/4 C. orange juice
4 C. sweetener
2 tsp. cinnamon
1 tsp. allspice
2 tsp. nutmeg
1 tsp. cloves
1 tsp. salt
1 C. walnuts or pecans, diced

Bring all ingredients to a boil in a large kettle.  Stir frequently.
Turn heat down and simmer ingredients uncovered for an additional 1 hour,
or until thick.  Pack in hot, sterilized jars, and process in hot water bath for 20 minutes.
Makes 5-6 Quarts.  It can be used immediately for making mincemeat pie.

**TO MAKE MINCEMEAT PIE:** *See page 199 for piecrust recipe.  Fill unbaked pie shell with 1 quart of mincemeat.  Cover with top crust, cutting a couple of slits in center of crust.  Bake at 450° for 10 minutes, using foil or a metal ring to protect the fluted edge.  Lower heat to 350° and continue baking for 40-50 minutes, or until done.*

---

*Growing your own food is one of the most rewarding experiences; from the planting, caretaking, harvesting, eating and storing, to the processing for wintertime enjoyment.  When you grow your own veggies and fruits, you can harvest them when they have reached just the right stage of maturity for eating, canning, drying, freezing or storing in a cool pantry or root cellar.  By growing organically, one can eliminate harmful chemicals and learn to garden with the natural elements; planting at appropriate times for better growth, and to reduce the possibility of insect infestation.  Astrological principles can be incorporated, whereby planting is done at moon phase times that assist with fertility, or for better harvesting and storage. Companion planting is another method whereby various plants and herbs assist each other with growth and disease resistance.  If you live in the city, or don't have enough room to grow a garden, try growing veggies in pots on your patio, or in a sunny window, join or start a community garden project, or buy organic produce from local growers.*

# DILL PICKLES & OTHER VEGGIES

*It's quite easy to turn any surplus garden veggie into a gourmet dilled treat; or buy veggies from an organic vendor at your local farmer's market. Pack whole or sliced veggies in hot sterilized canning jars, and pour the following brine solution over the veggies. Seal jars in a hot water bath for 5 minutes after the water comes to a boil. Take jars out of bath immediately, being careful not to process too long, or the veggies will be overcooked and not crispy.* **Tip for crisper pickles:** *If the jars, lids and brine are boiling hot, you can eliminate the 5-minute water bath. As the liquid and jars cool down, the lids should seal naturally, and you avoid the possibility of over cooking the veggies.*

## PICKLING BRINE:

| | |
|---|---|
| 6 C. apple cider vinegar | 3/4 C. sea salt |
| 9 C. water | 2 TB. pickling spice mix. |

Bring the above ingredients to a boil. Reduce heat and simmer for 5-10 minutes. This is enough for about 8 quarts of veggies. In each jar of veggies, (cucumbers, beans, mixed veggies, etc.) fill with the brine and optional ingredients, leaving a half inch headspace, then seal as per above information.

**Optional Ingredients:** 1 or more cloves of garlic, 1-2 heads of dill weed, (especially for dill pickles) 1/2 tsp. cayenne pepper, (or a few slices of fresh, hot pepper)

## SWEET N' SOUR CURRY PICKLES

| | |
|---|---|
| 6 large or 12 small cucumbers* sliced thin, or in chunks. | 1 C. water |
| 10 medium size onions, sliced | 1 ½ C. dry sweetener |
| 2 large sweet red peppers, sliced | 3 TB. mixed pickling spices |
| 1/2 C. sea salt | 2 TB celery salt |
| Soaking water | 1 tsp. curry powder |
| 2 C. apple cider vinegar | |

1. Mix sliced cucumber, onions and peppers in a large pot, and sprinkle with salt and enough cold water to cover veggies. Let soak 4-6 hours or overnight. In the morning, drain but don't rinse.

2. To the veggie mixture add, vinegar, 1 C. water, sweetener, spices tied in cheesecloth or in tea ball, and celery salt. Heat to boiling and simmer 15 minutes. Remove from heat and add curry powder and stir well. Ladle into hot, sterilized canning jars. Process in boiling water bath for 5 minutes after water comes to a boil, or eliminate bath and let lids seal naturally as the jars cool. Makes 6 pints.

**OTHER IDEAS:** <u>Sweet n' Sour Curry Zucchini Pickles</u>: *\* Bumper crop of zucchini? Use zucchini instead of cucumbers.*

## AGGIE'S MUSTARD PICKLES

2 quarts (about 24 small) green tomatoes
2 quarts (about 24 small) cucumbers
2 heads (about 2 quarts) cauliflower
2 quarts (3 lbs.) small white onions, left whole (the marble size ones)
1 ¼ C. pickling or sea salt
water for soaking
4 C. apple cider vinegar
2 C. water
2-4 C. dry sweetener, (depending on your sweet preference.)
1 C. flour
6 TB. dry mustard
2 TB. turmeric
1 ½ oz. celery seed

1. Cut up tomatoes, cucumbers, and cauliflower into bite size pieces. Mix in a large pot along with onions. Cover the veggies with the salt and enough water to come to top of veggies. Soak overnight in a cool place. Next morning drain off the salt water, but don't rinse.
2. Combine the remaining ingredients in a saucepan. Bring to a boil, and then simmer slowly for 10-15 minutes. Pour this mixture over the veggies and bring everything to a boil. Turn heat down and simmer for 5-15 minutes. Pour mixture into pint jars and process in a hot water bath, for 5 minutes after the bath comes to a boil. Makes 12-16 pints

## ZUCCHINI PICKLES

*What to do with all those zucchini?!*

2 C. apple cider vinegar
1/2 C. dry sweetener
1/4 C. sea salt
1 tsp. celery seed
1 tsp. turmeric powder
1/2 tsp. ground mustard powder

8 C. thinly sliced unpeeled zucchini
   (or cut in bite size pieces)
2 C. onions, sliced
2-4 garlic cloves, minced

Bring vinegar, sweetener, salt, celery seed, turmeric, and mustard to a boil. Pour mixture over sliced zucchini, onions and garlic. Set aside for 1-2 hours. Bring everything to a boil and simmer for 2-3 minutes. Fill pint jars and process in boiling water bath for 5 minutes, to seal the jars. Makes 4 pints.
**VARIATION:** Dilled Zucchini Pickles: *Add or substitute 2 tsp. dill seeds for the turmeric.*

# GREEN TOMATO RELISH

1 gallon (about 40 small) green tomatoes, finely chopped or ground
2 medium size onions, minced
2 large red peppers, seeded and finely chopped
4 large green peppers, seeded and finely chopped
1/2 C. sea salt
1 tsp. pickling spice mix
3 C. apple cider vinegar
1 C. water
1 C. maple syrup or other sweetener

Chop and mix veggies.  Mix in the salt, and let stand in a cool place 4-6 hours, or overnight.  Place pickling spices in a tea ball or cheesecloth.  Combine spices and all remaining ingredients along with veggies, and simmer 30 minutes or until mixture is thick.  Ladle hot mixture into canning jars, and process in hot water bath for 5 minutes after the water comes to a boil. Makes 6-8 pints

# SWEET CORN N' CABBAGE RELISH

8 C. fresh or canned corn (about 10-12 ears)
4 C. green or red cabbage, finely chopped or shredded
1 C. each of green & red peppers, seeded and diced
1 C. onions, finely chopped
4 C. apple cider vinegar
1 C. dry sweetener
2 TB. dry mustard
2 TB. sea salt or pickling salt
1 TB. turmeric
1 C. water

In a large pot combine all of the ingredients, and bring to a boil over high heat.  Reduce heat and simmer for 10-20 minutes. Fill canning jars within an inch of their tops.  Hot water process for 5 minutes after water comes to a boil.  Remove jars and set on a towel to cool. Makes 6-9 pints.

> "To own a bit of ground, to scratch it with a hoe, to plant seeds, and watch the renewal of life-this is the commonest delight of the race, the most satisfactory thing a man can do."
>
> - Charles Dudley Warner

## SWEET ZUCCHINI RELISH

9 C. finely grated or ground zucchini
2-4 C. grated onions
4 TB. sea salt
2½ C. apple cider vinegar
2-3 C. dry sweetener
1 TB. dry mustard powder
3/4 tsp. each of ground nutmeg & turmeric
1½ tsp. celery seed
1/2 tsp. ground black pepper
3/4 TB. cornstarch
1 red and 1 green pepper, finely chopped

Mix finely grated zucchini and onion with 4 TB. salt, and let sit covered overnight. In the morning rinse the ground mixture in cold water and drain well.

In a large kettle mix vinegar with sweetener, spices and cornstarch and bring to a boil. Turn heat down and simmer about 10 minutes. Add zucchini and onion mixture along with green and red peppers. Cook for another 30 minutes, or until mixture is thick. Fill hot jars with relish. Clean tops of jars before screwing ring and lid in place. Process jars in hot water bath for 5 minutes after water comes to a boil. Makes 5-6 pints.


## NEW MEXICO SALSA

3-4 lbs. (12 medium) ripe tomatoes, chopped
3-4 jalapeno or other small hot pepper, minced
1/3 C. onion, finely chopped
10-12 cloves of garlic, minced
1/2 C. green pepper, finely chopped
1/4 C. fresh cilantro, minced
1 tsp. cumin powder
1/3 C. fresh parsley, minced
2 tsp. sea salt
1/3 C. lime juice

Cook all ingredients until the mixture is of desired thickness. Pour into pint jars, and seal in hot water bath, processing 5 minutes after water comes to a boil. Makes 2-3 half-pints.
**Note**: *Adjust hot peppers to your heat preference.*

## GARDEN FRESH TOMATO/SPAGETTI SAUCE

60-80 medium size tomatoes
1–2 large onions, chopped
6 or more cloves garlic, minced
1/3-1 C. fresh oregano, chopped (1-3 TB. dried)
2-3 TB. fresh thyme (1-2 tsp. dried)
1/4–1/2 C. fresh basil, chopped (2-4 tsp. dried)
1/8 C. fresh dill weed (1 tsp. dried)
salt and pepper to taste

There are two ways to make this sauce. One way is to use your electric juicer. If you don't have an electric juicer, you can put the tomatoes in a large kettle with a little bit of water in the bottom. Bring the tomatoes to a boil, then simmer until they are soft. Put this mixture through a hand operated food mill, to remove the skins and most of the seeds. Put the juice from the food mill or the electric juicer back in the large kettle. Add all of the remaining ingredients in the proportions that you prefer….more spices for more tomatoes, or for a spicier mixture. Simmer the mixture until it has reduced in quantity and is of the desired thickness. Taste for seasonings and salt and pepper to taste, adding more spices if necessary. This sauce can be used immediately over your favourite pasta, or sealed in canning jars for later use. Makes 4-6 quarts

> **TIP: THREE WAYS TO REMOVE TOMATO SKINS: 1.** *Drop whole tomatoes (very briefly) in a pot of boiling water until skins soften. Remove from pot and skins can be easily removed.* **2.** *Cook chopped tomatoes until soft, and then put them through a hand operated food mill. The sauce will come out the bottom, and the peels will stay in the mill.* **3.** *Use an electric juicer.*

## DEBBIE'S CHILI SAUCE

30 - 40 medium size ripe tomatoes
  (peeled and chopped)
2 ½ lb. medium size small onions (chopped)
1 bunch of celery (chopped)
2-3 hot peppers (chopped)
2-3 sweet peppers (chopped)
1 ½ C. apple cider vinegar
1 tsp. allspice
1-1 ½ C. dry sweetener

2 small cans tomato paste
3-4 large cloves of garlic (minced)
1 tsp. dry mustard
1-2 tsp. ground cloves
1-2 tsp. regular or seasoned salt
1 tsp. each of nutmeg, cinnamon, mustard
  seeds, worcestershire sauce
1 tsp. cayenne pepper (optional)

Cook the tomatoes until soft, before adding the rest of ingredients. Simmer until thick. Test for taste and adjust seasonings if necessary. Seal in pint jars in a hot water bath for 5-10 minutes, after the water comes to a boil. Makes 4-6 pints.

## PICKLED GARLIC

*You will need a lot of garlic heads to fill a half-pint jar. This recipe makes enough brine for 3-4 pints or 6-8 half pint jars.*

10-15 heads of garlic
1-2 red peppers, sliced in slivers (optional)
2 C. apple cider vinegar

1/2 C. dry sweetener
1 tsp. mustard seed
1 tsp. celery seed

1. Fill 1/2 pint or smaller jars with peeled garlic cloves and strips of red pepper.
2. In a saucepan bring vinegar, sweetener, mustard and celery seed to a boil. Turn heat down and simmer 10-15 minutes.
3. Strain hot vinegar mixture to remove seeds and pour over garlic, leaving 1/2" between garlic and top of jars.  Process jars in hot water bath for 5 minutes, or to avoid the possibility of over cooking the garlic, eliminate the water bath, and let the jars seal naturally as they cool down.

## SAUERKRAUT

5 lbs. shredded cabbage

3 TB. sea salt (not iodized)

1. Mix cabbage and salt in a large bowl.  Let the cabbage wilt, and then transfer it to a medium size ceramic crock or glass container.  Tuck a clean piece of cotton cloth, such as muslin, over the cabbage and down the sides.
2. Place the largest plate you have that will fit in the crock, on top of the cloth and cabbage.
3. Put a quart jar filled with water on top of the plate. This acts as a weight.
4. Cover the crock with a towel, so that the kraut is protected from dust but can still breathe. Place kraut in a cool room, around 68 degrees. The cooler the room the slower the kraut will ferment, and the better tasting the kraut will be.  If you have a room that stays just above freezing, the kraut can stay in the crock over the winter, once it has fermented, where you can scoop it out for eating. Otherwise it will need to be sealed in pint or quart jars to stop the fermentation process.
5. Check the kraut the next couple of days to see that the liquid is reaching the top of the plate.  If not, increase the weight on the plate by adding more jars of water.  Continue to monitor the process a couple of times a week, adjusting the jars weight if the liquid rises above the plate. Skim any film off the top of kraut and wash and re-apply the cloth.
6. Fermentation will stop after 2-6 weeks, depending on the temperature of the room.  A temperature of 68-72° is best for the fermentation process.  When the fermentation is finished, move the crock to a room that is at least 50° or lower, but not freezing.  You can scoop your kraut directly from the crock.  If you don't have a room that will consistently stay at this cool temperature, pack kraut in clean, hot, sterilized jars to 1" of top.  If the kraut lacks enough juice, you can make a weak brine by mixing 1 quart of warm water and 1 ½ TB. salt, and pour this into the jars.  Process in hot water bath for 10 minutes.   Fresh kraut will keep for weeks in the refrigerator without being processed.   Makes 4-5 pints.

## OLD FASHIONED APPLESAUCE

*Quick and easy to make for serving immediately, or can or freeze for later.*

Wash, core and peel at least 8-10 large apples.
Chop apples into small pieces, and cook with enough water in bottom of a pot, to keep fruit from sticking to pan. Stir and simmer until apples are soft. Add sweetener to taste, and sprinkle with cinnamon. Eat now or can in hot water bath, or freeze for later.

**Note:** *If you like a smoother applesauce, put the cooked apples through a food mill or in a blender. If using a Foley food mill, or similar device, the apples can be cooked without peeling, as only the sauce will go through the food mill screen.*

## APPLE BUTTER

10 lbs. apples (a mixture of varieties makes a great flavour)
2 C. apple cider or water
1/2 tsp. each of cinnamon, & allspice (optional)
1/4 tsp. cloves (optional)
1/4 tsp. salt

Cut up cored and peeled or unpeeled apples and place in a large kettle with water or cider. Cook mixture until apples are soft; then put them through a food mill, or puree in a blender. Test for sweetness and adjust by adding preferred sweetener. Stir in spices and salt. Pour the mixture into a roasting or baking pan, and place in a 250° oven for 2-3 hours, or until thickened to desired consistency. Stir every half hour or so. Pour into canning jars and seal, or store in freezer. Makes 5-6 pints.

PEAR BUTTER : Use same amount of pears as apples, and continue as with apple butter, adjusting sweetness.
GRAPE BUTTER : Use 1 gallon of grapes to 1/2 C. water in kettle. Heat and mash grapes, and cook until grapes are soft. Put mixture through a food mill or press, to remove the seeds and skin. Fill a baking pan with the grape mixture, and cook the same way as apple butter. (No spices are necessary.)

> *"Our daily lives, the way we eat, drink, walk, all has to do with the world situation."*
> Thich Nhat Hanh -Buddhist Monk & author

## BERRY JAM

9 C. washed raspberries, strawberries or other berries
3 C. dry sweetener

Bring fruit and 1½ C. dry sweetener to a boil. Reduce heat and simmer and stir for 5 minutes. Add remaining 1½ C. sweetener and continue to simmer and stir until desired thickness is reached. Pour jam into canning jars and freeze or process in hot water bath to seal lids.
Makes 4 pints or 8 -1/2 pints.


## VERY BERRY TOPPING     *A great topping for "cheese" cake or pudding.*

9 C. berries (raspberries, strawberries or blueberries, or a combination of fruit)
1½ C. dry sweetener

Combine berries and sweetener. If using strawberries, slice or chop them first. Bring mixture to a boil; reduce heat and simmer, without crushing the berries, just long enough to dissolve the sweetener. Store in the refrigerator or freezer for later use, or pour into pint canning jars, and process in a hot water bath, for 5 minutes, to seal the lids. Makes 3-4 pints.


## RHUBERRY JAM

*The rhubarb gives this jam a very creamy texture without affecting the berry taste.*

2 C. crushed berries (raspberries or strawberries)
6 C. rhubarb, diced or ground  (scalded in boiling water, then drained)
2-3 C. dry sweetener or 1½ -2 C. maple syrup

Bring fruit and 2 C. sweetener to a boil. Boil and stir 5 minutes.
Test mixture for sweetness and add more sweetener if necessary.
Lower heat and simmer and stir for 10-15 minutes, or until thick.
Pour into jars and process in boiling water bath for 5 minutes, or store in the freezer.
Makes 3-4 pints.

---

**TIP**: To speed up the thickening process for jam making---add a couple slices of apple to the mixture, for natural pectin.

---

# FRESH CANNED BLUEBERRIES

*This is a quick and easy way to preserve the summer's crop, for use in pies and other baked Goods. Any fresh berry can be canned this way. When making pies, use the liquid too.*

Fill hot pint or quart jars with berries, shaking jars and gently pressing the berries down to make room for more. Add about 1/2 C. boiling hot water to each jar.
Seal jars in hot water bath for 5 minutes after water comes to a boil.

**Note:** *Sweetener is not necessary. If you prefer to add it during canning, rather than in the pie or baked goods, add approximately 1/2 C. to each cup of boiling water.*

# GINGERED PEARS

16 C. pears (approx. 5 lbs.) peeled and chopped
1/2 - 1 C. fresh ginger, very finely diced
    (if you really like ginger, use a full cup)
3/4 C. lemon juice (fresh squeezed or bottled)
1 C. dry sweetener
1 C. water
1/2 C. apple cider vinegar

Soak ginger in lemon juice for at least 2 hours.
While this soaks, prepare pears. Cover chopped pears with sweetener.
Pour the ginger, lemon juice mixture over the pears.
Cook all ingredients except vinegar in an un-lidded pot, until pears are soft and clear. Stir to prevent sticking, and cook until the liquid is slightly thick. At last 5 minutes of cooking add apple cider vinegar. Pour mixture into hot sterilized jars and seal in hot water bath 10-20 minutes, or freeze in appropriate containers, or store all or part of pear mixture in the fridge. Makes 3-4 pints.

---

Although vegetarian Issac Singer appreciated the health aspects of vegetarianism, he states very clearly that the ethical consideration is primary. "Even if eating flesh was actually shown to be good for you, I would certainly not eat it."

---

## OVEN DRIED APPLE SLICES

Core and cut apples into ¼" slices. Place apple slices on a fine wire or plastic mesh screen. There are four ways you can proceed from here. 1. Place screen inside your gas oven, on the rack, and let the warmth of the pilot light do the job of drying. 2. Place screen in a preheated 100° oven. 3. Place screen in an electric oven, or without the gas pilot on, and replace the interior oven light bulb with a 100 watt bulb. This bulb will keep the oven at a consistent temperature for drying the apples. 4. Use a dehydrator specifically designed for food drying. A simple dryer can be made, by using an oven that no longer works. Set it up in your basement, spare room or corner of a room, with a 100 watt light bulb inside. Apples will dry in 2-3 hours, or when dry and firm to the touch. **Note:** *Most fruits, vegetables and herbs can be dried in this manner.*

## AIR DRIED APPLE SLICES

If you have a wood stove or a dry and warm area in your home, you can string sliced apple rings above the stove or in a warm area. They will take 1-3 days to dry, depending on your areas humidity. You can also lay apple slices on a fine wire or plastic mesh screen, cover with cheesecloth so that the cloth doesn't touch the fruit, and place the screen in a dry, shady area outside, or in a dry warm attic. Make sure that air can circulate under and all around the screen. Drying apples or any other fruit outside in this way can be tricky. Keep a close eye on them, and bring the fruit in at night, to avoid damp evenings or hungry animals. Hanging the fruit in a dry, warm room or above the wood stove, should bring consistently good results. **Note:** *herbs and other cut up produce can also be air dried.*

## SOLAR HERB VINEGARS

*Almost any herb can be used to season vinegar. Some suggestions are: tarragon, basil, oregano, rosemary, mint, lemon balm, sage and dill.*

**TO PREPARE:**
To each cup of apple cider vinegar add 2-4 Tb. or a sprig or two of fresh herbs, using only a single herb in each jar. Set the lidded jars in the sun for 2-3 weeks, or until vinegar is nicely flavoured. Check jars periodically for desired aroma, and then store in a cool place. Strain vinegar if desired, before using. **Note:** *For those lacking sunlight at the time of harvest: Put 2 TB. herbs in stove heated vinegar, and let stand for at least 1-3 weeks for the herbs to infuse the vinegar.*

---

Live as if you will die tomorrow, but garden as if you will live forever.

---

# Personal Care
## & Household Cleaning Products

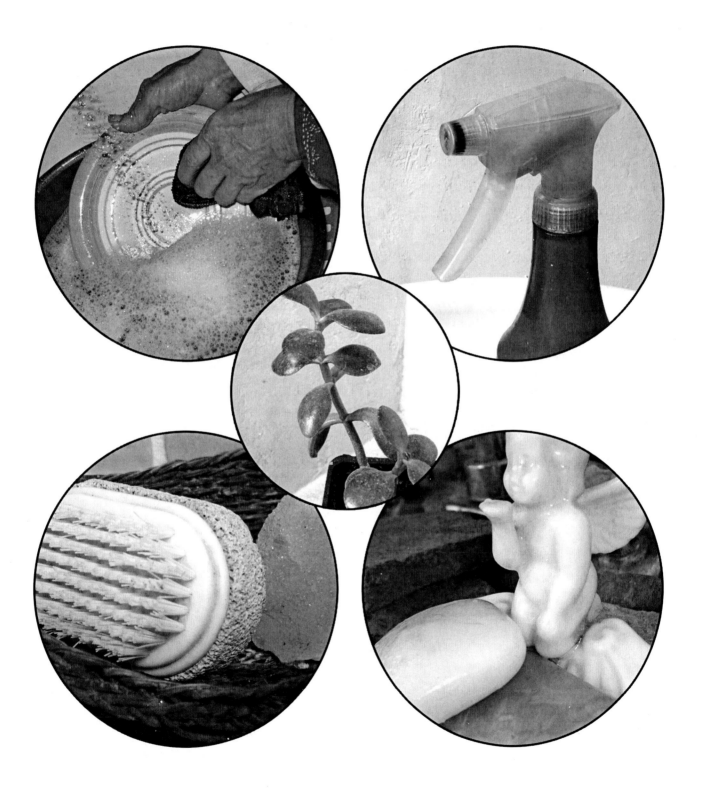

# PERSONAL CARE PRODUCTS

## Facial Astringent

1 C. witch hazel
15 drops tea tree oil
10 drops rosemary oil
12 drops lavender oil
7 drops birch oil (optional)

Shake all ingredients together in a small bottle. Spray or dab on face. This is a great astringent for acne or oily skin conditions.

## Dry Skin Night Time Moisturizer

3 drops lavender oil
2 drops sandalwood oil
2 drops patchouli oil
1 drop rose oil (optional)
3 TB. apricot oil, or a mixture of almond and wheat germ oil.

Shake all ingredients in a jar, and apply liberally to your face before going to bed. This moisturizer is also good for dry feet.

## Relaxing Massage Oil

12 drops sandalwood oil
6 drops lavender oil
6 drops roman chamomile oil
1/4 C. almond oil

Mix all ingredients in a small jar or container.

## Invigorating Clay Mask

Mix a small amount of green, or other clay powder with enough water to make a smooth paste. Add a drop of mint or lavender essential oil. Pat the mixture on your entire face, avoiding the tender area just around the eyes. Lay back and relax as the clay hardens. This mask will help firm and tighten and pull toxins out of the skin, and is especially helpful with acne and skin rashes. Wash off with clean, warm water.

## Gentle Eye Oil

*For the skin around the eyes*

1 tsp. wheat germ or almond oil
1 drop lavender oil
1 drop lemon oil

Mix together well and apply at bedtime to the tender skin around the eyes.

## Sunscreen Oil

*Protect the skin from the drying affects of the sun with this gentle oil.*

1/4 C. plain sesame or almond oil
4 TB. aloe vera gel
1 tsp. vitamin E oil
8 drops lavender oil

Shake all ingredients together in a small bottle. Apply to skin when needed.

## Aloe-E Sunburn Oil

1/4 C. aloe vera gel
1 tsp. vitamin E oil
10 drops lavender oil

Shake or mix everything together until well blended, and apply when needed.

# Apple Cider Vinegar for Sunburns

This is simply the easiest and generally the most available ingredient when it comes to a mild to severe sunburn. It works almost instantly to remove the pain and red colour. Just dab pure, organic, apple cider vinegar, wherever the skin is burned. **Other suggestions for any type of burn:** *Apply pure vitamin E oil, aloe vera gel or essential oil of lavender.*

# Healing herbal salve

*Use this light green salve on stiff, aching joints and tired muscles. It's also great for sore feet and skin conditions such as eczema.*

1/4 C. fresh chickweed herb
1/4 C. fresh St. Johns Wort flowers
3/4 C. olive oil
1/3 C. coconut oil
Several drops of essential oils of: tea tree, rosemary, and lavender.

Simmer herbs with olive oil, in the top of a double boiler, for 1 hour. Strain the mixture. Clean the top of the double boiler of any herbs, and return olive oil mixture to the pot, along with the coconut oil. Heat just long enough to melt the coconut oil. Remove from heat, and add several drops of each essential oil, mixing well. Pour mixture into a small container and cool in the refrigerator. This salve is best if stored in the refrigerator, as it liquefies at room temperature.

**Note:** *If Chickweed is unavailable, use 1/2 C. St. Johns Wort, although the healing properties will be different. Dry herbs can be used if fresh are not available, although the potency may be affected.*

# Protective Oil Blend

*This essential oil blend has anti-viral properties. It works well on cuts, sores and infections. Don't get it near your eyes or on tender skin areas. Apply to bottoms of feet or on your wrists. It has a pleasant scent, which along with a healthful, immune building diet, will help protect you from contagious illnesses.*

Mix the following oils in a small bottle. Shake well before using.

1 tsp. essential oil of clove
1/2 tsp. essential oil of cinnamon
1/4 tsp. essential oil of eucalyptus
1 TB. almond or sesame oil

Nose Drops    *Put a drop in each nostril, at bedtime, to clear sinus passages and heal infections.*

Fill a one once dropper bottle with plain sesame oil. Add 3 drops of essential oil of oregano and 3 drops of grapefruit seed extract, available at natural food stores. Shake bottle and use when needed.

## Herbal Bug Spray

3/4 C. water
1/4 C. witch hazel
3 TB. aloe vera juice or gel
16 drops thyme oil
16 drops lavender oil
16 drops peppermint oil
32 drops lemongrass oil

Mix all ingredients in a small spray bottle. Shake and spray generously when needed.

**Tips on Natural Bug Protection:** *(for flies, fleas, mosquitoes and ticks) Apply essential oils of citronella, eucalyptus, cedar wood, peppermint, or lavender. Basil growing or hung to dry at the door is purported to detract insects. Avoid consuming alcohol and sugar before going into mosquito territory. Eating serotonin rich foods such as bananas and nuts may <u>attract</u> insects. Vitamin B-1 taken for a month during mosquito season, may be helpful, as insects are often repelled by the taste and odor.*

## Bee Sting and Bug Bite Potion

*This is a foolproof and easy remedy for preventing the discomforts of numerous stings and bites from insects. It has a drawing power like nothing else, and should be in every camper and hikers backpack, especially for the emergencies regarding poisonous snakes and spiders. It's also very affective in cases of food poisoning.*

<u>PURE ACTIVATED CHARCOAL POWDER</u>
*It comes in powder or capsules...the capsules are easier to purchase and to pack.*

Break open a capsule and mix the charcoal with enough water to stick together into a very thick paste. Apply mixture to the wound and cover with a bandage.
Swallow three to six charcoal capsules as well, to work internally.... especially in the case of poisonous bites and stings. In the case of a rattler or poisonous spider bites, seek medical help as soon as possible.

## Minty Toothpowder

*This toothpowder makes your teeth feel sparkling clean.*

1 ½ TB. green clay powder
1 TB. sea salt (not iodized)
2 TB. baking soda
5 drops peppermint oil
8 drops lemon essential oil

Shake all ingredients together in a jar or dispenser bottle. Leave it overnight for the oils to combine well. Put a small amount of powder in the palm of your hand, and dip your wet toothbrush into it as needed. Peppermint oil can be replaced with tea tree or cinnamon oil.

**Tip:** *To help prevent plaque build up, rinse your mouth with a dilute solution of food grade hydrogen peroxide, or essential oil of tea tree oil and water.*

## Relaxing Bath Salts

1/2 C. sea salt (or Epsom salts)
1 TB. baking soda
1 TB. borax
1/4-1/2 tsp. lavender oil or your favourite essential oil

Mix dry ingredients first, then add oil. Store in a zip lock bag or airtight container.

**VARIATIONS:**  Invigorating Bath Salts--- *Use peppermint oil instead of lavender*

## Bulk Bath Salts

1 ½ C. Epsom or sea salt
1 ½ C. baking soda
10 or more drops of your favourite essential oil
   or a combination of oils: such as orange, lavender and mint

Combine all ingredients in a large jug or a zip lock plastic bag. Shake to combine the ingredients. Use 1/2-1 C. of mixture in your bath.

## Healing Bath

Pour 1-3 C. **apple cider vinegar** in your bath water, or 1 C. 35% food grade **hydrogen peroxide**, or 1-2 C. **baking soda**.  Soak for 25-40 minutes.  This bath helps ease conditions related to itchy skin, Candida, uric acid, poison ivy, chickenpox and other ailments.

## Natural Hair Rinse

* The herbs **sage or nettles** can be used as a rinse, to nourish and brighten the hair, and to help with growth.  Sage also helps control or reduce dandruff. Steep a tablespoon of dried herbs in a pint of boiling water, for at least a half hour.  Strain liquid and rinse hair with the solution after shampooing.  Don't rinse it off.
* Pure **apple cider vinegar** can be used to rinse after shampooing.  It helps with dandruff conditions and leaves the hair sparkling clean.

## Herbal Eye Wash

1/2 tsp. goldenseal powder
1/4 tsp. sea salt

Dissolve the goldenseal and salt in a 1/2-pint jar (1 cup) of purified and boiled water.  Shake the mixture well, and let the herb settle.  Strain through fine cheesecloth or muslin before using.  Apply cooled solution with a dropper or eyecup. **Note:** *The herbs eyebright, red raspberry leaf or chamomile can also be used for an eyewash.  Strain the herbs well before using.*
**Other eye wash ideas:** Specifically for infections and itchiness: 10 drops of onion juice or apple cider vinegar in 1-2 tsp. pure water.  The drops will initially sting.  Try a drop or two of colloidal silver or pure aloe vera in each eye.  For sore and tired eyes: try a compress of black tea or apple cider vinegar.  Be careful not to get the vinegar in your eyes.

## Disinfectants
*For cuts, abrasions and punctures.*

Clean wound well, and then apply **tea tree oil**, a **3% peroxide** solution, or the **"Protective Oil blend"** pg. 246

> " You know, you asked me what I attributed my long life to, and I would like to tell
> you in a very short sentence.....It's inward calm."
> Li Chung Yun, died in 1930 at age 256

## The Facial Sauna

*For head colds and sinus congestions. Also helpful for skin conditions such as acne.*

In a large bowl containing steaming hot, boiled water, add 3-5 drops essential oil of Eucalyptus. Have a large towel and a box of Kleenex at your side. Lean over the bowl and cover the bowl and your head with the large towel. Breathe in the strong fumes. Come up for air if necessary, but as the pungency of the oil lessens, you will be able to stay under the towel for longer periods of time. This is a great mucus eliminator, and can help with lung congestion and headaches. It is also helpful for opening the pores, softening the skin, and for conditions such as acne.


## Herbal Moth Repellent

Mix together equal parts of the following dried and crushed herbs. Place mixture in small cloth bags and secure tops with ribbon or string. Hang the bags in closets or tuck in drawers. This is a fragrant mix, even if moths aren't a problem.

bay leaf, thyme, rosemary, mint, pennyroyal, lavender.

**Other Ideas:** *If fragrance is what you're after, for hanging in closets or vehicles; try equal portions of dried rose petals, lavender flowers and crushed mint leaves.*

> "I know enough about food to nourish my body properly and have excellent health. I enjoy my food, but I eat to live. I do not live to eat, as some people do, and I know when to stop eating. I am not enslaved by food. People can still be hungry after eating large quantities of wrong foods. In fact, you can suffer from malnutrition even though you consistently overeat wrong foods. You can begin a healthy diet by having only good, wholesome foods available. Eat slowly and chew your food well, as I do. Then make food a very incidental part of your life by filling your life so full of meaningful things that you'll hardly have time to think about food."
> Peace Pilgrim - Her Life and Work In Her Own Words

# HOUSEHOLD CLEANING AIDS

**These are non-toxic, environmentally safe recipes, using products that are commonly found in the house.**

## Fruit and Veggie Spray or Soak
*To help remove parasites and germs.*

1. Use a few drops of **grapefruit seed extract** (available in small, squeeze-type bottles, at health food stores) to a sink of water. Soak food for 10 minutes, then rinse.
2. Mix 1/4 –1/2 C. **apple cider or white vinegar** in a sink of water, and soak veggies for 10 minutes, then rinse.
3. Mix 1/4 C. 3% or 1 tsp. of 35%, food grade **hydrogen peroxide** in a sink of cold water. Soak light skinned produce for 20 minutes. Soak thicker skinned for 30 minutes. Rinse with clean water. **Note:** *35% hydrogen peroxide is available at some independently owned natural food stores. It should be handled and stored carefully.*

## Vinegar and cornstarch Window Cleaner
*This is the best homemade preparation.*

Combine the following in a spray bottle: 2 C. pure or distilled water, 1/2 C. white vinegar, and 1 tsp. cornstarch. Shake bottle well every time you spray the windows. Wipe the windows clean with newspaper or a clean cloth. **Note:** *The water must not contain many minerals. Distilled water works best.*

## Natural scouring powders

*Use these simple ingredients just like any commercial brand scouring powder or household cleaner. They can be sprinkled on the surface and scrubbed, or mixed with water; or for tougher jobs, mix with vinegar and soak over night. Use for everything from cleaning pots and pans, ceramic tile, refrigerators, stoves, toilets and sinks.*

**Baking Soda**: A great all purpose cleaner. It doesn't scratch enamel surfaces. It also removes coffee and tea stains from cups and pots.
**Borax**: For mold and mildew problems on tile or grout, add some borax to baking soda.
**Vinegar**: Wipe or spray plain white vinegar on all your mineral deposit problems—on faucets, in sinks, tubs and showers. Soak a couple of hours or overnight before scrubbing clean. Or mix vinegar with baking soda for a mild abrasive cleaner.

## General All purpose Cleaners

* Fill a spray bottle with water and a few squirts of your favourite, **scented liquid soap.** Shake well before using.  You can also use plain, unscented liquid soap, and add a few drops of essential oil… such as mint, citronella, lavender, lemon or a woodsy scent.

* Use full strength **vinegar** to wipe kitchen work surfaces, and to wipe down wooden cutting boards to eliminate odors.  Also use it to clean up mineral buildup on metal, and to remove soap scum from shower walls.

* Keep a spray bottle of 3% hydrogen **peroxide** in the kitchen and bathroom to disinfect counters and appliances, and to clean the refrigerator.  (To make a 3% solution: combine 1 oz. 35% peroxide with 11 oz. of water.)

## Lemon Furniture Polish
***Also for cleaning wood floors.***

1/2 C. lemon juice
1/4 C. water
1 tsp. olive or flax oil

Mix all ingredients in a small spray bottle or container.  Shake before using. Spray or rub on wood furniture and wipe with a dry cloth.

## Metal Cleaner

* Mix 1/8 cup **baking soda and enough white vinegar** to make a paste.  Rub the foamy mixture on the metal.  On especially tarnished metal, leave it on for a few minutes before scrubbing clean.  Wash the solution off with clean water.  Discoloured stainless steel pots, pans and bowls clean up nicely with baking soda dampened with vinegar.  Use a stainless steel scrubber pad for especially stained areas.

## Old Fashion Silver, Copper & Brass Cleaner
*This is simply the best polish.  If you heat with wood, the ingredients are easy to come by.*

Make a thick paste of cooled **wood ashes and water**, or just dip a wet cloth into the wood ashes.  Rub the paste on the object, then rinse for a sparkly clean finish.

## Herbal Air Fresheners
*Keep a small spray bottle in the bathroom, or near the cat litter box.*

* Fill a small spray bottle with water and 10-20 drops of your favourite **essential oil.** The amount will depend on how big the spray bottle is. Peppermint is especially nice, or a combination of lavender, mint and clove oil. Shake before each use.
* **Vinegar/herbal air Freshener.** Simmer 1/2 cup vinegar on the stove, to clear the kitchen of unwanted odors. Add a few drops of cinnamon or mint essential oil to the vinegar.


## Incredible Drain Cleaner

Put 1/2-1 C. **baking soda** down the drain. Follow with l C. **vinegar.** Let the mixture sit for at least l5 minutes; then run hot water down the drain.


## Floor Cleaner   *For ceramic tile, stone, and linoleum.*

Mix 1/4 C. **liquid soap** and l/2 C. **white vinegar** in a 2 gallon bucket of water.


## Dish Water Grease Cutter

Add 1/2 C. **white vinegar** to the dishwater.


## Laundry Aids

* Add 1/4 C. **vinegar** to the washing machine, to help inhibit mold and fungus, or to help eliminate odors of new clothes. Vinegar will also help remove fruit, grass and tea stains, when used full strength on the stain. Soak tough stains over night.
* Add 1/2 C. **borax or baking soda** to wash, as a cleaning and softening agent.


## Plant Spray   *For all your house and garden plants*

To assist growth: Mix 4 oz. of 3% food grade **peroxide** or 1 tsp. dry **seaweed** with 1 gallon of water, and spray plants or apply to soil.

# HERBS

HOW TO GROW, GATHER AND USE IN COOKING

PLANTING AN HERB GARDEN

Planting an herb garden is easy and fun. It's pretty special to walk out to the garden or patio for some fresh herbs to use in the kitchen. Herbs will easily grow and multiply in most soils, whether you create a simple round bed bordered by rocks, or a large bed with paths and benches for sitting. Lacking the space, beds can be formed close to the house, along driveways and sidewalks, and near the kitchen door, making it more convenient for using herbs in your daily meals. For apartment dwellers or those with limited planting space, herbs can be grown in pots on the patio, or inside on a sunny window ledge, where leaves can be picked throughout the winter to embellish salads and cooked foods.

Although herbs are often found growing in what appears to be the poorest ground, soil can be enriched with organic matter such as composted kitchen scraps. To help reduce weeds and to prevent the soil from drying out, mulch around the herbs with grass clippings, straw or pine needles.

Many herbs will come back year after year. Annuals like borage, cilantro, dill, and parsley often re-seed themselves, sprouting up between stone patio pavers, or along pathways. Perennials like mint, sage, lavender, thyme, chervil, chives and oregano come back year after year. Sensitive to cold plants, such as some varieties of rosemary and white sage, will do better if brought inside before the first freeze, and replanted when spring arrives. Some herbs such as mint, wintergreen and oregano can be found growing wild in forests, or on the banks of lakes and rivers, and medicinal plants such as chaparral grow prolifically in dry desert areas.

> " The ancient Greeks and Romans valued plants for various uses: as medicines, symbols and magical charms, food seasonings, cosmetics, dyes, room scenters and floor coverings...Hippocrates advocated the use of a few simple herbal drugs, along with fresh air, rest and proper diet---to help the body's own "life force" in eliminating the problem."
>
> John Lust - The Herb Book.

# COLLECTING HERB LEAVES & FLOWERS

Herbs should be gathered when the plants are in their prime. Don't wait until they dry on the stalk or are hit by a freeze. Pick them in the morning after the dew is off the plants, and in dry weather. With many herbs two or more cuttings can be made in one season.

Herbs can be broken or cut at the base of the stem, or the leaves can be removed individually for immediate use in teas or cooking. Tie a bunch of stems together with a piece of string, and hang the herbs upside down in a place in the house that's out of direct sunlight. Herbs also dry well if put in a paper bag and left to dry in a shady area of the yard, or in a pantry or dry storage area.

When the herbs are dry, strip the leaves from the stems and store them in a closed container. Make sure that the herbs are dry before storing them; otherwise they could spoil. When using the herbs in cooking, they can be crumbled by hand or ground fine in an electric grinder.

Fresh picked herbs will keep for a number of days in a plastic bag or container in the refrigerator, or a cool room. To prolong freshness, many herbs such as cilantro, which loses its potency when dried, can be stored in zip lock bags in the freezer, for immediate use in cooking.

# USING HERBS IN BAKING AND COOKING

*Here are just a few ideas for using herbs in cooking and baking.*

**Note:** *Use approximately ½ tsp. dried crushed or ¼ tsp. ground herbs to 1TB. of fresh.*

ANISE: Cookies, cakes and applesauce.

BASIL: Tomatoes, tomato sauce, soups, stews and pesto.

BAY LEAVES: Soups, stews and beans.

BORAGE: Leaves in soups, stews and beans. Flowers in salads.

CHERVIL: Salads and soups.

CHIVES: Salads, soups, stews and stir-fry.

DILL: Potatoes, soups, stews, pickles, salads and dressings.

FENNEL: Beans and tomatoes.

GARLIC: Sauces, soups, stews, beans, salad dressings.

MARJORAM: Soups, stews, salads, sauces, veggies.

MINT: Tea, cookies, cakes, icing, sauces, salads.

NASTURTIUM: Salads, embellishments for cooked dishes.

OREGANO: Sauces, pizza, tomatoes, meatless loaves, stews and soups.

PARSLEY: Soups, stews, salads, potatoes, rice, veggies, salads.

ROSEMARY: Soups, stews, potatoes, salad dressings.

SAGE: Meatless sausages, patties and loaves, stuffing, salads, teas.

SAVORY: (Resembles thyme) Soups, stews, and salads.

TARRAGON: Beans, soups, salads and dressings, tomatoes.

THYME: Soups, stews, stuffing, meatless sausage, tomatoes.

# HERBAL TEA BLENDS

*The dry herbs for these teas can be found in most health food type stores that sell bulk herbs and spices, or at an herb shop. Each recipe makes one quart of tea. Adjust liquid for a stronger or weaker brew.* **If you are pregnant, breastfeeding, or have any dis-ease, and are unfamiliar with herbs, consult an herbalist or health care practitioner prior to using herbs.**

**TO PREPARE TEAS:** *Steep, don't boil the herbs in each recipe in 4 C. boiled water, for at least 5- 10 minutes; then strain. Enjoy hot or cold. Add more water for a milder blend. For a single cup of tea: Use 1- 2 tsp. herb mix per cup of water.* **TIP FOR MAKING ICED TEAS:** *To speed the chilling process - Steep herbs or tea bags in 1-2 cups of boiling hot water. After a minimum of 10 minutes, remove bags and add desired quantity of ice-cold water.*

CALMING TEA

*Helpful for headaches, arthritis, mucus and night sweats.*

2 tsp. blessed thistle
2 tsp. spearmint
1 tsp. blue vervain
1 tsp. hyssop

COLD CARE TEA

2 tsp. peppermint
1 tsp. hyssop
1 tsp. pennyroyal
1/2 tsp. sassafras

CIRCULATION TEA

*Also soothing for the stomach.*

2 tsp. spearmint
1 tsp. hyssop
1 tsp. St. John's wort
1 tsp. blue vervain

DIGEST TEA

*Also helpful for Candida problems.*

2 tsp. peppermint
1 tsp. chamomile
1 tsp. pau d'arco

## HEADACHE TEA NO. 1

2 tsp. peppermint
2 tsp. blue violet
3/4 tsp. ground willow

## HEADACHE TEA NO. 2

2 tsp. peppermint
1 tsp. pennyroyal
1 tsp. blue violet
3/4 tsp. ground willow

## LYMPH TEA

2 tsp. peppermint
1 tsp. nettles
1 tsp. St. John's wort
1 tsp. blue violet

## LONG LIFE TEA

1 tsp. peppermint      1/2 tsp. sarsaparilla
1 tsp. hyssop          1/2 tsp. passionflower
1 tsp. nettles

## MONTH-EASE TEA

*For symptoms related to PMS.*

2 tsp. spearmint
1 ½ tsp. St. John's wort
1 tsp. red raspberry leaf
1/2 tsp. passionflower

## SLEEP AID TEA

*For a good night's sleep.*

2 tsp. spearmint
1 tsp. chamomile flowers
1 tsp. hops

## MOON-PAUSE TEA

*Specifically helpful during menopause.*
*Eliminate the licorice if you have problems with high blood pressure.*

2 tsp. spearmint
1 tsp. passionflower
1 tsp. blessed thistle
3/4 tsp. licorice powder
1/2 tsp. chaste berry

---

**Steep herbs in each recipe in 4 C. boiled water, for at least 5-10 minutes.
(Or use 1-2 tsp. of herb blend per cup of water.) Don't boil.  Enjoy hot or cold.
Adjust water if necessary for a stronger or weaker brew.**

---

## PAIN RELIEF TEA

3 tsp. spearmint
1 tsp. wood betony
1 tsp. St. John's wort
1 tsp. blue vervain

## RELAXING TEA BLEND

2 tsp. spearmint
1 tsp. passionflower
1 tsp. blue vervain

## SENSUAL N' RELAXING TEA

2 tsp. spearmint
1 tsp. hyssop
1 tsp. damiana
1 tsp. blue vervain
1/2 tsp. chamomile

## SKIN & NERVE TEA

*A calming tea, which also nourishes the skin.*

1 tsp. shave grass (or oat grass)
1 tsp. blue violet
1 ½ tsp. pennyroyal
3/4 tsp. ground willow
3/4 tsp. ground black cohosh

"Herbal healing was the first system of healing that the world knew...Why use herbs? They are nature's remedies..........There is an herb for every disease that a human body can be afflicted with. The use of herbs is the oldest medical science."
Jethro Kloss - Back to Eden

*This is just a short reference for various ailments...and in no way covers the wide scope of herbs and natural therapies that could be of assistance. Refer to the <u>Recommended Reading</u> list at the back of the book, for further information on the subject. Check the <u>Nutritive Food Source guide</u> following this section, for some remedies listed in brackets.* **Note: Pregnant or nursing mothers, or those with certain health problems, should always consult a health care professional regarding the use of some herbs.**

**Aches:** arnica cream, ginger, mint, comfrey (calcium, E, magnesium, potassium)

**Acne:** red clover, sassafras, buchu, apply tea tree oil or witch hazel. Do a Candida cleanse, blood cleansing herbs, facial saunas, (B vitamins, clay masks, vinegar)

**Adrenals:** echinacea, ginseng, licorice, (B6, calcium, iodine, phosphorus, sulphur, zinc)

**Age spots:** use herbs for the liver, (antioxidants, exercise, limit sun exposure, apply apple cider vinegar, or 2 parts vinegar to 1 part citrus or onion juice)

**Aging:** gingko, ginseng, (Kombucha tea, phosphorus, potassium, selenium)

**Alcoholism:** liver-cleansing herbs (vitamin Bs, magnesium, zinc)

**Allergies:** goldenseal, blood and lymph cleansing herbs, (colon cleanse, faulty digestion)

**Anemia:** burdock, comfrey, dandelion, nettles (iron: blackstrap molasses, beets, kale, raisins)

**Anger:** (manganese, sulphur.) *consistent and out of control*--possible lack of magnesium

**Anxiety:** chamomile, St. John's wort, (B vitamins, chlorine, sulphur)

**Appetite Stimulant:** ginger, ginseng, mint

**Arthritis:** alfalfa seed tea, cayenne, chaparral, devils claw, ginger, yucca, (alkaline the diet, apple cider vinegar, calcium, hydrochloric acid, hydrogen, magnesium, msm, zinc)

**Asthma:** garlic, ginger, licorice, mullein, (cranberry juice, vitamin B, oxygen therapy)

**Athletes Foot:** pau d'arco, apply tea tree oil (apply apple cider vinegar)

**Back Pain:** nettle, uva ursi, apply ginger pack. Apply thyme oil for sciatica (calcium, magnesium, manganese, stretching exercises.)

**Bad Breath:** laxative teas, licorice, fennel, parsley (colon cleanse, dental work)

**Baldness:** sage tea as hair rinse, (kelp, headstands, vinegar hair rinse, vitamin B, use only natural hair products, avoid products with sodium laryl sulphate.)

**Bed Wetting:** buchu, St John's wort, (avoid stimulants at bedtime.)

**Bee stings:** (vitamin C internally, apply charcoal paste and take capsules internally)

**Boils:** apply fresh garlic or tea tree oil (apply cooked onions or castor oil)

**Bones:** comfrey (Vitamin C, calcium)

**Bowels:** dandelion, sanicle, senna, (flax seeds, psyllium seed, salt purge cleanse, wheat bran, slant boarding, yoga and stretching exercises.)

**Bladder:** buchu, oat straw, spearmint, uva ursi, (cranberry juice)

**Bleeding gums:** (vitamin C)

**Blood Pressure, high:** black cohosh, garlic, hawthorn, (kelp, calcium, potassium, selenium, colon cleansing, relaxation techniques, celery, vitamin C, olive oil.)

**Blood Pressure, low:** ginseng, goldenseal, licorice, (Iron: black strap molasses, beets)

**Blood Purifying:** chaparral, dandelion, pau d'arco, red clover, sassafras, yellow dock, (Beets, cleansing fast)

**Body Odor:** (baking soda or cornstarch as a dusting powder, eat magnesium rich foods)

**Body Temperature:** Low (silicon) High: (hydrogen)

**Brain Function:** ginkgo, gotu kola

**Breast Lumps:** lymph-cleansing herbs (oxygen therapy)

**Breast Milk:** *to encourage:* catnip tea   *to decrease:* sage tea

**Bruising:** apply arnica cream (vitamin C deficiency)

**Burns:** apply aloe vera or lavender oil  (apply apple cider vinegar or vitamin E gel)

**Cancer:** chaparral, Essiac tea, pau d'arco, (parasite cleanse, alkaline system, oxygen therapy)

**Candida:** chaparral, garlic, pau d'arco, tea tree oil, (charcoal caps, acidophilus, blood purifying herbs, grapefruit seed extract, lower sugar intake, oxygen therapy, colloidal silver)

**Carpal tunnel:** (B6)

**Chickenpox:** raspberry leaf tea. Use blood-purifying herbs (apple cider vinegar, peroxide or baking soda in bath water, apply vitamin E to alleviate itching and spreading)

**Cholesterol:** (**high**): garlic, ginseng, (lecithin, shitake mushrooms, seaweed, green tea)

**Chronic fatigue:** burdock, cayenne, echinacea, pau d'arco, (vitamin B, potassium, oxygen)

**Circulation:** cayenne, garlic, ginger, hawthorn berries, rosemary, sasafrass, (Vitamin B, calcium and magnesium, bowel cleansing, exercise)

**Coldness:** cayenne, catnip, mint (could be thyroid problem)

**Colds/Coughs:** blue violet, fenugreek, licorice, mint, sage,  (vitamin A & C, zinc, salt water gargle, facial sauna, inhale eucalyptus oil, avoid dairy!) *Susceptibility to:* lack of iron.

**Cold Hands and Feet:** apply hot pepper salve, and use herbs internally for circulation.

**Cold Sores:** chaparral, pau d'arco, red clover, sage tea, (acidophilus, lysine caps and cream)

**Colic:** catnip, chamomile, mint.

**Colon:** (acidophilus, charcoal caps, flaxseed, psyllium seed, salt water purge, wheat bran)

**Constipation:** cascara sagrada, senna, (colon cleansing, flax seed, wheat bran)

**Cramps:** ginger, thyme (calcium and magnesium)

**Cravings:** for *chocolate:* may need chromium, *Sweets:* may need magnesium, *Salt:* may have weak adrenal gland or have hydrogen deficiency.

**Cuts:** apply essential oils of lavender or tea tree. (hydrogen peroxide)

**Cystic Fibrosis:** aloe vera products, use herbs for the lungs (vitamins A, B, C, D and E, selenium, zinc, facial saunas with eucalyptus oil, avoid dairy and mucus forming foods,)

**Dandruff:** rinse hair with sage or nettle tea (vitamin B, silicon, apple cider vinegar rinse)

**Depression:** St John's wort, apply oils of lavender or jasmine, (B 12, chlorine, iron, silicon)

**Diabetes:** red clover, pau d'arco, turmeric (artichokes, chromium, kelp)

**Diaper Rash:** (apply cornstarch to prevent, or vitamin E to heal)

**Diarrhea:** red raspberry leaf, slipper elm, (acidophilus, charcoal caps, magnesium)

**Digestion:** aloe Vera, chamomile, mint, parasite cleanse, (acidophilus, calcium, oxygen)

**Dizziness:** See Anemia.

**Ears: Infection:** apply mullein, garlic oil or apple cider vinegar. *Ringing:* apply clove oil.

**Eczema:** blood-cleansing herbs, (sulphur, apply vitamin E)

**Emotions:** chaste berry, St John's wort (have hormone levels checked) Women-also see PMS and Menopause.

**Eyes:** eyebright, chamomile or goldenseal used in *eyewash.* (vitamin A, sodium, or zinc) For *twitching:* B6. *Night blindness:* vitamin A, potassium. *Nearsightedness:* chromium. *Farsighted:* vitamin B. *Itchy:* vitamin B. (parasites) *Double vision and crossed eyes:* vitamins A, D and zinc. *Styes:* chamomile eye wash, hot compresses. *Tired:* chamomile, black tea or apple cider vinegar compress (*don't get the vinegar in your eyes*)

**Eyes Continued:** _Dry:_ take evening primrose or flax oil internally. _Dark Circles under:_ Adrenal exhaustion, allergies or insufficient water intake. _Swollen:_ grated potato compress

**Fatigue:** see herbs for adrenals, (B vitamins, kelp, magnesium, nitrogen, potassium, sodium, zinc, oxygen therapy) _Heat exhaustion-_ drink grape juice

**Feet, burning:** (B vitamins, pantothenic acid, silicon) _itching:_ apply tea tree oil or vinegar

**Fever:** blue vervain, mint, passion flower (increase fluid intake, hot bath with ginger)

**Fibroid Tumors:** milk thistle, burdock, (castor oil compress, Vitamin A, C, selenium, zinc, possible hormonal imbalance)

**Flu:** pau d'arco, mint tea, eucalyptus oil in bath

**Food Poisoning:** (take charcoal capsules internally)

**Fractures:** apply ginger, lavender, or thyme oil. (fluorine for fragile bones)

**Frostbite:** apply ginger or lavender oil

**Fungus:** apply aloe vera, tea tree oil or (apple cider vinegar or peroxide solution)

**Gallbladder:** cascara sagrada, licorice, nettles, wood betony, yellow dock, (vitamin B & C)

**Gallstones:** cascara sagrada, nettles, wood betony, yellow dock (olive oil, vegetables)

**Gas:** asafetida, ginger, mint, nutmeg, sassafras, valerian, (food enzymes, papaya, charcoal caps, magnesium, colon cleansing, check for parasites or Candida)

**Gout:** alfalfa tabs, blood purifying herbs, buchu, chaparral, ginger compresses, uva ursi, (alkaline the system, drink distilled water, hydrogen, kelp, manganese, silicon, sodium)

**Growth (slow):** (B vitamin, kelp, thyroid problems, zinc)

**Gums, infected:** rub with cayenne pepper and olive oil mixture or tea tree oil (vitamin C)

**Hair, Nails & Skin:** horsetail herb, oat straw tea, rinse graying hair with sage or nettle tea, (vitamin B, Kombucha tea, silica, sulphur, zinc, hormonal imbalance)

**Hair Loss:** (kelp for under active thyroid, fluorine, silicon, vitamin B, zinc)

**Hay Fever:** herbs for adrenals and blood and lymph purifying

**Headache:** blessed thistle, blue violet, passionflower, willow, wood betony, essential oils of peppermint or lavender rubbed on forehead and temples, (soak feet in hot water, colon cleanse, magnesium) _Frontal:_ sodium _Motion_ headache: manganese

**Heart disease:** cayenne, hawthorn berries, (calcium, lecithin, magnesium, potassium)

**Heartburn:** mint, sarsaparilla, wood betony

**Hemorrhoids:** blood-purifying herbs, aloe vera juice (apply apple cider vinegar, bath containing baking soda)

**Herpes:** goldenseal, Oregon grape leaf, apply tea tree oil (vitamin C, lysine cream/caps, panthothenic acid, zinc)

**Hiccoughs:** (a spoonful of peanut butter, orange juice or hold the breath)

**Hives:** see blood-purifying herbs, sassafras tea, apply catnip tea on hives, (hot bath with baking soda and salt)

**Hormones:** chaste berry, sarsaparilla, see menopause or PMS

**Hot Flashes:** licorice, passionflower, (avoid caffeine)

**Hypoglycemia:** licorice, (balance acid and alkaline in body)

**Immune System:** blood-purifying herbs, (Vitamin A, B, C, E, kelp, Kombucha tea, zinc)

**Infection:** echinacea, goldenseal, white oak tea, apply tea tree oil or garlic poultice

**Inflammation:** cayenne pepper poultice, sage, willow (ginger, garlic, charcoal poultice)

**Insomnia:** catnip, chamomile, gotu kola, hops, nutmeg, valerian. (calcium, magnesium, silicon, melatonin, relaxation techniques, avoid caffeine)

**Itch:** apply tea tree oil, witch hazel or peroxide, (soak in water containing 1-2 C. baking soda)

**Jaundice:** see herbs for liver

**Jet Lag:** ginger internally, apply lavender or mint oil, (melatonin, Vitamin B)

**Joints** (swollen): willow (manganese)

**Kidneys:** buchu, corn silk, hyssop, nettles, oat straw, saw palmetto, uva ursi (potassium)

**Lack of confidence:** (phosphorus)

**Leukemia:** use blood and parasite cleansing herbs, thyme oil on thymus gland

**Lice:** apply tea tree oil with olive oil on head at night and comb out in morning.

**Liver:** cascara sagrada, dandelion, milk thistle, Oregon grape root, St. John's wort, (beets)

**Lungs:** comfrey, hyssop, licorice, mullein, pennyroyal, sage, (calcium, manganese, phosphorus, silicon, oxygen therapy,)

**Lymph:** blue violet, echinacea, nettles, red clover, red root (exercise on mini trampoline; also called a rebounder, massage, fast paced walking, avoid dairy!)

**Measles:** yarrow or red raspberry leaf tea

**Memory:** see herbs for brain (calcium, iron, manganese, nitrogen, oxygen, sodium)

**Menopause:** black cohosh, blessed thistle, chaste berry, motherwort, (calcium, vitamin D and F, evening primrose oil, flax and soy products, bio-identical plant based hormone products, exercise, have hormones checked, avoid caffeine)

**Menstruation,** problems: calcium, Painful: blue cohosh, pennyroyal. Delayed: ginger

**Metabolism & poor appetite:** ginger, cayenne (chlorine, iodine, Kombucha tea, exercise)

**Miscarriage,** to prevent: red raspberry leaf tea

**Morning Sickness:** red raspberry leaf tea

**Motion Sickness:** ginger, apply oil of peppermint to forehead

**Muscles,** Sore: apply ginger or peppermint oil

**Nails, brittle:** (vitamin A and calcium)

**Nausea:** ginger, goldenseal, mint, red raspberry leaf (Vitamin B, lemon juice, lysine)

**Neck Ache:** apply lavender or mint oil (magnesium) Stiff: (silicon)

**Nerves:** chamomile, hops, skullcap, St. John's wort, valerian, (vitamin B, calcium, iodine, magnesium, manganese, phosphorus, potassium, silicon, sodium, sulphur)

**Night Mares:** blood-purifying herbs, catnip, hop tea before bedtime, peppermint

**Night Sweats:** hyssop, nettles, oat straw, sage

**Numbness:** (vitamin B6, phosphorus, silicon)

**Osteoporosis:** (calcium, vitamin D, magnesium, manganese)

**Pain:** chamomile, catnip, mint, (Apply: lavender, peppermint oil, arnica or tiger balm ointment)

**Pancreas:** dandelion, goldenseal, uva ursi, (zinc)

**Parasites:** black walnut, garlic, wormwood, (pumpkin seeds, citrus seed extract, colonics)

**Perspiration:** Lack of- (chlorine, sodium, sulphur)

**Pituitary:** chaste berry. (iodine, phosphorus, sulphur)

**PMS:** for cramps: black cohosh, for delayed menses: vervain, for depression, bloating and headache: chaste berry, for cramps, and nausea: Don qui and ginger, for bloating: Uva Ursi (calcium, magnesium, iron) to decrease blood flow: red raspberry leaf or sage tea. To increase blood flow: Ginger, St. Johns Wort, thyme

**Pneumonia:** comfrey, sage, vervain

**Poison Ivy and Oak:** tansy tea on rash (Epsom salt bath)

**Prostate:** burdock, corn silk, pau d'arco, peppermint, saw palmetto, (pumpkin seeds, magnesium, silicon, zinc, alkaline the system)

**Rash:** blood cleansing herbs, apply aloe vera, lavender or tea tree oil, (MSM cream, Vit. E)

**Restless Legs:** nettle tea (calcium, magnesium, silicon)

**Ringworm:** apply tea tree oil or (apple cider vinegar) Drink blood purifying herbs.

**Scars:** apply peppermint oil or (vitamin E, sandalwood powder mixed with rosewater)

**Sciatica:** Apply oils of tansy, wintergreen, or thyme, (keep back limber, invert- to stretch spine, yoga stretches such as the twist.

**Sinus:** garlic, goldenseal, hyssop, mint, sage, hot facial sauna with eucalyptus oil, herbal nose drops-see index (nasal purge with Nettie pot, using mild salt or peroxide solution)

**Skin:** sasafrass internally, apply witch hazel, aloe vera or vitamin E (avocado mask)

**Slow healing power:** (silicon)

**Smell, loss of:** (zinc)

**Snake bites:** black cohosh, hyssop (charcoal - poultice and internally)

**Snoring:** colon-cleansing herbs (B vitamins, allergies?)

**Spleen:** goldenseal, hyssop, wood betony (iron, sodium, potassium, magnesium)

**Sprains:** rub with essential oil of mint (hot vinegar poultice.)

**Stomach:** blue vervain, chamomile, ginger, goldenseal, mint, (enzymes, parasite cleanse)

**Stuttering:** (B vitamins, especially B l)

**Styes:** chamomile or eyebright tea eyewash, hot compresses, (clay poultice)

**Swellings:** burdock, comfrey, apply lavender oil

**Swollen ankles:** see herbs for kidneys

**Taste, loss of:** (B vitamins, zinc, poor thyroid function)

**Teeth, grinding:** Could be parasites- see herbs for parasites, (calcium, iodine, magnesium, silicon) **health of:** (vitamin D, calcium, fluorine)

**Throat:** blue vervain, garlic, hops, sanicle *Tonsillitis:* gargle with and drink sage tea

**Thyroid gland:** (B vitamins, iodine, kelp, potassium, zinc)

**Tiredness:** (could be dehydration-drink more water, see thyroid, B vitamins, molasses)

**Toothache:** apply oil of cloves.

**Tumors:** red root, blood cleansing herbs,(alkaline salts, magnesium, oxygen therapy)

**Twitching:** (B vitamins, could be from parasites)

**Ulcers:** aloe vera, comfrey, licorice, goldenseal (cabbage, bananas, garlic, green tea)

**Urinary:** buchu, uva ursi, juniper

**Uterine trouble:** blessed thistle, motherwort, St. John's wort, squaw vine

**Vaginal infection:** see Candida (douche with acidophilus, apple cider vinegar in bath)

**Varicose veins:** purify blood, use herbs for circulation. (slant board or head stands)

**Vomiting:** ginger, mint

**Warts:** apply garlic, mullein, milkweed liquid, or thyme oil (apply wood ash paste, peroxide or raw potato)

**Weakness:** calcium *constant:* (phosphorus)

**Wrinkles:** apply lavender or patchouli oil (use facial creams containing vitamin A, E, C, aloe vera,) hydrogen, iron, take flax oil and evening primrose oil internally, drink plenty of pure water, head stands or slant boarding, vegetable salts and avoid prolonged exposure to sun)

**Vitamin A:** Carrots, dark green vegetables, some fruits.

**Vitamin B:**  B1 - Nutritional yeast, whole grains and unrefined cereals, oatmeal, peanuts, vegetables.

B2 - leafy greens, yeast.

B6 - Black strap molasses, brown rice, cabbage, melon, nutritional yeast, oats, peanuts, soy beans, walnuts, wheat bran and germ.

B12- fermented soy products, nutritional yeast, sea vegetables.

**Vitamin C:** Berries, citrus fruits, green and leafy vegetables, peppers, potatoes, and tomatoes.

**Vitamin D:** Sunlight.

**Vitamin E:** Brussels sprouts, leafy greens, nuts, soybeans, spinach, wheat germ, whole wheat and whole grain cereals and flours.

**Vitamin F:** Avocado, almonds, peanuts, pecans, sunflower seeds, vegetable oils, walnuts, wheat germ.

**Vitamin K:** Alfalfa, kelp, leafy green vegetables, safflower and soybean oil.

**Calcium:** The highest sources: Dulse, greens, kale, kelp, nuts, sesame seeds, unrefined grains, cauliflower, celery, lemons, nettles, rhubarb, whole wheat bread. Others include: almonds, avocados, barley, beet greens, beans, blackstrap molasses, bran, broccoli, brown rice, cabbage, carrots, coconut, cornmeal, figs, lentils, millet, onions, parsnips, prunes, rice polish, rye, soymilk, walnuts, watercress, whole wheat.

**Carbon:** The highest sources: Breads, grains, most proteins, starches, wet fruits. Others include: Almonds, avocados, coconut milk, olive and peanut oils, pinions, pistachios, popcorn, walnuts.

**Chlorine:** asparagus, avocados, bananas, beets, blackberries, carrots, cucumbers, celery, dates, eggplant, kale, kelp, oats, raisins, spinach, strawberries, sunflower seeds, tomatoes.

**Chromium:** dried beans, corn and corn oil, mushrooms, nutritional yeast, potatoes, whole grains.

**Fluorine:** The highest sources: sea plants. Others include: avocados, Brussels sprouts, cabbage, cauliflower, dates, endive, garlic, greens, juniper berries, lemon grass, licorice, mother's milk, parsley, spinach, tomatoes.

**Hydrogen:** The highest sources: water, citrus fruits, fruit and vegetable juices. Others include: apricots, asparagus, blackberries, blueberries, broccoli, cabbage, carrots, celery, chard, cherries, eggplant, horseradish, juniper tea, mangos, muskmelon, okra, papaya, parsley, peaches, pineapple, prunes, radishes, sauerkraut, spinach, strawberries, tomatoes, watercress, watermelon.

**Iodine:** The highest sources: kelp, dulse, and sea plants. Others include: artichokes, asparagus, beans, blueberries, Brussels sprouts, carrots, chives, coconut, cucumber, eggplant, garlic, kale, lettuce, mustard greens, okra, oats, onions, peanuts, peppers, potatoes, rutabaga, seaweed, strawberries, summer squash, tofu, tomato, turnips, watercress, watermelon.

**Iron:** The highest sources: dulse, kelp, dried un-sulphured fruits, black cherries, greens, liquid chlorophyll, blackberries, blackstrap molasses, rice polishing and bran, spinach. Others include: almonds, apricots, cashews, dates, figs, kale, lentils, limas, millet, mung beans, parsley, peas, hot peppers, pinto beans, prunes, pumpkin seeds, radish, rye, sesame seeds, soybeans, sprouted seeds and beans, sunflower seeds, Swiss chard, wheat bran and germ, white beans.

**Magnesium:** The highest sources: Cornmeal, greens, nuts, wheat germ, whole grains. Others include: apples, avocados, dried bananas, beans, black walnuts, cabbage, cashews, coconuts, dates, figs, lentils, oats, okra, parsley, peanuts, pecans, prunes, pistachio nuts, prunes, rice, wild and brown, (note: brown rice has eleven times the magnesium content of polished white rice.) soy milk, spinach, sunflower seeds, Swiss chard, tofu, turnip greens, watercress, whole wheat.

**Manganese:** The highest sources: Nuts and seeds. Others include: acorns, almonds, apples, apricots, beans, blackberries, blueberries, butternut, celery, chestnuts, English walnuts, leaf lettuce, mint, oats, olives, parsley, pineapple, rye, watercress, wintergreen.

**Nitrogen:** The highest sources: High protein foods, condiments, nuts, pasta, spices. **Others include:** almonds, beans, butternuts, lentils, peas, walnuts.

**Oxygen:** The highest sources: Greens, iron foods and tonics, nuts and seeds, watery vegetables and fruits. Others include: beets, blueberries, carrots, figs, grapes, horseradish, leeks, mustard green, olives, onions, parsnips, raisins, spinach, tomatoes.

**Phosphorus:** The highest sources: Almonds, lentils, pumpkin and squash seeds, rice bran and polishing, soybeans, sunflower seeds, wheat bran and germ. Others include: barley, beans, cabbage, carrots, cashew nuts, dulse, kelp, millet, oats, olives, pecans, sesame seeds, walnuts.

**Potassium:** The highest sources: Dulse, bitter greens, Irish moss, kelp, sun-dried black olives. Others include: almonds, apples, apple cider vinegar, apricots, bananas, beans, beets, beet greens, black cherries, blueberries, broccoli, carrots, cashews, cucumbers, dates, dulse, figs, grapes, Jerusalem artichoke, kale, kelp, lentils, limas, parsley, peaches, pears, pecans, raisins, rice bran, sage tea, sesame seeds, soy milk, soybeans, spinach, Swiss chard, tomatoes, turnips, walnuts, wheat bran and germ.

**Selenium:** Broccoli, onions, tomatoes, wheat bran and germ.

**Silicon:** The highest sources: Barley, kelp, nuts, oats and oat straw tea, rice polishing and bran, seeds, whole grains and cereal. Others include: apples, apricots, asparagus, bananas, beans, beets, cabbage, carrots, cauliflower, celery, cherries, corn, cucumbers, dates, figs, greens, millet, parsnips, plums, pumpkin, sprouted seeds, strawberries, tomatoes, turnips, watermelon.

**Sodium:** The highest sources: Black mission figs. Others include: apples, apricots (dried), asparagus, barley, beets, cabbage, celery, chickpeas, coconut, dandelion greens, dates, dulse, horseradish, kale, kelp, lentils, olives (black), okra, parsley, peas, peppers (hot), prunes, raisins, sesame seeds, spinach, strawberries, sunflower seeds, Swiss chard, turnips.

**Sulphur:** The highest sources: Brussels sprouts, cabbage, cauliflower, horseradish, kale, watercress. Others include: almonds, avocados, black currants, brazil nuts, corn, cucumbers, horseradish, leeks, lima beans, mustard greens, okra, oats, onions, parsnips, snap beans, turnip.

**Zinc:** Nutritional yeast, pumpkin seeds, wheat germ.

---

"When I realized that white flour and white sugar were bad for your health I stopped eating them. When I realized highly seasoned things were bad I quit them. And when I realized all processed foods contain substances that are bad for the body I quit eating them. Even most water out of the tap is a chemical cocktail. I would suggest bottled or distilled water."

*Peace Pilgrim - Her Life and Work In Her Own Words*

# SPROUTING

Sprouts are easy to grow and afford one of the most concentrated sources of enzymes, vitamins, minerals and protein. They are a live food offering vital energy for your body. When you eat sprouts you are getting the very best of what that seed has to offer in terms of nutrition. Each seed is filled with energy just waiting for the right environment to grow. When the seeds sprout an incredible flow of energy is released. The sprouts provide us with an inexpensive and easy way to incorporate the essential enzymes needed for good digestion. Enzymes are destroyed when foods are cooked. One of the most important nutrients in sprouts is chlorophyll. Chlorophyll has been researched for its nutritional and healing properties, and has been found to carry oxygen to the cells throughout the body, and stimulates the body's inherent self-cleaning and self-healing attributes.

## HOW TO SPROUT

Sprouts don't require a lot of space. They grow indoors in any season, reaching a mature and edible stage in only a few days. Growing an indoor sprout garden is easy and fun. Sprouts can be grown in jars with mesh lids, in sprouting bags, on trays in soil, or with automatic sprout units.

## WHAT TO SPROUT

All beans seeds and nuts can be sprouted. Alfalfa, radish, clover and mung beans for home sprouting are commonly available at natural foods stores. Lentils, mustard, sunflower seeds and wheat can also be sprouted easily.

## GETTING STARTED

Find a location to sprout that is close to your water source, for ease in rinsing the sprouts. Next to the kitchen sink is an ideal spot. The sprouts should be rinsed once or twice a day depending on the weather. On warm days they may need to be rinsed at least twice, depending on the sprouting method. I've used both the bottle and bag method, but prefer the stacked sprouting trays. They eliminate the risk of the sprouts being jiggled around too much. Keep the sprouts out of direct sunlight, which could overheat them. Indirect lighting is adequate. If you're using sprout jars with screened lids, the seeds will first need to be soaked 4-6 hours for small seeds, and 12 hours for larger seeds and beans. The water is then drained off and the jars set at a 45° angel to allow draining between rinses. Sunflower seeds are ready in 1-3 days, pumpkin and almonds in 1, and most others in 3- 6 days. My *Biosta "Miracle Sprouter"* requires no pre-soaking, and uses 2-3 TB. large seeds and 1TB. small seeds such as alfalfa, clover, and radish, per tray. The larger seeds like mung beans require rinsing each day until harvest, where as the smaller seeds are rinsed only on day l and day 4, and every day there after until harvested. If you're sprouting in quart jars, use 2-4 TB. small seeds and approximately 1/2 cup large seeds and beans per jar, and rinse at least once a day, every day, until harvest time, when they should then be eaten or stored in the fridge.

**SPROUTING GUIDE**   *Note: dry measure is per quart sprouting jar or mesh bag.*

| Variety | Soak | Dry Measure | Harvest Length | Days Ready |
|---------|------|-------------|----------------|------------|
| Adzuki | 12 hrs. | 1/2 C. | ½ - 1" | 3-5 |
| Alfalfa | 4-6 hrs. | 2 TB. | 1-1 ½" | 4-6 |
| Almonds | 12 hrs. | 1/2 C. | 0" | 1 |
| Clover | 4-6 hrs. | 2 TB. | 1-1 ½" | 4-5 |
| Lentils | 12 hrs. | 1/2 C. | 1/4 –3/4" | 3-5 |
| Mung | 12 hrs. | 1/4 C. | 1/2 –1 ½" | 3-6 |
| Mustard | 4-6 hrs. | 2 TB. | 1" | 4-5 |
| Radish | 4-6 hrs. | 2 TB. | 1" | 4-5 |
| Sunflower | 8 hrs. | 1 C. | 0-1/2" | 1-3 |
| Wheat | 12 hrs. | 1/2 C. | 1/4 –1/2" | 2-3 |

"Sprouts and immature greens are the most nutritious and live, raw organic foods that are available on this planet."
      Victoras P. Kulvinskas, M.S. – Survival into the 21st. Century.

# SOLAR, WOOD & PRESSURE COOKING

## SOLAR COOKING

You've probably heard of solar steeped teas…a jar of water containing a few herbal tea bags, placed in a sunny spot, with the sun as main contributor to a delicious cup of tea. The sun can help with much more than tea.

We built our first solar oven ten years ago. It's a simple wooden box with a glass door, and aluminum foil lining the inside. It has four metal side wings that can be folded in for ease in transporting, but which also serve to help magnify the heat of the sun to the food inside the oven. It was simple to make. The directions for this cooker and others can be found in *Beth and Dan Halacy's book, "Cooking with the Sun."*

Solar cooking is not only easy and fun, it's a wise use of our natural resources, helps protect our environment, and is a great way to cook on camping trips where wood fires may be restricted. As well, cooking with the sun takes the heat out of the kitchen.

You can bake or cook anything in a solar oven that you normally would bake in a gas or electric one. It may take longer if the oven temperature is lower or fluctuates. This can often happen if a cloud even temporarily blocks the sun, or if a cold breeze sweeps across your solar oven. Most bread, cookies and some desserts will not be significantly affected by being baked at a lower temperature, for a longer period of time. Cookies can be baked at 200°. It takes an hour or longer, but they're still delicious. Pizza crust can be baked at 200-250° in about one hour, and then removed from the oven, sauce and veggies added, and put back in the solar oven for 30-40 minutes, or until the veggies are hot. Cakes generally do better if baked no lower than 350°. (especially at higher altitudes)

On a sunny day a solar oven can reach temperatures as high as 350°- 400°. The trick is to "track" the sun by pointing the oven right at it, and to place it where it is sheltered from the wind. Air temperature is not as important as sun exposure, but a strong wind can slow the cooking process.

There are many advantages to cooking with solar energy. Solar cookers are not a fire hazard and can be used safely in areas closed to fires. There's no fuel to buy, no smoke or other pollution, and no ashes to clean up. Best of all, using a solar cooker is fun.

Use dark coloured casserole dishes, which will absorb more heat and help the food to cook more quickly.

Preheat the oven for baked goods. It may take 30-40 minutes, depending on the weather conditions. The sun is hottest at mid-day, but depending on the location of the oven it can be set up as early as 9 a.m.

Place a thermometer in your oven so you can know the exact temperature. Experiment until you come up with your ideal setting and time of day for cooking in your particular area.

Always work with the weather. Plan your solar cooking and baking on a day that's mainly sunny. You'll find it easier to bake during the summer when the sun is higher in the sky, and your oven gets hotter. Although the days are shorter in the winter, it's still possible to cook with the sun. The temperature of your oven is determined more by the amount of sunshine than the outside air temperature.

If the pots have glass lids, you can check on the food more easily and avoid reducing the temperature if you have to peak under a solid lid.

Use hot pads when going in and out of the solar cooker.

Plan the time you eat your meal around the time your solar cooked food will be ready. Otherwise, you will find yourself eating overly cooked food, or having to warm it up on your gas or electric stove, defeating the whole purpose of solar cooking in the first place.

## WOOD STOVE COOKING

*Using a wood cook stove is somewhat like a relationship or love affair. You have to watch and tend it carefully. Unlike an electric or gas stove where the dials are set to various degrees of heat, a wood stove functions by the quantity and type of wood it's fed, and the changing of drafts and dampers. If you don't have a wood <u>cook</u> stove, but you have a wood stove that is used to heat your home, you can set a portable oven on top of the stove. These are lightweight, metal boxes with a door and a rack inside. It's big enough to make biscuits and desserts and for small casserole dishes. <u>Lehmans of Kidron, Ohio</u> 877-438-5346 advertises these in their mail order catalog, or you might find one at a flea market or antique store. Boiling and sautéing can also be done on top of a wood heat stove, using metal trivets as devices for adjusting the heat.*

<u>Here are a few tips for the beginner wood cook stove user.</u>

Start by making a fire in the firebox. Use crumbled newspaper and small sticks. Open the side draft and damper. The damper handle is usually on the side or top of the stove. Sometimes there will be an arrow to indicate which way is open or closed. If you take the back round stove plate off and look inside the stove, near the stovepipe, and move the damper handle, you should see a vent (called the damper) moving back and forth. The vent should be open so that a good draft is produced when first starting the fire. If it isn't marked with arrows, note which way creates an open or closed vent and write it down for future reference.

Continue adding wood to the firebox. The smaller and dryer the sticks, a hotter fire will result more quickly. This is helpful when you want to use the cooking surface of the stove right away. When the fire really gets going, add larger pieces of wood to the firebox. In 15 to 30 minutes you can close down the damper and side draft, so that the wood burns slower, and the heat will go directly towards the oven.

The built-in door thermometer on most wood cook stoves is seldom accurate. You're lucky if yours is. Place a small oven thermometer inside the oven as a second or more accurate gauge. When baking in the oven, watch the placement of the oven racks. Some stoves have them placed too high and too close to the top of the oven, where baked goods could brown too quickly. If this happens, move the rack to a lower setting, or place the rack on a very shallow pan on the floor of the oven. If it's not hot enough, continue adding more wood to the firebox until it is. If it gets too hot, which can happen right in the middle of baking, open the door of the oven to cool it down some, stop filling the firebox with wood and open the damper all the way to release some of the heat.

As water and food cooks on top of the stove, move them around to decrease or increase the heat. Every spot on the stovetop will be different. Right over the firebox is the hottest. To simmer something after it has come to a boil, move it to a place farthest from the firebox. Cooking on a wood cook stove takes experimentation. Every stove is different, and some firewood such as well-dried oak and juniper, will burn hotter than others. Wood stove cooking not only adds warmth to the kitchen, but when well tended, can produce great meals and delicious baked goods.

## CAMPFIRE BAKING

*Here's a few tips on how to never be without home-made breads and baked goods, while on extended camping trips, and if you don't have a portable solar oven to take with you.*

Build rocks up around the campfire, close enough together for a large oven size rack to be placed securely on them. When the fire burns down to hot coals, place a very large stainless steel bowl upside down on the oven rack. You can set an oven thermometer inside the bowl area. Remember to use hot pads, as the bowl will get quite hot. The bowl acts as a domed oven. It can also be used for mixing the baked goods before washing and setting over the hot coals. Place a pan of biscuits, bread, cake, or other baked goods underneath the bowl. Use large oiled juice cans to bake breads in. Breads such as tortillas, English muffins and biscuits can be baked slowly on a hot griddle without the domed oven. Watch the baked goods carefully. Don't allow flames to touch the pans, or the bottom of baked goods could burn. If you're concerned about the temperature of this make shift oven, it's always better to have the temperature lower than normal, than hotter. Baked goods do better when baked longer than flash cooked. If the temperature is too hot, the outside of the baked good could become dry and hard and brown too quickly, and the inside could end up under baked and mushy. **Note:** *For a permanent outside wood-fired oven, a horno (pronounced ore-no) could be built. It's a simple dome shaped structure, made with earth, and typically seen in Mexico and the southwest United States.*

## HIGH SPEED PRESSURE COOKING

A pressure cooker can make fast work out of foods like beans and rice, which normally take a long time to cook. It also helps save our natural resources. Many of us raised in the fifties remember the fear that pressure cookers engendered. "It's going to blow" was a common household phrase. But, most pressure cookers are now made with a back up mechanism for releasing excess steam.

Pressure cookers cook foods at temperatures much higher than standard methods. Follow the instructions that came with your cooker, which usually contain amounts of water needed, and cooking times for various ingredients. Also, see the Cooking Times for legumes chart on page 18. Make sure to buy a pressure cooker that is stainless steel, not aluminum. Six to eight quarts is an ideal size, since you can only fill a cooker about two thirds full, in order to leave room for the pressure to rise.

Remember, once the high pressure is reached, lower the heat just enough to maintain the pressure. After the allotted amount of time has elapsed, take the pressure cooker off of the heat and let it cool naturally, or place it under the cold-water faucet, allowing the water to run over the lid. The cooker cannot be opened until it cools down and the pressure valve opens. If you have an older cooker with a jiggle top, a teaspoon or two of oil may need to be added, to control the foaming of split peas.

# GUIDELINES FOR A WHEAT FREE DIET

*Wheat and products containing gluten sometimes produce allergic type reactions in some individuals; such as excessive mucus, stomach aches, indigestion and gas. Sometimes a person can eat wheat products, if exposure is far enough apart, or some form of treatment is used to block the reaction. If you want to experiment with a wheat free diet; follow the guidelines below. Almost all the recipes in this book can be converted to wheat free. Also, check the index for specific wheat free recipes.*

\* Substitute a mixture of potato starch (not flour), rice, bean and tapioca flours for wheat flour. Mix it up ahead of time for future baking: 2 parts rice or bean flour, (garbfava flour-a flour made with garbanzo and fava beans) or a combination of both, and 1 part each of potato starch and tapioca flour. Mix together well, and store in a lidded container.

\* Add ¼ - 1 tsp. xantham gum to baked good recipes, or approximately ¼-½ tsp. per cup of flour.

\* Substitute pasta or other wheat or gluten containing products, (such as oats, rye, barley, spelt and kamut) with products made with amaranth, corn, millet, quinoa, rice, or soy. Arrowroot, gluten free baking powder, corn and potato starch, and tapioca flour can also be tolerated. Sprouted grains are usually tolerated, because the chemical structure is changed when sprouted.

\* Watch out for the following products, which could contain wheat and wheat derivatives: TVP, baking powder, condiments such as mustard, ketchup and mayonnaise, salad dressings, sauces, cereals, candies, desserts, breads and crackers, tamari, prepared or canned foods, meat substitutes, and products containing gluten.

" We should reduce the amount of food we eat, and not be so fussy about its taste. We should try to live simply and economically, eat simple and healthy food, and not overindulge just for the taste. Try not to be fussy or over-particular, nor attached too much. Control your eating, i.e., eat only when necessary and just the right amount. Eating more than necessary fetters, blemishes, and degrades the mind. If we live moderately and adequately, the mind will be elevated and advanced."

*Phra Ajahn Yantra Amaro, Buddhist Monk & Author - Look Into The Mind*

*A healthy lifestyle is not often taught in schools. Television, radio and magazine commercials bombard the public with products that often produce just the opposite of a healthy lifestyle. Many junk type "foods," cigarettes and alcohol are often glamorized, making such products seem in vogue, or the proper things to indulge in to acquire acceptance by peers. When illness or dis-ease strikes, a person might start looking into a healthier way of being, but why wait until then? Why not take the approach from the East, where people generally make appointments with Oriental Doctors in order to stay healthy, not always to remedy a sickness. Dr. Elson Hass states, in his book* Staying Healthy with the Seasons, *"much health improvement takes real work on your part, and daily care. Healing is a process, not a destination. Illness is usually not imposed on or separate from us. It's more our own lack of self-control, moderation and direction which endangers our health, though environmental and economic factors are certainly concerns." Take the first step to maintaining a healthy lifestyle, by adding at least one new beneficial change to your daily routine. You'll find that through discipline true serenity will follow.*

**FOOD:** Eat an abundance of organically grown, fresh fruits and vegetables, every day. Include greens such as lettuce, spinach, beet tops, cabbage and sprouts. Remember to soak them in a solution to remove bacteria and parasites. Attempt to eat many of your foods as close to their natural state as possible. Health is found in natural, pure and whole foods. We cannot live well on foods grown on artificial soils. If you shop at regular supermarkets and buy non-organic foods, you have to watch that your shopping cart isn't filled with biochemical deficiencies. Grow your own vegetables by converting all or part of your lawn into an organic veggie garden. Lacking space, join or start a community garden, or grow sprouts in your kitchen, herbs in a sunny window, vegetables in pots on a patio, and buy organic produce at local farmer's markets. Eat whole grains and avoid white flour and white sugar products. Minimize your intake of salt, fat, caffeine and processed foods; and eliminate food additives, preservatives and colourings. Adapt to the changes of the seasons. In the Chinese system of healing, every season is connected to a particular part of the body, and associated with various foods and diets. Chew your food 25-100 times per mouthful, depending on the type of food. Eat only when you're hungry, and eat a variety of foods in order to obtain all of the elements your body needs. Eat to live rather than live to eat. Eat a diet of at least 70% alkaline forming foods and 30% acid producing foods. Colds, infections, excess mucus and many illnesses are directly related to an overly acid diet and body. (See the acid and alkaline chart in this section.) We can't necessarily stay well on nutrition and food alone, but it should be one of the first things that we learn about.

**DRINK:** at least six to eight cups of water a day, between meals, less if you eat high water content foods. Drink only pure water. If you live in the city where water is fluoridated and chlorinated, or your water source is questionable, invest in a purification system, such as distillation, reverse osmosis and ozonating, or purchase purified water from a reputable source. Cold water or drinks with meals disrupts the digestive process. Drink pure juices or herbal teas instead of soda pop and caffeinated beverages, and drink them between meals, not with them.

**EXERCISE DAILY:** Find an exercise program that suits you, whether it's aerobics, yoga, tai chi, exercising on a mini trampoline, or fast paced walking, and get into a regular routine. Join a fitness club or gym. Get out of bed every morning and stretch, touch your toes, keep your body limber. Invest in a body inverter or a headstand stool. By inverting up side down, the body gets a rest from the downward pull of gravity. This is a great aid for prolapsed organs. If you don't have an inverter, or standing on your head scares you—buy a slant board, or turn an ironing board or a wooden plank into an inexpensive slant board, by propping it up on a bed or chair. Lie on it for 10-20 minutes a day. Take a steam bath or sauna for relaxation, as well as to help release toxins from your body.

**SLEEP IN A WELL VENTILATED ROOM:** Drink Chamomile or other relaxing teas, to help induce a restful sleep. Don't eat or drink too close to bedtime, as your body will be spending time digesting the food, when it should be relaxing for the night. Get adequate and restful sleep every night. Invest in a good mattress and sheets and blankets made of natural fibers. If insomnia is a problem, consider natural healing alternatives, such as putting a few drops of lavender on your pillow. Melatonin or an herbal sleep supplement might also be helpful, or practice a few tension taming exercises or relaxation techniques, such as yoga or meditation, before retiring. As well, avoid too much stimulation right before bedtime.

**CONNECT WITH THE EARTH:** Spend time every day connecting with the Earth and being close to nature. Create a flower and organic vegetable garden and get your hands into the soil. Take walks and hike in quiet places away from the busyness of city life. Breathe in the fresh air and observe the wild life around you. Rent a canoe or kayak and float peacefully in a local lake or river. Give thanks for all that the Earth Mother offers you, and remember that famous quote; *"All things are connected. Whatever befalls the Earth befalls the sons and daughters of Earth. Man did not weave the web of life. He is merely a strand in it. Whatever he does to the web, he also does to himself."* By becoming more in tune with nature, or practicing living in conscious harmony every day, we greatly enhance our life force and our connectedness with all beings. We may start to consider more seriously the two R's in the recycling symbol that are often neglected, but of most importance; reduce and reuse. By simplifying our lives, lowering our consumption, and enacting practices that reduce the use of our natural resources, we not only save money, we contribute to the health of our world and all beings. The simple acts of using power saving compact fluorescents, taking shorter and fewer showers, redirecting bath water to feed outside gardens or inside house plants, supporting second hand stores, incorporating old but usable items into building and craft projects, can make important contributions. The sun is a powerful vehicle for cooking, heating water and homes, and in the process reduces gas or electric use. Car pooling or making fewer trips by careful planning and list making, walking or riding a bike, buying a hybrid or electric car, or at least an energy efficient vehicle, are all wise choices for contributing to a healthier Earth. When we can view ourselves in the great circle of life as part of the sacred web, where all life is connected and related, we take more seriously the choices that we make each day, and embellish on those that contribute to a energizing life and a healthier planet. We have to be looking at and taking care of what's on our own plate, because all that we can really change is ourselves. Perhaps what's on our plate will be an inspiration to someone else.

**PRACTICE DEEP BREATHING:** Remember to breathe. Watching the breath--breathing in peace and harmony, breathing out tension and disharmony, can ease many stressful situations.

**CLOTHING:** Wear comfortable clothing made of natural fibers that breathe, and shoes that don't constrict your feet. Avoid high-heeled shoes and tight fitting clothes.

**AVOID TOXINS:** It's often difficult to escape the pollution of automobiles and industrially polluted air, especially if you live in or near a city. But we can control, to some degree, the environment in our homes, by choosing household products which are safe and environmentally friendly. Buy furnishings with non-synthetic fibers, or low or no VOC paints for your walls. In building projects use non-treated, non-formaldehyde woods and insulation. Use cleaning and personal care products which are safe for you and the environment. Remember that your skin is like a sponge. Our health is determined by what we put on our bodies as well as what we put in it. Eat organically grown foods. Soak produce in a fruit or veggie spray, or in one of the solutions found in the *Household Cleaning Section* of this book. This will help to reduce or eliminate bacteria and chemicals. If working with toxic materials or dusty projects is unavoidable, protect your hands and face and wear a good dust mask or respirator. Use foam ear protectors around noisy work places. Rather than pop an over the counter or prescription drug when minor discomforts arise, such as head and muscle aches, consider relaxation techniques, a hot bath, herbal teas, or natural pain relieving creams and supplements. Therapies and techniques such as: aromatherapy, acupressure and acupuncture, ayurveda, homeopathy, iridology, kinesiology, naturopathy, reiki, colonics, ozone and periodic fasting from solid foods, are just a few of the many holistic alternatives to chose from for health care and self healing.

**ATTITUDE:** A positive attitude can assist with good health. The immune system is greatly jeopardized by states of stress, depression, anger, sadness and worry. If any of these emotions creep into your day, find time to relax, take a walk, breathe harmony in and breathe disharmony out. Meditate at the end of the day or when you need a break. Find time to be in the silence, free of talking. Every day spend time relaxing the mind and body, and loosen up by stretching your muscles. When we enlighten our outlook with the understanding that all obstacles that come into our life have a purpose, we can come to an acceptance and peace with what we have been gifted with, instead of holding on to resentment and malice and being a victim to our past. There's an old saying, that it isn't necessarily how a person falls that counts, it's how we get up. Stay in tune with your personal needs and what you're hungry for. There are many types of hunger in life---hunger for delicious food and good health, for friendships or to be of service to others, for time to be alone or spent with family and loved ones, for music, travel and artistic pursuits. Learn to make contact with your own intuitive knowledge for better health and well being. Follow your hearts desires and do those things that you really love to do. Avoid procrastination. It's far better to start and complete something than to worry about the perfection of an outcome. Even if the end result is not satisfactory to you, at least by giving it your full attention, you ended up learning from your mistakes, rather than to not have started at all. In most endeavors, whether it's self-healing, gardening, arts and crafts or building projects, it's often through trial and error that we can perfect anything. Sometimes we just need to come to terms with perfection not being that necessary for our happiness. If things aren't working out the way you want for your life, make changes. Change comes from letting go of attachments to people, things, values and practices that no longer serve us. Take steps to bring about the life you envision. We cannot just fill our heads with thoughts and ideas; we must put those ideas into action. Limit your exposure to negativity from people, television, radio, newspapers and movies. As much as possible put your time and energy into uplifting and positive environments and endeavors, and with people who exhibit an optimistic and cheerful attitude. We are responsible for our own life. Don't expect your happiness to come from other people. Develop your own inner peace and happiness. The challenge is to keep ourselves well enough, so that as we get older, we will still be young and healthy enough to enjoy life without illness or dis-ease.

**VIEW STAYING HEALTHY IN A PREVENTATIVE MANNER:** Benjamin Franklin said, " An ounce of prevention is worth a pound of cure." Endeavor to improve your physical, mental and spiritual bodies by right living, and avoiding injurious habits. By eliminating unhealthy habits such as smoking, heavy alcohol use, drugs and refined and adulterated food products; and by incorporating a healthful diet and positive attitudes and actions, such as relaxation, meditation, exercise and educating oneself on nutrition, we can achieve well being and prevent illness. Remember, if money isn't spent on good food and healthful practices, it'll end up being spent on doctors and medical bills. If illness or dis-ease does occur, look at it as a message that changes need to be made. Take steps to make those changes, rather than bring fear and tension into your body, or mask the symptoms with chemical drugs. Keep your life force or Chi energy high, by eating good food, drinking pure water, getting fresh air, exercise and adequate sleep. By maintaining a positive and calm mind, we can access the direction to take in our lives, and develop the dedication, discipline and stamina to carry it through.

*Also read the section on Weight Control, pg. 280*

---

Earth Mother

I close the book
Turn off the radio, computer,
Telephone and television,
Shut myself off
From any kind of information.
From Nature: feel all.
Surrender myself like a seed
Extract from its womb
Put down roots and
Renewed by the elements
Re-assume my divinity

Terezinha Fialho, Brazilian poet

---

# ACID & ALKALINE FOODS

| ACID | ALKALINE |
|---|---|
| Meat, fish & Eggs | Most fruits & vegetables |
| Dairy Products | Mushrooms |
| Most beans and nuts | Fruit and vegetable juices |
| Most seeds | Millet, amaranth, quinoa |
| Most grains | Sprouted grains & seeds |
| Candy & carbonated beverages | Almonds |
| Alcohol & Drugs | Soy & lima beans |
| Coffee & coffee substitutes | Herbal teas |
| Most sweeteners | Brown rice syrup & succanat |
| Starches & proteins | Miso, salt, seaweed |
| Blueberries, cranberries, plums | Mu and Bancha tea |
| | All cold processed oils, except nut |

**Signs of an overly acid body:** Over tired, slow nerve action, (not thinking or acting quickly or clearly) excess mucus in body, congestion, colds, headaches, sinus problems, skin trouble, infections and dis-ease.

**To reduce excess acid in the body:** Eat miso soup, cucumbers, grated radish, lots of veggies and fruit. Reduce consumption of acid producing products.

**To neutralize extreme situations of acidity quickly:**
Drink either 1 tsp. baking soda in 8 oz. of water, or drink some fresh lemon juice in water every 15 – 30 minutes, until the acidity passes.

**Tips on what makes blood overly acidic:** Eating too many acid type products, stress, hot showers and baths, nutrients too much in pill form.

**How to keep our bodies in a balanced state:** Eat at least 70 percent alkaline foods, and 30 percent acid. One to two teaspoons apple cider vinegar in water, just before meals, will increase hydrochloric acid in the stomach for better assimilation of food. Eat as many foods as possible in their natural raw state. Chew foods 50-100 times per mouthful. Sprits with cold water after hot showers, and avoid stress. Use natural healing modalities and products such as: herbs, supplements, massage, acupressure and acupuncture, chiropractic, and naturopathic. Monitor your PH level with testing strips, available at most natural food stores.

# WEIGHT CONTROL TIPS

*Eating healthful foods is the first step for losing, gaining or maintaining your ideal weight. Since you're reading this book you are already on the path to eating healthier foods, free of unhealthy fats and artificial ingredients.*

*There are many causes for over and underweight conditions, including: glandular, emotional, metabolic, nutritional, psychological, over or under eating, and lack of exercise. Chronic over or severely underweight conditions can contribute to numerous health problems, including: fluctuations in blood pressure, heart disease, diabetes, hardening of the arteries, circulatory problems, strain on the joints causing osteoarthritis, poor adjustment to temperature changes and premature death.*

*Also read the section: <u>Tips for a Healthy Lifestyle, pg. 275</u>*

* <u>**Avoid products with empty calories**</u>…. such as junk "food". They might fill you up, but, they can also fill you out, without adding nourishment to your body. Instead, munch on raw sunflower seeds, low-fat rice crackers or non-sulphured dried fruit. Keep fresh cut carrots, celery and cucumbers in the fridge, for a healthy snack. Drink herbal teas or fresh fruit and veggie juices instead of carbonated beverages and soda pops.

* <u>**Eat less if you're intention is to lose weight, and chew your foods completely:**</u>
Every mouthful should be well masticated, in order for the food to be properly digested and capable of nourishing your body. (At least 25-100 chews per mouthful, depending on the type of food.) By chewing foods more completely, and by eating in a slower manner, you will feel satisfied more quickly, and it'll be easier to cut back on the quantity of foods you normally eat.

 * <u>**Eat whole grains and foods**</u> containing natural fibers, such as wheat, and oat bran, veggies and fruit. Avoid breads made with white flour. Eat real whole wheat bread. If it says "wheat bread" or the ingredient list does not list whole wheat, it's nothing more than dyed white bread. Stay away from overly processed and sugared foods. Eat organically grown foods as much as possible, to reduce chemicals in your diet, and the stress they can cause on your body. Be aware that you may experience *withdrawal and detoxing symptoms* when you switch to a healthier diet. As with caffeine withdrawal, most symptoms last only a couple of days. Assist the detoxing by using products that help clean the colon and blood stream, such as colon cleanse teas and fiber rich powders that can be mixed with juice; or herbs such as pau d'arco or red clover, which help purify the blood.

\* **Eat your largest meal at mid-day**; eat your last meal before 7 p.m., and if weight gain is a problem, make it light. You're usually least active in the evening when calories need to be burned off. Besides, you'll sleep better when you're body isn't working so hard to digest a large meal. If excess weight is a problem, consider fasting from solid foods, at least one day a week, and include colon cleanse teas and enemas to help clean out your digestive tract. For those unable to gain weight, consider adding digestive aids and enzymes, as well as herb teas for parasites and blood cleansing.

\* **Keep your body hydrated** by drinking at least half your body weight in ounces of pure, unadulterated water a day. For instance-- if you weigh 160 pounds, you would drink approximately 80 ounces of water a day, or 2 ½ quarts. Herbal teas and pure juices can make up part of this liquid, but not soft drinks, black tea or coffee. This is just a guideline. If you live in a drier climate, are out hiking or working in the hot sun, you might require more. If you're eating a lot of raw fruits and vegetables, you probably require less. Often people think they are hungry, when really they are just thirsty. For better digestion, drink your liquids between meals, not with them.

\* **Exercise,** stretch, walk, do daily yoga asanas, or attend a yoga class, walk or bicycle to work or school. If you *must* watch television, exercise while doing so. Find a friend to go on daily fast paced walks with. Buy a rebounder or miniature trampoline for exercising inside. They are small enough to slide under your bed, when not in use. A rebounder is not only a great form of exercise, especially when the weather is not conducive for outside walking, but, it also helps to keep your lymph fluids moving. Find an exercise program that suits you. Some people do better with fast paced aerobics; and others with slow moving yoga or Tai Chi. Fast paced exercises generally work better for burning calories, while yoga and stretching help to tighten and reduce bulge and keep your body limber and relaxed. Whatever exercise you choose, let it become a passionate and consistent part of your life.

\* **Relax and enjoy life**; maintain a positive attitude. Don't beat up on yourself if you get off your diet or exercise routine. Note it and get back on the path to a healthier you. Remember, it's not so much what you do some of the time, but what you do most of the time, that really counts. If you don't notice any changes within a few months, consider making an appointment with a Naturopath or a clinic or consultant that uses non-evasive testing techniques that can easily pin point areas of concern; such as metabolic disturbances or hormonal problems. Don't give up on any routine too quickly. As Rome wasn't built in a day, your body didn't get to its present condition overnight. Be persistent and as consistent as possible.

> "... one of the three rules that they have for long life is never to get overweight, and they're all the same weight at age 153 as they were at 20. They never overeat and they never retire. They never quit working. These things I find definitely in all the old men and all the old people."
> Bernard Jensen PhD. - Food Healing for Man

It is possible and easy to cook nutritious meals, when you live alone or have a busy schedule. To simplify the process, cook a large pot of rice, beans or pasta to last a few days. You can vary each days meal by adding different items to the pre-cooked foods. For instance, a pot of bean soup can be turned into a veggie bean soup by adding chopped up veggies or a handful of small pasta shells. With a fresh salad, your dinner can be nutritiously balanced and the prep time is greatly reduced.

If you have leftover veggies from one meal, consider using them in a cream soup base, or adding them to rice for a quick stir-fry. Spice up left over beans, and serve them over rice. Pasta with a simple sauce, such as olive oil and vegan parmesan, a few crushed herbs and sautéed veggies, is another easy meal to prepare. Variety is the spice of life, so vary rice, potato, pasta and soup dishes during the week. Also use quick cooking grains, such as millet and bulgur, or couscous and orzo pasta, which looks similar to rice, but cooks up quicker.

Consider pre-cooking casseroles on the weekend, when you may have more time, and freezing them for later use. Make sure you bring the cold dish to room temperature before putting it in a hot oven; otherwise, you risk the dish breaking. Breads and desserts can also be prepared and frozen or refrigerated for later use. Slice the bread before freezing, and then when you want toast, just take individual slices out of the zip lock freezer bag, and put them directly into a toaster or toaster oven.

A small pressure cooker can assist with cooking meals quicker, especially with raw beans, which take a long time to become soft when cooked in the conventional stovetop manner. In the summer time turn those cooked beans into a salad, or toss with some cooked pasta and veggies. Use a simple lemon and oil dressing mixed with garlic and some herbs. A nutritious meal can be put together first thing in the morning, and left to simmer slowly in a crock pot, while you attend to your business or are off at work. If your mornings are too busy, put everything together the night before, refrigerate, and then add to the crock-pot before leaving for work.

Sprouting seeds such as alfalfa, radish, clover and mung requires very little time, and can add lots of enzymes and nutrition to your meals. All they require is to be rinsed once or twice a day. If you grow more than you can eat, put some in little zip lock bags, and give them to friends or neighbours. Growing sprouts in your kitchen, especially during cold, winter days when outdoor gardening has been put to rest, can be fun, and provide the means of acquiring fresh, local greens packed with so much nutrition.

If you live alone, consider preparing a meal and having a neighbour or friend over to share it with, or start a weekly or monthly vegan potluck. Specify to those who eat meat and dairy that the dishes should be meat and dairy free. Some guests may find this request to be somewhat of a challenge, but once they see and taste the diversity of vegan foods, they'll be looking forward to the next potluck. The potlucks could be hosted at a different home each time. In the process of good food and company, you'll be exposing and educating family and friends to the fine art of vegan cooking, and providing a space where other healthy lifestyle ideas can be shared.

There's no need as a single or busy person, whether you are still actively working outside the home, or are retired and living a relatively sedentary life, to live on TV dinners and processed food. We can keep our good health no matter what our schedule. It just takes dedication and pre-planning. For additional information, read the sections: <u>Tips for a Healthy Lifestyle</u>, pg. 275, <u>Acid / Alkaline & Weight Control tips,</u> pg. 279 & 280.

"Thomas Edison once remarked, "Well....I made 4,000 experiments before the electric light was accomplished." Someone said, "Oh, my goodness, what a waste of time!" Tomas Edison said, "but you know, I know 3,999 things not to do."
"That's elevation" - Bernard Jensen  - Food Healing for Man

There's no need to change your eating and cooking routine, when having dinner guests or company on extended visits. Hosting friends and family provides the opportunity to introduce healthful vegan dishes, and to serve delicious meals and desserts, that will nourish and please guests with a wide variety of food preferences and diets.

Older guests, or those with cholesterol or heart and circulation problems, will appreciate your low fat cooking and dishes containing stimulating herbs and spices. College students visiting with friends, and accustomed to fast food diners, convenience foods and dorm cafeterias will generally appreciate any effort you make in the kitchen, let alone a nutritionally balanced and attractive vegan meal. Meat eaters of all ages will be amazed and delighted with recipes using vegan meat substitutes. In fact, many meat eaters might be really surprised to see that a vegan diet just doesn't consist of salads and steamed veggies. If you've ever attended a banquet where you made arrangements in advance for a meatless meal, and were served a baked potato, with limp, overcooked broccoli and a few pieces of head lettuce, you'll understand what I mean. I'm not implying that we shouldn't be accepting of such efforts, or be grateful that we get to eat at all; it's just that vegan cooking can comprise far more than that.

There are a few practices that may be helpful when serving company. Never apologize for what you serve at the dinner table, or for any mishap in the kitchen. Just do the best you can and realize that hardly anyone but you will realize what the finished product could have looked like. Never talk about the meat or dairy substitutes you used, unless you're asked. In some cases an entirely lovely and delicious meal can be ruined by exuberantly and innocently exclaiming that the sauce was made with pureed tofu, or fake rice cheese, or what looks like burger is really a weird dry concoction called TVP, that before cooking looks similar to cat kibble. Also, go light on the hot pepper. Some people really don't like their food spicy hot. Let them add their own, or ask their heat preference before adding hot ingredients.

Consider having guests over for breakfast or brunch, or what I call Slunch, (in between lunch and supper) rather than the traditional dinner hour. Ever since we spend some time at a Thai Monastery and Vipassana Meditation Retreats, we've switched from the traditional three meals a day to two. We usually eat our second meal by mid afternoon, and save any dessert for early evening. Our extended guests, whether family or friends, usually adapt to this routine; although they often appreciate snacks of fresh fruit or cookies, and the occasional bowl of popcorn in the evenings. You might want to consider a festive potluck type dinner party, and plan a meal based on a particular country or culture. Have the guests bring one of the planned dishes; or host a meal such as nacho salad pg. 64, Pizza pg. 115, or tostados pg. 101, where everyone contributes by bringing one of the ingredients. Whatever you organize, careful planning and preparation will be necessary, to assure plenty of time for the cook to relax and visit with guests.

#1  Greek

Savory Miso Soup Pg. 77
Greek salad Pg. 68
Spanakopita Pg. 117
Dessert:  Lemon bars Pg. 171

#2  Italian

Autumn Harvest Salad Pg. 65, 68
Ricotta Stuffed Shells Pg. 95 OR
Mushroom Spinach Lasagna Pg. 96
Herbal Whole Wheat Rolls Pg. 29
Dessert:  Lemon Pudding Cake Pg. 183

#3  Mexican

Spinach or lettuce Salad Pg. 68
Enchiladas Pg. 104
Steamed brown rice Pg. 129
Dessert:  Orange Mango Sherbet Pg. 218

#4  American

Spinach Salad Pg. 68
Scallop potatoes Pg. 128
Oat Loaf Pg. 138 with Brown Gravy Pg. 158
Steamed Carrots
Dessert: Apple Pie Pg. 201
Or Blueberry Pie Pg. 203

#5  Oriental

Fresh Spring Rolls Pg. 56
Oriental Hot n' Sour Soup Pg. 77
Coconut Stir Fry Pg. 110 OR
Pad Thai With Veggies Pg. 88
Dessert:  Lemon Ginger Ice Cream Pg. 215

#6  Middle Eastern

Spicy Cucumber & Tomato Salad Pg. 69
Dolmas Pg. 57
Tabooli Salad Pg. 59
Hummus Pg. 150
Pocket Pita Bread Pg. 31

BREAKFAST IDEAS

*Ideas for overnight visitors and extended company*

#1  Scrambled tofu with veggies Pg. 43, Spicy Sausage Patties Pg. 44, Potato Cakes pg.127
#2  Pancakes Pg. 42 with maple syrup & fruit topping and Spicy Sausage Patties
#3  Veggie Breakfast Wraps Pg. 44
#4  Porridge (hot cereal) Pg. 50, with toast and jam
#5  Granola Pg. 50 with sliced bananas and soy milk
#6  Other ideas for a lighter breakfast: Scones Pg. 46, blueberry coffee cake Pg.49,
     Bran Muffins Pg.52

*Here are some suggestions on how to survive and not jeopardize your good health, on vacations and trips away from your vegan kitchen.*

When you travel by car, pack a cooler, especially on trips that are longer than one day. Stock it with fresh fruit, soy yogurt, zip lock bags of raw, sliced veggies, such as carrots, radishes and celery, and a container of dipping sauce, such as hummus. A hearty potato or pasta salad and veggie sandwiches can be made the night before a trip, and carried in the cooler inside lidded containers. Hearty muffins or a box of soymilk and a supply of dry cereal or granola can be packed for a quick breakfast. Don't forget to pack a bowl and spoon. In fact, a simple wooden bowl and spoon could be used for all of your out-of-the-cooler eating. Other handy food items are: granola bars, sliced whole wheat bread or pita and peanut butter, trail mix, (a mixture of nuts and dried fruit) a bag of corn chips and a bottle of salsa. As you travel the highways and byways, keep your eyes open for health food type stores and natural food markets; and stock up on deli items, produce, nourishing snacks, and a bag of ice.

When traveling by bus, or train, or on hikes longer than a day, you can take a lightweight insulated backpack or cooler with ice packs, to keep your "survival" food cold. On longer air and train trips you can request vegan meals. You can almost always find some salad, fresh fruit, herbal teas and pasta-hold the cheese, on train dining cars.

In large cities it's generally easy to find a restaurant that is vegan friendly. There are many Asian and Indian establishments that serve non-meat dishes, minus the fish or meat broth. Always ask if a particular dish contains any meat products, dairy or eggs, before ordering. Many Mexican restaurants no longer use lard in their refried beans. Best of all, is that there are many vegan and organic establishments popping up in cities across the world. You can always count on some organic fare in the deli section of a large natural food store. Check the yellow pages when you get into a city, or purchase a book or vegetarian guide, which lists places to eat, sleep and shop veggie. There is no reason to jeopardize your vegan principles when traveling locally or abroad. **Suggested Reading:**
Vegetarian Restaurants & Natural Food Stores in the U.S., by John Howly,
Vegetarian Britain, by Alex Bourke & Katrina Holland
Vegetarian Europe, by Alex Bourke

---

" The tragic truth is that most folks treat their automobiles better than their own bodies. If it was definitely proved that smoking cigarettes in an automobile would instantly corrode the engine, every smoker would quit smoking in his car. No automobile owner would pour refined sugar into the gas tank, or stuff a steak in the carburetor, or shove wet, soggy white bread into the radiator. Automobile owners would refrain from such things because they know it would damage their precious machines."

Dick Gregory – Natural Diet for Folks Who Eat- Cooking with Mother Nature.

---

# RAISING HEALTHY CHILDREN

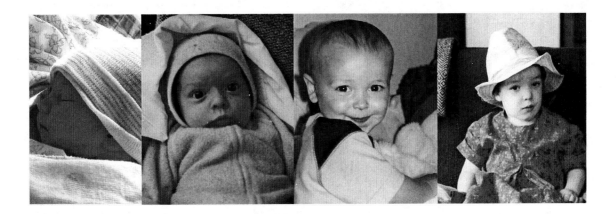

Your children can be vibrant and healthy on a meatless diet.  The National Academy of Sciences vouched for the health of children eating meatless diets, as far back as 1974.  The American Academy of Pediatrics and the American Dietetic Association both issued positive papers in the mid nineteen nineties, asserting the nutritional adequacy of vegetarian diets for children.

Studies have been conducted on vegetarian children, the largest by the Center for Disease Control and reported in Pediatrics (Sept. 1989), following children at the "Farm" community in Tennessee.  They found that children raised on a strict vegetarian (vegan) diet, achieved adequate growth.

Doctors and scientists agree, that mother's milk is still the best food for a baby.  It has two to three times more absorbable calcium than cow's milk, five times more absorbable iron, and is three times higher in vitamin C.  As well, studies have shown that nursing mothers are less likely to get breast cancer later in life.  Children can get adequate protein and calcium with a balanced and varied diet containing enough calories.  Protein is not just in meat and dairy products, it's in grains, vegetables and legumes.  For growing children, leafy greens, broccoli, kale, tofu, beans, almonds and sesame seeds are high in calcium.  There is growing evidence that these are better forms of calcium than any dairy product, and that the high protein content of animal dairy actually causes a loss of calcium in the body.

A diet devoid of junk "food" and containing lots of fresh and dried fruits, vegetables, and whole grains and beans will supply an adequate iron intake for growing children.  Studies conducted in both England and the U.S., have shown that vegan children get plenty of iron and vitamin C, which enhances iron absorption.  B12 is available in the breast milk of healthy moms, and is found in products such as nutritional yeast, fermented soy products and sea vegetables. Research has shown that non-meat eaters do not need B 12 in as high quantities.

287

Home schooling is one way to make sure your children are getting good wholesome foods during the day. Stock your cupboards and pantry with healthy snacks, such as seeds and nuts, dried fruits and fresh vegetables and fruits. Instead of the highly processed and overly sugared cereals, make your own granola or hot cereals. Have cold herbal teas and natural fruit juices in the refrigerator, instead of pops and sugary beverages. If they attend school away from home, you can send them off with a packed lunch. Buy a sturdy lunch box and thermos, so that the meal will be protected on route. Hot soups and stews can be put into wide mouth thermoses, or an ice pack can be included in the box to keep a salad or sandwich cool.

Start early in their childhood talking about health and nutrition, but don't make a big fuss over food. Children will generally choose the foods their bodies need at any given time, as long as those healthful foods are available. A particular food that they might find disagreeable one day, may be perfectly acceptable on another. Many children who dislike certain vegetables, change their opinion if they get involved in the families vegetable garden, or if the vegetables are served in a different way; such as raw instead of cooked, or vise versa. As well, foods should never be used as a form of bribery or be forced upon a child. Mealtimes should be happy times, where the family can get together and share the days events, eating food in a relaxed manner. Making a fuss about a child's eating, or giving them excessive attention or praise in that regard, or attempting to hurry them through their meals, can contribute to unpleasant childhood memories, or food phobias when they become adults. A few words of thankfulness said before a meal, can help to instill gratefulness for the sustenance received through food, and show appreciation for not only the cooks, but, all the energies that brought the food to the table.

Inform those close to you that you are feeding your child a healthful diet, and would appreciate that they don't bring sugary treats when they visit. Grandparents, family and friends are generally responsive to this request, and more so if they observe hyperactive behaviour in a child, after they consume sugary and artificially flavoured products.

Although it is the responsibility of the parents to know which foods are the best for their growing children, it is only one aspect of maintaining good health. Albeit food is certainly one of the most important elements, a positive and cheerful environment is also a vital condition. If a television set *must* be in the home, children should not be allowed to watch unlimited, unsupervised programs. They should also be encourage to limit over-stimulating toys and games; and to fill their days playing or just being in the natural elements, or pursuing creative endeavors; and taught at a young age to develop patience, tolerance and positive, beneficial attitudes and actions. Parents can set good examples for choices and behaviour that enrich and nourish their children's lives, and that contribute to a peaceful atmosphere filled with mutual respect and compassion.

The key to a child's good health is: adequate calories, quality and variety of food, avoiding junk "foods" with empty calories and high sugar content, drinking pure water for adequate hydration, regular exercise, adequate sleep, avoiding chemicals and drugs, and a harmonious living environment.

**Suggested Reading**:

<u>Every Woman's Book</u>, by Paavo Airola N.D. Ph.D.
<u>Vaccines; are they really safe & effective?</u> By Neil Z. Miller
<u>Pregnancy, Children & The Vegan Diet</u>, by Michael Klaper, M.D.
<u>The Successful Homeschool Family Handbook,</u> by Dr. Raymond & Dorothy Moore.

PLAY CLAY

| | |
|---|---|
| 1 ½ c. flour | 1 C. water |
| 1 C. cornstarch | 1 tsp. dish soap |
| 1 C. sea salt | natural colourings (optional) |

Combine flour, cornstarch and sea salt.  Add water, soap and natural colouring.  Knead the dough until it is smooth and elastic.  Add more flour or water if necessary.  Dough can now be formed into shapes.  Keep the dough in a closed container in the fridge.  Shapes can be hardened by baking at 250° for approximately 1-2 hours.  Once they are cooled, they can be painted or drawn on.

# THE VEGAN PET

Dogs and cats can live a long and healthful life on a vegan diet. Besides eating vegan canned or dry food, dogs especially are quite accepting of table scraps, such as, tofu, cereals, vegetables, beans and avocado. Seaweed can be included with their food for added iodine. Garlic powder and bran, if added to their food, will help prevent or eliminate intestinal parasites. Bran can be included daily for good bowel elimination. Dogs and cats generally enjoy the taste of nutritional yeast, when sprinkled on their food, and it supplies them with added B vitamins. It's generally recommended that dry kibble food be moistened, especially for male cats, to help prevent urinary tract infections.

Most commercial meat based pet foods contain diseased animals or by products, that can't be sold for human consumption, but are allowed in pet food. Hormones and antibiotic residues are found in commercial pet foods containing meat. Hormones are given to the animals to increase growth rates, not to increase the health of the animal. Unfortunately, even the premium brands of pet foods use slaughterhouse waste and diseased animals and or parts. They spend their money on advertising, not ingredients. The fact is, that growth hormone residues actually increase the rate of infection and cancer; not only in slaughtered animals, but also in the people and pets that eat them.

It's relatively difficult to find a vegan pet food, even in a natural foods market. Occasionally you can find a vegetarian dog food. Vegan pet foods can be ordered through a few mail order companies. Our vegan cat food is shipped across the country, from Minnesota, *(Evolution Diet- 1-800-659-0104 or www.petfoodshop.com.)* We like their products not only because they are vegan, but also because they contain no growth hormones or antibiotics, and use pure polyunsaturated vegetable oil instead of animal fat, which can cause clogging of arteries, cholesterol and heart and joint diseases. Because the dry kibble is so nutritious and satisfying, it goes further than most commercial cat foods, thus balancing out the additional cost of shipping the food.

Survey results on vegetarian dogs, following the health of 300 dogs over a period of one year, stated, " there also appeared to be a health advantage to veganism over vegetarianism. 82% of dogs that had been <u>vegan</u> for 5 years or more were in good to excellent health, while only 77% of dogs that had been <u>vegetarian</u> for 5 years or more were in good to excellent health." *(From People for Ethical treatment of Animals - Vegetarian Health Survey Results.)*

How do cats and dogs fit into a vegan household, where wild life are also honored and enjoyed? First, by supplying them with a nutritious vegan diet, so that your principles and philosophy are not jeopardized. Second, by not allowing pets, especially cats, outside and unattended, where they can freely harass little critters and our flying friends. Most cats can easily get used to going outside on a leash, or enjoy staying inside, and sitting in a sunny window. It may be part of their inherent mindset or memory to sneak up and kill birds and other wild creatures, but they really don't need them for supplementing their diet. They can just as easily chase or play with a toy or ball, and get all the nutrients they need from their pet food.

---

Nutritious Pet Formula: *Shake the following together in a jar and store in a cool place.* Mix ½-1 tsp or more, in your pet's meal daily.
1 ½ C. nutritious yeast, ½ C. kelp powder, 1 C. lecithin granules, 2 C. wheat bran, 1 TB. garlic powder, (optional) ½ C. calcium powder (optional)

Homemade Cat Litter: *Mix the following in a bucket, or directly in the litter box.*
4 cups sawdust, (fine to coarse) 8 cups sand, 1cup baking soda, or well-sifted wood ashes. With 1-2 cats, the litter will need changing at least twice a week. Consider providing a covered litter box, to keep it more easily contained and out of young children's reach. *(Make sure that the sawdust is dry and not from treated lumber.)*

**TIP:** When you leave your cats at home for extended periods of time, and you want to make it easier for your friend who comes over to check on your pets; make up cat box liners full of fresh litter, and secure them with a bag tie. When the box needs to be changed, the old litter can easily be picked up inside the liner, and disposed of, and the new liner can be put into the litter box.

---

*"The more we come in contact with animals and observe their behavior, the more we love them..." Immanuel Kant - German Philosopher, 1724-1804*

# ANIMALS IN OUR SOCIETY

**BULL FIGHTS:** There is no fair challenge when it comes to this tourist attraction. The bulls are handicapped from the start; by having Vaseline smeared in their eyes, their horns filed blunt, irritants rubbed on their legs, and their nostrils stuffed with cotton.

**CIRCUSES:** Physical punishment has long been the standard training method for animals in circuses. Animals might also be drugged and have their teeth removed.

**DOG RACES:** The cruelty in greyhound racing begins with the dogs training. Each year approximately 100,000 small animals, mostly rabbits, are used as live bait to teach young dogs to run around the track. These animals may be used repeatedly throughout the day, whether alive or dead. The legs of bait animals are sometimes broken, their cries often exciting the dogs. Guinea pigs are used because they scream. Those dogs that are not so aggressively inclined are sometimes placed in a cage with a rabbit or other animal, and released only after it has killed the animal.

**FARM ANIMALS:** People often say that as long as animals are raised and killed humanely, they don't have a problem eating them. With the high volume livestock industry of today, and the demand for inexpensive meat, the vast majority of animals are <u>not</u> raised or killed humanely. Animals used for food are also excluded from anti-cruelty laws. Livestock have no protection from abuses that would normally be criminal offenses if done to dogs or cats. Today most animals do not live on traditional farms. They are raised in confinement as though they are objects, often being crowded together with as many animals that can fit in a building. The animals feed is mixed with hormones, designed for faster growth and larger production than their skeletal systems can tolerate.

Slaughterhouse animals can often hear and sometimes see the animals ahead of them being killed. All animals, whether humanely or organically raised or not, fight for their lives, and struggle with their remaining strength to get away.

Dairy cows in the U.S. are intensively confined. Their calves are usually taken from them immediately following the birthing, causing distress for both. The cow's milk production is continued non-stop by repeated impregnation, and since 1993, increased in volume by the ingestion of the bovine growth hormone BGH. This, along with the electronic vacuum extraction of the milk, produces a great physical stress to the cows. The weight of the milk stresses their joints and increases the risk of udder infection, known as mastitis. Industry test have shown, that BGH can actually cause enlargement of internal organs and intolerance to heat. Under normal conditions cows can live 25 years or longer, but dairy cows in our present times are usually slaughtered after only five years of milk production.

The veal industry has been created by the high consumption of dairy products. Most veal calves live in confined stalls, sometimes without sunlight, and often being tied to a short rope or chain, where they are unable to move. Their diets are deficient in iron, which produces a pale flesh and the instinct of the calf to try to get iron by chewing on their cages. Up to 20% of calves raised for veal die before reaching the slaughter age of 15 weeks.

**HUNTED ANIMALS:** Hunted animals sometimes escape with injuries and end dying a slow and painful death. Mothers are killed and their young end up starving to death. If hunting was really done for population control, as is often claimed, more females would be hunted than males. Many animals such as the bison and grizzly bear have been hunted to the brink of extinction.

**LAYING HENS:** Laying hens in the U.S. are also intensively confined. Four or five hens might live in one cage that is so small that they can't turn around. The cages are stacked one on top of the other, where excrement from above falls on those hens below. Their automated feeding and watering systems sometimes break down. Male chicks are of no use to an egg hatchery. These birds are simply discarded and die from suffocation, gassing, drowning, or being ground up alive.

**MARINE PARKS:** Orcas and dolphins swim up to 100 miles a day; but captured dolphins are confined to tanks as small as 24 x 24 feet and only 6 feet deep. More than half of all dolphins die within the first two years of captivity. The remaining dolphins live an average of only 6 years. In the wild, orcas stay with their mothers for life. A Canadian research team found that captivity shortens the orca's life by as much as 43 years, and a dolphin's by up to 15 years.

**PRODUCT TESTED ANIMALS:** Every year millions of animals are killed testing personal care and household cleaning products. Rabbits, mice, rats, dogs, cats, primates and guinea pigs are the usual subjects. Tests done often produce: blindness, skin irritation, and poisoning, causing a slow and painful death. Fortunately, there are now many companies who no longer do animal testing. Look for the no animal testing labels, when making purchases.

**RACE HORSES:** Eight hundred and forty race horses suffered fatal racing break downs in American racetracks in 1992, while 3566 were injured badly enough that they could not finish the race, just to create another form of entertainment and gambling for humans.

**RODEOS:** Calf roping often causes broken bones, torn ligaments and other internal injuries to the animals. The animal's are often subjected to electric prods, caustic ointments, sharp spurs, and bucking straps, which dig into the animals abdomen to incite the bucking.

**ZOOS:** Many people defend zoos as a way of promoting education and awareness, as well as preserving threatened species. However, most zoos are tourist attractions containing only non-endangered animals. Many zoo babies are produced to increase public draw, with the excess animals killed once they are no longer cute. The goals of education and preservation cannot justify forcing an animal to live in captivity. The main lesson taught, is that animals are important only in their value to their captors. If one is concerned with endangered species, the effort should be to preserve habitat, not to imprison more animals.

**Resources:**     *Fact sheets from People for Ethical treatment of Animals,*
*The pamphlet; And Justice for all-Animal Liberation Action.*
*Animal Factories, by Jim Mason & Peter Singer*
*Diet for A New America, by John Robbins*

"....Every animal that walks the earth or swims or flies is precious beyond description, something so rare and wonderful that it equals the stars or the ocean or the mind of man."
          James Michener 1902-1997 - American Author and Novelist -

"When will we reach the point that hunting, the pleasure of killing animals for sport, will be regarded as a mental aberration? We must reach the point that killing for sport will be felt as a disgrace to our civilization."......"We must fight against the spirit of unconscious cruelty with which we treat the animals."
          - Dr. Albert Schweitzer

"We stopped eating meat many years ago. During the coarse of a Sunday lunch, we happened to look out our kitchen window at our young lambs playing happily in the fields. Glancing down at our plates we suddenly realized that we were eating the leg of the animal who had only recently been playing in a field herself. We looked at each other and said, "wait a minute, we love these sheep---they're such gentle creatures. So why are we eating them?" It was the last time we ever did."
          - Sir Paul McCartney, English musician, singer and songwriter.

# DICTIONARY OF NON-VEGAN PRODUCTS & INGREDIENTS

*This is just a short list of some common products, which may contain animal products or byproducts.*

**Boar Bristle:** Hair from hogs, found in natural hairbrushes and natural toothbrushes.

**Bone Meal:** From animal bones. It's in some supplements.

**Calcium carbonate:** May come from oyster shells.

**Casein:** Protein of cow's milk. It's in *most* soy cheese and *some* cosmetics.

**Chocolate:** May contain milk. Read the label and eat dark chocolate instead of milk chocolate.

**Collagen:** Unless otherwise stated, is derived from animal tissue. Found in cosmetics and personal care products.

**Commercial Produce & Non-Organic Products:** Not only were they grown with harmful chemical fertilizers and sprays, the chemicals are responsible for the death of many insects, birds and wild life and cause major health hazards for farm workers.

**Cosmetics and Personal Care Products:** May contain dairy or animal products.

**Emus oil:** From birds that originated in Australia, now being factory farmed in the U.S.

**Gelatin:** Is protein dissolved from animal bones and skin. Found in jello and marshmallows. Most capsulated supplements are made of animal gelatin, unless stated otherwise. Look for vegan-caps or "suitable for vegetarians," printed on the label.

**Glues and Adhesives:** Are often made from animal by products.

**Honey:** Although a byproduct of bees, a valued insect for crop pollination, many beekeepers manage their hives in a humane manner, and make every effort to keep the bees alive throughout the winter.

**Ivory:** Comes from tusks of elephants, whales and walruses.

**Lactose:** Milk sugar from mammals. Used in food and cosmetics.

**Leather, Suede and Fur:** All obtained from animals that are killed in the process, unless noted as imitation or man-made. A number of companies are now manufacturing vegan shoes and accessories.

**Marshmallows:** Contain animal gelatin, unless clearly stated as vegetarian.

**Musk oil:** Unless it's artificially made, comes from genitals of deer, beaver and civet cats.

**Premarin:** Female hormone product – is urine from pregnant horses. Natural vegetarian creams are now available, as an alternative for women in menopause.

**Rennet:** The lining of calves stomach, used in cheese making.

**Soy cheese:** May contains casein, a milk derivative, unless clearly stated vegan.

**Soy or vegetarian Burgers:** May contain dairy, unless stated as vegan.

**Steric Acid:** Can be fat from cows and sheep. Used in some personal care products.

**Supplements:** Unless stated "suitable for vegetarian," or contains vegetarian gelatin, most supplements in capsule form are animal based. Some tablets also contain animal based items.

**Tallow:** Rendered beef fat. Used in some candles, crayons, soaps and cosmetics.

**Whey:** Derived from milk. Found in some protein powders, supplements and processed foods.

**White Sugar:** May have been processed with animal bone.

**Woolen Goods:** Although the outer coat of sheep and other furry animals, the animal is not generally killed for the wool, unless it is for the skin as well. Sheep and other animals *can* be raised on small farms, purely for the wool, and not for meat production.

---

### It's Time for a Change

"Anyone who is sick knows it is time for a change. One thing we have to change is our eating habits. But, food is not an easy problem to tackle because most of us have well-established cooking habits and our past habits make it very difficult for us to make changes. While we are getting along in life, we never recognize that there is a relationship between our food and our health. We find it difficult to conceive of an actual relation between the food that goes into our bodies and what happens in our toes or hair or eyes. We have never had a training in this. We do not know that the bloodstream depends upon what we eat. We do not know that what we eat today is going to talk and walk tomorrow. We do not know that what we eat actually becomes the cell structure of the body. This is why if we do not change our faulty ways of eating, we can never expect a permanent turn for the better in our health."

Bernard Jensen PhD.  -  Food Healing For Man

---

# DICTIONARY OF INGREDIENTS

**AGAR - AGAR:** Made from sea vegetables, and used as a jelling agent in soups, salads and desserts.

**AMARANTH:** Tiny, cream coloured seeds, which were an important food in Aztec culture. Has an earthy flavour. Gluten free and high in protein, calcium, iron, phosphorus and lysine. Can be prepared like a hot cereal, or combined with other grains and cooked in puddings. To pop or cook amaranth for salads, heat seeds in a dry skillet until they pop, stirring constantly to keep them from burning. Remove from heat and cool.

**ARROWROOT:** A starch made from a West Indies root. Excellent for thickening low heat sauces. Can be used to replace cornstarch.

**ASAFETIDA:** Also known as Hing. It is a strong aromatic resin available in powder form, and traditionally used in East Indian cooking. Keep it in a tightly sealed container, as it has a very pungent odor. It can be used instead of garlic and onions in a recipe. Add a pinch to cooking beans, for better digestion.

**BAKING POWDER:** A leavening powder for non-yeasted baked goods. Buy the non-aluminum brands at your local health or natural food store.

**BARLEY:** A grain with an earthy taste. Can be substituted for rice. Often used in soups and stews.

**BRAGG LIQUID AMINOS:** A delicious, low sodium, unfermented alternative for tamari or soy sauce.

**BRAN:** Oat or wheat bran. The husk of the grain, which has been separated from flour. Used in breads and muffins. A great source of dietary fiber.

**BROTH:** Vegetable broth comes in liquid, powder, or in bouillon cubes.

**BUCKWHEAT:** Not a true grain. Seed of a plant related to rhubarb. Gluten free, high in protein, B's, E, iron and calcium. Has an earthy flavour.

**BULGUR:** Cracked whole wheat that is parboiled and dried. Used in cereals and salads.

**CAROB:** Nutritious chocolate substitute. Comes from the pods of an evergreen carob tree. Resembles chocolate, but has no caffeine and contains calcium, phosphorus, potassium, magnesium, silicon, iron and traces of vitamin A, Bl and B2. Naturally sweet and low in fat.

**CHILI FIESTA BLEND POWDER:** This is a Frontier Herb company blend, available through some natural food stores. It's a mixture of chili powder, cumin, garlic, oregano, coriander, cloves and allspice. (See pg. 102 for a similar homemade blend called, *Chili Medley Blend.*)

**CORNSTARCH:** Made from corn, and used to thicken puddings and sauces. It's best used with non-acid fruits.

**COUSCOUS:** A small granular pasta made from semolina or whole wheat flour. It can be found packaged or in the bulk department of a natural food store.

**DRY SWEETENER:** Raw (unbleached) organic sugar is used in all recipes in this book, unless otherwise stated. Other dry sweeteners include: Date sugar, from ground dehydrated dates, Succanat, a high quality evaporated cane juice sweetener, and powdered Stevia, from a Latin American herb; which must be used very carefully, as it is at least 200 times sweeter than the above sweeteners. Many commercially produced white sugars have been unnaturally bleached and filtered through animal bone char.

**EGG REPLACER POWDER:** A powdered mixture of starches, that when mixed with water acts as an egg replacer. Contains potato starch and tapioca flour. The package instructions state that; 1½ tsp. powder mixed with 2 TB. warm water = l egg. The recipes in this book use a higher proportion of powder.

**FLAX SEED, OIL OR MEAL:** Seeds or meal can be used as an egg substitute. Soak ¼ C. seeds with ¼ C. hot water and sit for 5 minutes. Replaces 1 TB. of egg replacer powder, or add flax to baked goods for fiber and unsaturated fatty acids. The meal or oil is delicious added to juice or smoothies and the oil can be used in salad dressings.

**GARAM MASALA:** An aromatic blend of warming spices, such as, cardamom, cinnamon, cloves, black pepper and ginger. It can be purchased in natural food stores and Indian markets.

**KAMUT:** A distant relative of wheat. It contains 40% more protein than wheat, and is less allergenic. Used in salads, pilafs and can be used instead of rice, in some dishes.

**KELP:** Seaweed in powdered form, which is salty and rich in iodine.

**LECITHIN:**  Food from soybeans.  It's called an emulsifier of cholesterol in the blood. Can be used in breads and baked goods, smoothies and other blended beverages,

**MAPLE SYRUP:**  It takes 40 gallons of sap from the maple tree to make one gallon of maple syrup.  The dark, less expensive grade contains higher quantities of minerals.

**MARGARINE:**  Use non-hydrogenated soy margarines, made by Earth Balance.  They have a buttery flavour and freeze well.

**MEATLESS SAUSAGES and substitutes:**  Meatless low fat *Smart Bacon* and *Gimme Lean sausage* by Lightlife foods.  *Meatless ground,* precooked and ready to heat by Yves or Lightlife foods.  *Meatless sausages* and *burgers,* made with soy protein, by Boca.

**MILLET:**  Millet was eaten in China long before rice.  It has also been used for centuries in India, Japan and Africa.  A small, yellow bead like grain, which is naturally alkaline and has a nutty flavour.  Excellent in: salads, soups and stews, and as a breakfast cereal.  Can replace rice in most dishes.

**MISO:**  A salty paste made from cooked, aged soybeans, and rich in B vitamins.  Used in stews, soups, sauces and gravies.

**MOLASSES:**  The end product in sugar processing.  Blackstrap molasses is high in iron. Use in baked goods, sauces and other dishes.

**NORI SHEETS:**  Dried sea algae, pressed into sheets for nori rolls/sushi.

**NUTRITIONAL YEAST:**  A yellow powder or flakes that are grown on molasses.  It is high in vitamin B, protein and minerals. It has a buttery, "cheesy" flavour.  Mix with blended beverages and sprinkle on popped corn. It can be used in many baked goods and veggie dishes.

**OATS:**  Commonly regarded as a breakfast food.  Rolled oats are also delicious in desserts, cookies and granola cereal. Oat groats and steel cut oats can be used as a cooked breakfast cereal, and when soaked, used in bread recipes.

**QUINOA:**  Pronounce this ancient grain keen-wa.  A small disc shaped seed, which was once a staple of Incan culture.  It has a light, nutty taste and fluffy texture.  Contains 50% more protein than other grains, and high levels of calcium, phosphorus, iron and B vitamins.  Replace cracked wheat or bulgur with quinoa, for a wheat free alternative.

**RICE:**  A staple food in Asia since 3000 B.C.  Brown rice contains more nutritional value than white rice, which has had the bran and germ polished off in the refining process. Brown rice is high in calcium, zinc, iron and B vitamins. Use long grain brown rice for a fluffier texture, and short brown rice when a stickier texture is desired.

**RYE:** A cultivated cereal grain, first grown during the Roman Empire. It has a hearty flavour and is moderately high in gluten. It is nutritionally similar to wheat, being high in minerals and B vitamins.

**SAFFRON:** Imparts a rich and distinctive taste, and gives food a yellow/orange colour.

**SEA SALT:** Used in all the recipes in this book. It is seawater that has been vacuum dried at low temperatures. It contains minerals, which are devoid in regular table salt, which may also contain aluminum as an anti-caking agent.

**SEITAN:** Is made from wheat gluten flour. It is an excellent source of protein, and can be purchased at natural food stores.

**SPELT:** A grain related to wheat. Beige kernels, similar looking to brown rice. Sweet nutty taste, which contains gluten, but is easier to digest and higher in protein and B vitamins than wheat. It is sometimes tolerated by those on a wheat free diet.

**SPIKE:** A seasoning containing salt, nutritional yeast and 35 herbs and spices. A salt free spike is also available.

**STEVIA:** A plant derived sweetener, from the leaves of a South American shrub, available in powder and liquid form. It's estimated to be 200-300 times sweeter than sugar, yet has no calories. It is tolerated by those on restricted diets and for Candida/yeast infections. One cup of sugar is equivalent to 1/3-1/2 tsp. powdered or 1/2-3/4 tsp. liquid stevia. The taste is not quite like that of other sweeteners, and some modifications will need to be made with recipes, if stevia is replacing the entire amount of sweetener.

**TAHINI:** Ground sesame seeds. Also known as sesame butter.

**TAMARI:** A soy sauce made from a mixture of soybeans, wheat flour and fermenting agents. It is naturally fermented over a long period of time. Many soy sauces are chemically fermented in a matter of hours and contain caramel colouring. A non-wheat tamari is also available.

**TAPIOCA:** Comes from the cassava plant. The pearls are used in puddings and for thickening. Tapioca flour can be combined with other flours in wheat free baking.

**TEMPEH:** Made from whole cooked soybeans, and infused with a culture to form a dense, chewy cake. Can be grilled, fried or steamed, and used in salads and sandwiches.

**TOFU:** Also known as soybean curd. Made by curdling fresh soy milk with a coagulant, such as nigari, lemon or vinegar. It is high in protein, minerals, B6 and B12 and has alkaline properties. It can be purchased in aseptic packs that keep in the cupboard, and work well with most desserts; or the refrigerator brands, which are preferred in cooking and some desserts.

**TURMERIC:**  A spice with a musky scent.  It can be used as a colouring agent.

**TVP:**  Textured vegetable protein.  It is a high protein food made from soy.  It can be used in place of meat in chili and other casseroles; added directly to soups and stews, or reconstituted by mixing with hot water, and sitting 5-10 minutes to soften.

**VEGETABLE OILS:**  Cold pressed and expeller pressed oils are recommended.  Most commercially produced oils are extracted using heat, and are refined by bleaching.  Expeller pressed oils are produced without chemicals.  A number of oils, such as olive and flax, have medicinal values, are easy to digest and are healthy additions to salad dressings.  Olive oil and coconut oil are the best oils for stir-frying or sautéing.  Safflower or sunflower oils are best used in baked goods.

**VINEGAR:**  Use non-pasteurized apple cider vinegar.  Rice vinegar and Ume Plum vinegar, which is very salty, are also recommended in some recipes.

**WASABI:**  Japanese horseradish.  It has a strong and hot taste.  It comes in powdered form.  Mix the powder with a little water for a hot dip for rice filled nori.  Some wasabi powder is artificially dyed.

**WHEAT GERM:**  The inner part of the wheat berry, containing the embryo of the new plant and many nutrients, including vitamin E.

**WHOLE WHEAT FLOURS:**  Hard wheat is used for bread.  Soft wheat pastry flour is used for pastries and other desserts.  Light textured baked goods, resembling ones made with white flour, can be obtained when the pastry flour is finely ground.  The end result will also be delicious as well as nutritious.  Enriched white flour is void of nutrients, all having been removed in the milling process.  If used at all, use the organic, unbleached variety, and use it sparingly, such as where an alternative thickening agent is required.

**WILD RICE:**  An aquatic grass often mistaken for a grain.  It has a distinct woodsy flavour and pleasant chewy texture.  It is very nutritious, being rich in protein, minerals and B vitamins.  It expands four times when cooked.  It is often cooked with other grains and rice.

**XANTHAM GUM:**  Derived from bacteria in corn sugar.  A very small amount helps thicken salad dressings, sauces and baked goods, in wheat free cooking.  It can be found in the baking section of natural food stores.

---

" I do not regard flesh food as necessary for us at any stage and under any clime in which it is possible for human beings ordinarily to live.  I hold flesh food to be unsuited to our species."    - Mahatma Gandhi

Acid & Alkaline  by Herman Aihara

Ageless Body Timeless Mind  A Quantum Alternative to Growing Old
     by Deepak Chopra, M.D.

Alkalize or Die  by Theodore A. Baroody, Jr. Ph.D.

Animal Factories  by Jim Mason & Peter Singer

Apple Cider Vinegar Health System  by Paul C Bragg & Patricia Bragg N.D. Ph.D

Ayurveda  The Science of self healing  by Dr. V. Lad

Back to Eden  by Jethro Kloss

Back Care Basics  A Doctor's Gentle Yoga Program for Back and Neck Pain Relief
     by Mary Pullig Schatz, M.D.

Baking with Stevia  by Rita DePuydt

Better Late Than Early  by Raymond & Dorothy Moore

Body Feng Shui  by Chao-Hsiu Chen

Carrots Love Tomatoes: Secrets of Companion Planting for Successful Gardening,
     by Louise Riotte

Conscious Eating  by Gabriel Cousens, M.D.

Cooking with the Sun  by Beth Halacey and Dan Halacey

Diet for a New America  by John Robbins

Don't Drink Your Milk! by Frank A. Oski, M.D. with John D. Bell

Don't Sweat the Small Stuff…and it's all small stuff  by Richard Carlson, PH.D.

Dr. Mandells 5 Day Allery Relief System  by Marshall Mandell, M.D.
     & Lynne Waller Scanlon

Eating From the Wild  by Anne Marie Stewart And Leon Kronoff

Essential Feng Shui  by Lillian Too

Every Woman's Book  by Paavo Airola, N.D. Ph.D.

Fasting Can Save Your Life  by Herbert M. Shelton

Fed Up! The Food Forces That Make You Fat, Sick and Poor  by Brett Silverstein

Feng Shui Today:  Earth Design the Added Dimension  by Jami Lin

Fit For Life  by Harvey & Marilyn Diamond

Food for Life: How the New Four Food Groups Can Save Your Life by  Neal Barnard, M.D.

Food Healing for Man   by Bernard Jensen, PhD.

Food- Your Miracle Medicine -  How food can help prevent and cure over 1000 symptoms
     and problems  by Jean Carper

Four Seasons Harvest  by Eliot Coleman

Fresh Vegetable and Fruit Juices - What's missing in your body?  by N.W.Walker, D.Sc

Healing Wise, Wise Woman Herbal  by Susan S. Weed

Healing with whole foods - Oriental Tradition & Modern Nutrition  by Paul Pitchford

Health Building - Conscious Art of Living Well  by Dr. Randolph Stone, D.O.,D.C.

Heinerman's Encyclopedia of Fruits, Vegetables and Herbs  by John Heinerman

Home Remedies  Hydrotherapy, Massage, Charcoal and other simple treatments
     by Agatha Thrash, M.D. & Calvin Thrash, M.D.

Homeschooling for Excellence  by David and Micki Colfax

Hopes Edge  by Frances Moore Lappe and Anna Lappe

How to Get Well  by Paavo Airola, Ph.D.

Kombucha How-To and What It's All About by Alana Pascal with Lynne Van der Kar

Letting Go of the Person You Used To Be -  Lessons on Change, Loss, And Spiritual
     Transformation by Lama Surya Das

Mad Cowboy  by Howard Lyman with Glen Merzer

May all Be Fed  by John Robbins

Natural Diet for Folks Who Eat - Cooking with Mother Nature  by Dick Gregory

Natural Healing with Herbs  by Humbart Santillo,  N.D.

No Work Garden Book by Ruth Stout

Nutrition Against Disease  by Roger J. Williams

Peace Pilgrim; Her Life and Work in Her Own Words  by Ocean Tree Books

Pregnancy, Children and the Vegan Diet  by Michael Klaper,  M.D.

Prescriptions for Nutritional Healing  by James F Balch, M.D. & Phyllis A. Balch, C.N.C.

Raising with the Moon - The complete guide to gardening and living by the signs of the
     moon  by Jack  R. Pyle & Taylor Reese

Sacred Space:  Clearing and Enhancing The Energy of Your Home  by Denise Linn

Spiritual Nutrition and the Rainbow Diet   by Gabriel Cousens, M.D.

Stalking  The Healthful Herbs  by Euell Gibbons

Staying Healthy with the Seasons  by Elson M. Haas, M.D.

Stocking Up  by Rodale Press

Survival into the 21st Century  by Viktoras Kulvinskas

Take Off Your Glasses And See - The mind/Body Approach to Expanding Your eyesight
     and Insight by Jacob Liberman, O.D., Ph.D.

The Asthma Self-Care Book  by Geri Harrington

The Book of Tofu by William Shurtlett &Akiko Aoyagi

The Chemistry of Man  by Bernard, Jensen, Ph.D.

The Complete Book of Essential Oils & Aromatherapy  by Valerie Ann Worwood

The Ecological Health Garden and the Book of Survival  by Edmond Bordeaux Szekely

The Encyclopedia of Alternative Health Care  by Kristin Gottschalk Olsen

The Encyclopedia of Common Diseases  by the Staff of Prevention Magazine

The Encyclopedia of Medicinal Plants  by Andrew Chevalier

The Feng Shui Garden  by Gill Hale

The Good Life  by Helen and Scott Nearing

The Healing Mind of Man, Arise & Shine  by Bernard Jensen Ph.D.

The Herb Book  by John Lust

The Herbal Drugstore by Linda B. White, M.D., Steven Foster and the staff of Herbs for
     Health

The Master Cleanser  by Stanley Burroughs

The McDougall Plan  by John A. McDougall & May A. McDougall

The Miracle of Fasting  by Paul C. Bragg, N.D. Ph.D.

The Natural Remedy Book for Women  by Diane Stein

The One Straw Revolution - An introduction to Natural Farming  by Masanobu Fukuoka

The Old Farmers Almanac  published yearly since 1792, by Robert B. Thomas

The Organic Way to Plant Protection  by The Editors Of Organic Gardening

The Parasite Menace - The complete guide to the prevention, treatment and elimination of parasitic infection by Skye Weintraub, N.D.

The Rodale Book of Composting by Rodale Press

The Sprouting Book by Ann Wigmore

The Staying Healthy Shopper's Guide by Elson M. Haas, M.D.

The Successful Homeschool Family Handbook by Dr. Raymond & Dorothy Moore

The TVP Cookbook by Dorothy R. Bates

The Ultimate Guide to Homeschooling by Debra Bell

The Way of Herbs by Michael Tierra, C.A., N.D.

The Way We Eat: Why Our Food Choices Matter by Jim Mason & Peter Singer

The Wisdom of Menopause - Creating Physical and Emotional Health by Christine Northrup, M.D.

There Is A Cure For Arthritis by Paavo O. Airola, N.D.

Touching Peace, Practicing the Art of Mindful Living by Thich Nhat Hanh

Tissue Cleansing through Bowel Management by Bernard Jensen, D.C. Ph.D.

Using Energy to Heal by Wendell Hoffman

Vaccines; are they really safe & effective? By Neil Z. Miller

Vegan Nutrition: pure & simple by Michael Klaper, M.D.

Vegetables on the Grill, A menu Cookbook by Kelly McCune

Vegetarian Britain by Alex Bourke & Katrina Holland

Vegetarian Europe by Alex Bourke

Vegetarian Restaurants & Natural Food Stores In The U.S. by John Howly

Vipassana Meditation, as taught by S.N. Goenka, by William Hart

Vitamin Bible by Earl Mindell

Walden by Henry David Thoreau

What your Doctor may not tell you about Menopause by John R. Lee, M.D.

World Keys to Health & Long Life by Bernard Jensen, D.C. PhD.

Yoga 28 day Exercise Plan by Richard Hittleman

You Can Heal Your Life by Louise L. Hayes

# INDEX

ISBN 1425148190